MIND REVOLUTION

Unraveling Reality

(Manuals I & IV)

PHILLIP G. BOSCO

Table of Contents

DEDICATION

To Annie, for the life we lived together. Without you, your patience, your kindness, and your compassion, as well as the ups and the downs we had experienced together, I would not have encountered the difficult truths and realizations necessary to write this. Thank you, for everything, and the incredible life that we shared together.

To Paul, we started this deep-dive journey together, and I am eternally grateful to have you by my side all throughout, as you remained my trusted friend and ally during this immensely turbulent ride, which has all but ceased to continue. Thank you for your tremendous honesty, genuine character, and vulnerability. You are a true warrior.

To Mitch and Jon, for the countless hours of deep conversation as I tried to make sense of everything, along with my many attempts to formulate expressions and words to adequately share these intricate concepts and ideas about consciousness, choice, and our very existence. I know I'm long-winded and highly verbose, to say the very least, yet you've both been incredibly patient with me and have been more helpful on this journey than you can possibly know.

To Mom and Dad, for always believing in me and loving me through all of these unique, wonderful, painful, and sometimes outright scary phases of life. Thank you. I love you both very much.

NOTE FROM AUTHOR

As was the case for many, 2020 was a year unlike any other that came before it. In my experience, it was when my life and my concept of it forever changed. Like many others before me who have found themselves in the same trap after, somewhat unknowingly, dedicating their lives to chasing material things, possessions, relationships, and ego-gratifying titles and statuses, I found myself broken, empty, and unfulfilled. I craved external validation and fulfillment, always looking outward for satisfaction while blaming anyone but myself for the undesirable aspects of life and taking full credit (and then some) for the desirable and positive aspects of life. I saw myself as a victim of life, with much "evidence" to "conclusively" point to this personally derived classification.

Through a series of events at the hands of my poor judgment, inflated ego, and skewed version of the world, I lost nearly everything that I had relentlessly pursued and worked very hard for most of my life. I caused immense pain to those closest to me who would stand by me through thick and thin. In the earlier stages of this process, I experienced complete ego-dissolution, which can be summarized as a complete loss of subjective self-identity. I didn't know who I was, nor did I recognize myself anymore. For so long, I had identified so intimately with my core beliefs, my achievements, my statuses, finances, success, and so much more while forgetting the deepest version of myself that I left behind many, many years ago. I realized that I had built a sophisticated and disingenuous mask or persona to hide my insecurities and self-doubt. I did not believe that I had any value as a human on this planet, so I chased possessions and accomplishments, secretly hoping that others may find value in me as a result of the things I owned or achieved. This wasn't only to convince others, but myself also.

During this difficult journey through my very being, I uncovered suppressed memories from my early childhood whereby I was physically, emotionally, and sexually abused by a trusted family member for years. This had destroyed me and caused me to live life in a submissive manner, making me a prime target for my peers to tease and bully me throughout my years in school. In one standout instance, I was manipulated into following a "friend" into a field, only to be ambushed by others who leaped out from behind large bushes and threw stones at me as I tried to quickly escape. With experiences such as these, I realized that "trusted" family members and "trusted" peers could harm me. I learned that if I could make the bullies laugh, they wouldn't hurt me as much, either through distraction or by deferring their bullying to another. Humor proved to be an effective evasive maneuver that I leveraged as a defense mechanism to minimize the abuse and pain. I learned to be agreeable, to earn the acceptance of others who might have the capacity to harm me. Additionally, if I could demonstrate success through achieving great things, good grades, accomplishments, statuses, finances, and more through my adult years, I would no longer be the "lowest hanging fruit" for the bullies to harm, as I learned to create a persona that was more resilient to attacks. Still, this was only an illusion, one that I bought into nearly as much as anyone else outside of me. Though I once was the victim of many attacks, after many optimizing revisions to this illusory and fabricated persona that I created, I ultimately became the bully that caused harm to others through the employment of a superiority complex masked with humility and generosity. Perhaps I thought that should I appear superior to others and be the instigator of belittlement, I would not be the subject of it. Though I did not instigate physical attacks like the bullies of my life had done so to me, my attacks were passive, discreet, psychological, emotional, and mostly inconspicuous, fooling even myself as I justified every action, feeling, and manipulation tactic.

Upon realizing all of this in mid to late 2020, I became highly depressed and suicidal. I physically wrote at least three suicide letters, plus many more mentally, in excess of what I accurately count numerically. On several occasions, I held a loaded gun against my body. Many other days, I lived with the mindset of "It's Monday now, but Wednesday night is when it'll happen." On Wednesday, I'd wake up to my alarm sounding, thinking that it was truly the day I'd end this game of life that I no longer cared to play. At some point during an emotionally charged moment, an inescapable realization flashed before my mind's eye that posed the question:

"Why have you chosen to be in so much pain?"

In this moment, I realized that my pain and tears were a direct result of my perception of my life. But where did this perception come from? As I followed the threads of revelations and insights over the course of several months, I realized that my perception was a result of my choices, choices that I alone had the power to make. Through this journey, I began taking notes, journaling heavily, along with countless hours of audio diaries, as I relentlessly explored the depths of my consciousness and the power of choice that we all hold.

After feeling like I lacked purpose, passion, and identity through this painful process to rediscover myself, it was then that I felt what I only could describe as a tremendous "pull" to publish a book. I had never written a book before, nor had I ever considered myself an author of any sort, but I could not escape this strong feeling. Though hesitant at first to commit to this foreign objective,

I decided to put the pen to the page. Over the course of several more months in dedication and pursuit towards this undeniable pull that was filled with emotional and psychological ups and downs, I was finally ready to share the glimpses and abstractions of reality I have personally experienced with everyone, or at least, anyone willing to engage. The process of writing this book was not an easy one, as I continued to experience pain, confusion, and personal instability all throughout this journey. This book and its contents are just as much for me as it might be for others who decide to read it, for I must still work very hard to apply the concepts for myself as I continue my own journey to understanding them more deeply. This book does not contain the completeness of what I have experienced or continue to experience, as I am presently limited through my ability to communicate competently the other abstractions of my ongoing journey, which can only be shared in direct proportion with my capacity to internalize and process it within myself.

Some of the topics within may be difficult to read as they may challenge much of your current version of reality; please know that my truest intent is only to bring about more peace, love, and satisfaction in the lives of those who read this. It is not my intent to change your mind or opinions about any belief or opinion that you hold dear to yourself, but merely to understand yourself and how you might have arrived at such a belief more thoroughly. It may not always be an easy journey through, but should you persist, I'm certain you'll emerge with a stronger and more comprehensive understanding of not only yourself and your deepest-held core beliefs, but of others and their beliefs as well, leading to a more satisfactory and pleasant experience of life for all. Life is what you decide to make of it. You get to create your life and experience through it using your power of choice. I want to personally thank each and every one of you for your willingness to read this book, and I am honored at the opportunity to share much of my heart, mind, and soul with you. As I struggled with purpose and passion, this book has been my anchor in providing meaning to what once felt meaningless. Whether or not this book is ultimately part of your personal journey, I wish you all the greatest happiness and love possible in your lives.

With much love and respect,

Phillip

INTRODUCTION

Your entire life, such as your routines, your frustrations, your fears, your struggles, your money issues, your successes, and your perceived failures, have been created either consciously or subconsciously through your incredible power of choice. **You** have **decided** to make these **choices**.

No one else can ever make your choices for you, despite society's rules and norms, cultural expectations, or personal religious convictions. While there may be consequences or a cost for every choice made, whether we perceive it as "good" or "bad," we must not mistakenly conflate any associated consequence carried alongside a choice with an inability to make one freely. Developing an acute understanding of the differential between choices and consequences is both central and paramount to the principles shared within this book. No one can make you do anything, despite their efforts to convince you otherwise out of your own ability to exercise your free will.

You may think that you do not have an infinite array of

choices. Regardless, this is precisely where we can begin to dig into the depths of what we think, why we think it, and reawaken ourselves to truly the most powerful force in the universe that is at our disposal and under our complete control. This powerful force is our intrinsic ability to make real choices. This takes the willingness to step outside of the box that you have been conditioned to think within by influences like your upbringing, culture, laws, religions, family expectations, peer pressure, and governments. For most of us, this box resides largely in our subconscious mind, and we are not consciously aware of where it begins and ends. Not only must we step outside of this box, but we must also be willing to challenge and address every single ideal, belief, and assumption that we find within it. As we begin to unravel our consciousness, our core beliefs, and our perception of what we deem is good, bad, right, or wrong, we will find something that we have long forgotten. This "something" has been buried deep inside of us and actively suppressed by our life experiences and the influences of our culture, governments, and religions. This "something" is so unequivocally you that when you rediscover it, you won't be able to deny it. You'll recognize it. This "something" can never be taken from you, no matter what happens to you as a result of life's unpredictable circumstances, unfair treatment, attacks, imprisonment, or threats from others. This is something that is always yours and has never left you; it has only been misplaced.

This "something" is the power to make truly free choices in every single aspect of your life without the subjective bias of life experiences or the pressures of the many fabricated and illusory status quos of society. Depending on the country in which you reside, you may think you are mostly free to make your own choices or that you already are making every single choice consciously, though this is only an illusion even in the freest of countries. If you believe you are already free, you will not seek your freedom, as you believe you already have it and hold it. Further, the power of choice is not just about owning your choices or choosing between seemingly insignificant items like boxers or briefs, soup or salad, or the selection of a desired career path. This ability that we all possess in the deepest part of our being is greater than any of the many superficial choices that we all believe we are in control of making on a day-to-day basis.

- *Your ability to choose freely is more powerful than any other force in the universe.*
- *Your ability to choose freely is more powerful than any hydrogen bomb.*
- *Your ability to choose freely transcends religion, political parties, laws, and governments.*
- *Your ability to choose freely soars beyond your fears, insecurities, and personality.*
- *Your ability to choose freely can eliminate your stress, anxiety, and depression.*

- *Your ability to choose freely can disrupt the hierarchies of entire countries and social structures.*
- *Your ability to choose freely can free others from seemingly oppressive regimes.*
- *Your ability to choose freely can dismantle the entire human-trafficking industry.*
- *Your ability to choose freely can truly create positive change for every life form on this planet.*

Furthermore, if the ability to choose freely was widely understood and implemented by a mere fraction of the human race, it would have undoubtedly been powerful enough to stop World War II before it began, saving tens of millions of lives. As you continue to consume the contents of this book, you'll understand that even the examples provided here in the introduction are incredible oversimplifications of your power to make free choices. **This is intentional**. When we realize that we always have a choice, no matter the exterior circumstances, our entire perspective on life changes dramatically.

- *When in seemingly insurmountable debt, you still have a choice.*
- *When you are the victim of physical, emotional, or sexual abuse, you still have a choice.*
- *If you have lost your entire house and personal belongings in a fire, you still have a choice.*

- *If a drunk driver hits your car and requires your leg to be amputated, you still have a choice.*
- *When staring down the barrel of a loaded gun in a dark alley, you still have a choice.*

No one and **nothing** outside of you can **ever** make you do anything you don't choose to do. Period.

Certainly, there are things that happen to us in life that we believe to be out of our control and are unpleasant experiences, to say the very least. Additionally, this isn't to discredit anyone's experience or minimize the tragedy or pain experienced by anyone at all, especially when such experiences occur at the hand of a maliciously-minded individual with the intent to harm another human. Terrible and unexpected things happen to us, and there are things in your life that you may never be able to control. There is seemingly no escape from the many struggles and pains of life that result from the uncontrollable situations and traumas we've experienced. By embracing our true potential and the power of choice inside us, while not denying the internal turmoil we may feel at any given moment, we can become more aware of the things that we can and cannot control. Over time, and most often unbeknownst to us, we've blurred the lines of responsibility, choices, and control as a result of our influences, culture, and upbringing. The ability to actively observe every moment of our lives and understand the many choices available to us, should we choose to see them, is nothing but remarkably empowering. This heightened level of awareness is available to us only when we strip down the subconscious processes we are chronically burdened by, analyze our automatic reactions and feelings towards the things, situations, and people we encounter in life, while challenging our core beliefs and motivations for every single thing we say, do, act, interpret, or feel.

Without this understanding, our subconscious mind provides us a story, which is a subjective interpretation of our perceived world, riddled with the bias of your life experience up until this present moment. Once established in the earlier stages of life, we blindly follow this narrative without question and attempt to fit everything that we see, hear, think, and feel into this wildly incomplete and self-concocted model of "reality," which varies greatly from person to person. You may discover things that you once viewed as objective facts ultimately boil down to merely subjective opinions that vary greatly from one individual to another. This may be uncomfortable or unpleasant, as the manner in which you once viewed your reality for most of your life may be questioned or altered as it is dissected, analyzed, and reassembled. You may find yourself caught red-handed, making excuses for yourself, your behavior, and your core beliefs, as your inherent perceptual bias will reinterpret everything you see in the world and inside this book in a way that aligns with your current belief system and core values. You may find yourself disoriented, lost, or questioning everything you thought you knew to be true. This is **normal and expected**, and it may occur at varying degrees for certain individuals. Stay strong and stay present. It'll be worth the internal battle as you shake loose the very foundations of your reality. Ignorance may be "bliss" to a degree, but enlightenment brings peace, joy, and purpose that surpasses any potential or illusory bliss you may have been living in prior. Oftentimes, it takes getting through our own darkness and shadows before we allow ourselves to see the light and the greatness available to us on the other side. Approach this book with the mindset that you are ready for a change so that you may step into the incredible power that already resides within you and only needs to be rediscovered to access. **Only you** can take yourself there; this book alone cannot take you there on its own merit. It's always **your choice** and yours alone.

Be ready to challenge your deepest-held core beliefs, not for the sake of trying to change them necessarily, but to simply understand their origins and recognize the series of decisions and assumptions you've made along the way to accept them into the subjective reality that you've created for yourself. For anything in this book that arouses internal frustration, or should you find yourself getting offended or defensive, pay close attention to these feelings and observe them. Take notes on what triggered such feelings. Use these feelings as your personal guide to understanding what you hold dearly, your hesitations and limitations to see things another way, and the biased beliefs and subjective reality you may be holding onto. Throughout this process, you may begin to understand your deepest self and subconscious mind much better while identifying points of contention, perceived unworthiness, or other constraints that no longer serve you for you to step out of and remove from your being.

Many controversial topics will be shared throughout this book. **This is intentional**. The author does not intend to push any particular narrative, position, or ideology on anyone. On this, the author does not intend to diminish or disregard any particular view, opinion, or group of people. Should anything in this book be interpreted in a disparaging way towards any point of view discussed directly or indirectly, know that this is never the author's intention or the purpose of this book. The topics and questions shared are only to guide the reader to ask the difficult questions for themselves, as they analyze their own feelings along the way while opening themselves up to viewing the world differently. The author encourages you as the reader to dive deep within yourself, ask difficult questions, be willing to hear your truth that echoes back, and truly understand it.

There are many questions presented throughout this book for you to consider. They are intended to challenge your thought process and your firmly held beliefs to not only allow you to understand yourself more deeply but to understand the process responsible for the subjective realities created by others. Take your time going through the questions, and do not skim over them. Ask yourself the questions slowly and listen deeply for any answer, feeling, or reaction that arises. Sincerely asking yourself the questions posed are crucial to getting to the core of your deepest-held beliefs and the choices, subconscious or otherwise, that you've made throughout your life to create the reality of the core belief systems you currently operate within.

No one can tell you what to choose or how to choose it. This book's sole intent is to emphasize that you have this power to choose inside of you and to unblur the lines of responsibility of what you can and cannot control. You are in control of far more than you realize.

This isn't a new-age religion. This isn't a "new year, new you!" book, nor is it a guide on how to finally shed those stubborn 50 pounds or getting the promotion you want at work. This rediscovered awareness may very well lead you to these goals indirectly; however, you'll find something meaningful and much more significant on the other side. This is something much deeper than any accomplishment or life goal that can ever be attained, and it predates all laws, all societies, and all religious doctrine. It's something that has been here all along, inside of you, and inside of all of us. As you reawaken your conscious mind to this untethered power of choice you already possess, you'll inevitably discover true happiness, peace, and immense purpose for your life far beyond what any status, title, or income could ever generate.

You are the sole creator of your life and your beautifully unique and subjective view of reality.

Everything begins with a choice, and an awareness of your intrinsic ability to make one.

MANUAL ONE

(I)

1. THE BLUE SUNFLOWER

Imagine for a moment that you are a gardener who grows many flowers, and among the flowers you grow, your specialty is to grow sunflowers. You've been growing sunflowers for many years and have the process down to a verifiable and repeatable methodology to produce the greatest and healthiest sunflowers in the shortest possible time.

One day, you plant two sunflowers side by side at the same time, in the manner you normally would. However, one morning you awaken to find one of the sunflowers to be completely blue in hue. You pluck this strange sunflower from the ground, clear out the roots, and dispose of it completely while leaving the other yellow and healthy sunflower intact. You plant another sunflower in place of the recently discarded one, using a seed from your "known-good" collection of reliable and optimally bred seeds, only to find that this newly planted sunflower also turns blue after it grows. Baffled by this repeat occurrence, you discard the blue sunflower once again, then plant a new sunflower 137 feet away from the original one; however, the sunflower once again turns blue. Determined to find a solution to prevent this odd phenomenon, you plant a new sunflower in a pot using the highest quality and purest soil imported from another region. Further, you place the potted sunflower in an air-filtered, miniature greenhouse while using a separate source of nutrients and water than you use for the rest of your plants. Yet, the sunflower still turns blue.

Stunned and confused, you intend to remove all the flowers from your garden and begin to do so. Though, once you arrive at the original healthy sunflower, you notice that it has also turned a bright blue. Before you can pluck it from the ground, it changes to a bright and vibrant red before your eyes. Bewildered, the flower then changes to neon green, again before your eyes. You take a step back and look around to notice that all of the remaining sunflowers in your garden are changing in color to match the color of this sunflower only seconds after this single sunflower changes its own color. You begin shouting various colors at the sunflower, black, white, chartreuse, and scarlet, to not only find that the sunflower changes to the color you suggest to it, but the other sunflowers respond as well to your overt color suggestions.

Even for the most seasoned botanists and horticulturists, a situation involving a plant's ability to not only change its own color, but influence the hue of other nearby sunflowers, even the ones that do not share the same soil, nutrients, or air, would be mind-boggling. Further, for you to verbally suggest colors to the sunflowers to change their hue would leave you equally astounded. We would be shocked to discover this occurrence in plant life, or quite frankly, anywhere in nature with anything involving life on this planet. Yet, this is precisely how we as humans containing consciousness operate in every moment of every day within ourselves and in relation to other humans and forms of consciousness. By the very nature of life, we are both the gardener and the blue sunflower.

INSPIRING MATTER

As humans, we are products of the environment and grow from within it. On a material level, whether plant life, part of the animal kingdom, mycology, or human life, we are all made of matter on planet earth, which consists of the same subatomic particles: protons, neutrons, and electrons.

Close your eyes and imagine taking a bite of your favorite food or dessert. As you do this, imagine that the food or dessert of your choosing is perfectly prepared, perfect in consistency, and is the best version of that particular edible you've ever consumed. Imagine how it feels in your mouth as you chew with every single bite. Imagine how it tastes and how the texture of it feels against your tongue and cheeks. Is it sweet? Bitter? Salty? Soft? Cold? Warm? Spongy? Imagine the sensation experienced as you swallow it, allowing it to effortlessly slide down your throat as it makes its way to rest in your stomach so comfortably, leaving you with a great feeling of satisfaction and contentment. After much enjoyment, bite after bite, you finish your delicacy after consuming the perfect amount of it and rest comfortably in a cushy chair. As you sit in this chair, you feel an overwhelming sensation of gratification and fulfillment in your body, with the remnant taste of the food still detectable as your tongue glides around your mouth and through the spaces between your teeth. Leverage each of your five senses inside this visualization by asking yourself your own set of questions, relating to each sense individually, to impress the most realistic experience inside your own mind.

Throughout the visualization, how did your physical body outside of the visualization respond? Are there any effects you can continue to notice, even subtly, after coming out of this visualization exercise? Perhaps your mouth began producing an abundance of saliva. Maybe you became so immersed in the visualization that you felt a similar level of satisfaction in your physical body, akin to how the visualized version of yourself rested comfortably on the chair post-consumption with the imaginary food inside your belly. You might feel hungrier now and craving for the food than you did prior to the visualization, or even, you may feel content, satisfied, and full as if you had actually consumed it. The intensity of what you felt as you visualized consuming your favorite food or dessert is relative to your degree of submersion inside of the visualization you created inside your mind.

Let's visualize one more scenario together by placing ourselves in a situation that would elicit a fear response inside of us. Continue only as it is physically safe for you to do so without putting yourself in harm's way. For some, this may involve imagining yourself standing on a stage in the center of a large football area in front of 45,000 people and speaking to them all. The silence of the crowd is deafening, as you see countless camera flashes from audience members snapping pictures of you standing there, producing no words, as they hotly anticipate what you might say. In an act of unintentional procrastination, you shift your gaze upwards only to see a close-up of your face on several very large screens inside this arena, as well as on the giant screen carried by a blimp overhead, as the encircling cameras follow your every move from every angle imaginable. For those that don't fear public speaking, you may imagine something else, such as having to trek through a pit infested with countless 18-foot, poisonous king cobra snakes while barefoot. Regardless of the visualization you choose, imagine it with as much detail as you can do so safely. Imagine how the air smells. How does the air feel as it enters your nose or mouth? Is the air warm or cool? Are your palms sweating? Is your throat dry and scratchy? Is it dark or bright outside? If bright, does it cause you to squint due to the light source's intensity? What sounds do you hear, if any at all? Is your heart racing? Can you feel it pound through your chest and clothes? Are your extremities trembling? Are you short of breath? Ask yourself these questions, and any others of your choosing, to paint the picture of yourself inside this reality with as much detail as possible.

Through these visualizations, you were able to elicit various feelings inside of your own physical body, using your own imagination, through your conscious ability to manufacture the necessary scenes and stimuli, which all originate from the awareness of your choice to participate in such an exercise. As you imagined these acts deeply, your physical body responded in various ways as if you were engaged in the actual situation in the physical world at that very moment. As in, when you imagined the dessert, you felt satisfaction and pleasure inside your body, but when you imagined the fearful scenario, you felt your heart rate increase or, at a minimum, a general state of unease and anxiety. Was the satisfactory feeling that you felt after consuming the imaginary dessert part of your imagination, or did your physical body actually feel good? Surely, the excess saliva that might have been generated in your mouth wasn't only within the bounds of your imagination, as this effect breached into your physical reality. Similarly, did you imagine your heart race and your breath shorten only in terms of your imagination, or did your heart actually begin to race? Regarding the dessert and the feeling of satisfaction inside your physical body outside your imagination, this was caused by a chemical release of serotonin. For the fear situation, your imaginary act engaged your amygdala inside your brain, which alerted your nervous system, ultimately releasing a chemical cocktail of stress hormones, such as cortisol and adrenaline, causing the physical symptoms you experienced.

In short, by using your awareness to guide your conscious activity through various scenarios, you successfully altered the matter within your body. Your physical matter, consisting of the various subatomic particles, was effectively influenced through the thoughts and experiences inside of your own head, despite neither of these scenarios actually being experienced in your present physical world. These reactions can all be measured via brain-scanning equipment and blood sampling; thereby, they are not solely experienced within the imaginary visualizations but in the physical world within your physical body. In essence, you turned your sunflower blue by altering the matter there within through active awareness and recruitment of your consciousness alone. Though, through these recent visualizations whereby you affected your matter, are you the sunflower or are you the gardener? Sure, you affected your physical matter and state of being through thought alone, but where did these thoughts originate from? Did you engage in these thoughts on your own, or did these particular thoughts occur at this particular time that affected the particular parts of your matter due to the words you are reading on this page by the author who wrote them? In this way, have you turned yourself blue, or has the author of these words turned you blue?

After all, was it not the author that guided you through the experience of pleasure, contentment, and satisfaction by causing the release of physical chemicals within your own body? This wasn't simply a baseless thought experiment, as your physical-chemical composition and state of matter literally and materially changed as a result of your active participation in the visualization exercises. You may consider that it wasn't the author that changed your state but your own imagination and engagement of your consciousness that achieved this. Though indirectly, the author is, at a minimum, responsible for the suggestion to participate in such a visualization exercise, whereby the acceptance of the suggestion on its own alone altered your chemical composition to some degree before you ultimately made the choice to participate and intimately identify with the senses and visuals occurring within your own imagination. With this, even if you rejected the suggestion to participate in the visualization, the author has still effectively altered your thought through the mere broadcasting of the intended suggestion, which diverted your attention, your energy, and awareness. Thereby through the author's suggestion alone, whether you ultimately accepted or not, this caused various elements of your brain's physical matter to become engaged, enabling your neurons to fire and affecting your neurotransmitter receptors, resulting in various chemicals to release inside your body just to simply process the suggestion, as your own use of energy, awareness, attention, and consciousness was temporarily redirected, or arguably hijacked, during this process.

To revisit the prior inquiry, was it you who has turned yourself blue or the author?

CREATOR VERSUS CREATED

Within every moment, we are creating our own reality through our unique perceptions, chosen core beliefs, and interpretations of life. Though, is it us creating our reality and interpretation of it or another? Are we creating, managing, and controlling the emotions we feel, which are experienced through the release of various chemicals within our physical bodies, or is another doing this for us? If another can engage in an act that, through your interpretation and interaction with it as well as your observation of it, causes your physical state of existence to become altered, enabling a particular feeling, thought, or idea to cross your mind, are you in control of your own existence and your experience of life as you presently know it?

In the previous visualization examples, we may consider that you chose to engage in the exercises, but what about the rest of this book? Remember this as you continue through any moment where you might feel frustrated or flustered by the content you may read, or perhaps even enlightened as you receive an "a-ha!" moment. Attempt to be aware of what exactly is occurring as it takes place, whereby an external influence impacts your physical state of being. Surely, you've made the choice to pick up the book and read the words on the page, but who is in control of the chemicals released as you experience various feelings, thoughts, and concepts? Are you actively and consciously choosing frustration, joy, peace, or enlightenment, or are these feelings and ideas only happening to you? Further, consider the manner in which you became aware of this book that caused it to enter your conscious awareness in the first place. Did you first learn about it from a friend? By listening to a podcast? Or perhaps you saw it in an advertisement? With this, did some other external influence alter your body's physical and chemical composition in such a way that through the mere power of suggestion from another, it ultimately guided you here, right now, with your full attention present and focused, as you hold this book in your hands?

Are you the gardener or the sunflower?

As you move through this world, you are making an impact not only on yourself and your physical matter but on others and their physical matter. This occurs regardless of if you are engaging in this influence intentionally and consciously or unintentionally and unconsciously. Conversely, others can only be doing the same towards the world and the others they encounter in it, including you. When this realization is applied to one's own life, you may ask yourself what impact and influence you are having on your own life and on others, as you are undoubtedly making one. Should you choose to believe that you are not making an impact on others and the world, or your influence is so minuscule that it isn't worth spending time thinking about, this is your choice, and your experience and quality of life will be in alignment with the result of this belief. In other words, if you believe that others control your reality and experience of life through their actions, words, and influence, this is precisely the experience that you will consistently have. With that, you will always externalize the blame, guilt, and responsibility for your experience, emotion, and physical state of being, as you sway violently and seemingly uncontrollably in the winds and waves created by others. You create your life through your choices and perceptions, or you allow others to create you, your physical matter, your state of being, and your experience of your life by granting their choices, perceptions, and ideals to take root in your life. Would you prefer to be the creator of your own experience of life as the ultimate and singular authority, as you control your own state of being, chemical releases, energy flow, and physical matter? Or will you allow your experience of life and your present moment to be commandeered by an arbitrary other that experiences their life through their own subjective lens and biases? No one and nothing can ever create you unless you allow them to. When we are unaware of this process, to the various degrees to which it may occur and impact us, we unknowingly allow others and our environment to control our state of being and associated experiences and interpretations of life. When we become truly aware of it, we take back the control that we've always had access to. This is the power that has never left us, as we can only temporarily surrender it to another when we don't realize our infinite ownership and natural rights to it that are intrinsic to our very being.

We can operate from a point of intentional presence and fully conscious awareness, allowing us to create whatever it is we wish to create inside of our lives that stems from the depths of our being. When we operate proactively from this state of presence, living from the inside out, we create our reality and experiences of life that align with our truest passions and desires. However, when we operate reactively to life, we allow others and our environment to define what we feel, the thoughts we think, and the actions we take in our life. For example, when you awake in the morning and immediately check the notifications on your phone, you begin your day from a place of reactivity, allowing the actions, preferences, and ideals of others to influence the chemical compounds within your body. You are no longer living life intentionally and from the inside depths of your being or choosing how you want to feel or the exact way in which you will spend your time today. You have been hijacked, derailed, and redirected to the wind and waves of another. You have woken up as a naturally colored sunflower, in control of its own existence, but within seconds, have been turned blue in hue by others and will likely continue in that reactive state of being for your entire day, only to repeat it again tomorrow.

When another individual engages in something to make you feel angry, to what degree will you allow them to impact the hue that you intend to display to yourself and the world? Will you let them turn you blue, or will you choose another hue? No one can change your color for you, and this can only ever occur when you allow them to. Still, making this choice requires awareness, presence, and consciousness. In any case, their actions toward you will always impact your body's physical chemistry through the power of suggestion by implanting a choice, among many others, that you have available to you within every single moment. Though, the extent of their impact to alter your physical state ends here. At this point, they have not changed your color; rather, they have only added one to a vast palette of existing colors. You make the ultimate choice in the color that you choose for yourself. If you allow them to change your color, are you the gardener or the sunflower?

Is it ever the action of another that causes you to feel frustrated, or are your feelings a result of your perception of the action? If we externalize and blame another and their actions for "making us feel" a certain way, we have fully surrendered our power to them. We have also chosen to interpret the situation in a way that brings about internal turmoil, pain, and suffering. Should we choose to view the situation differently, we can either minimize the pain and suffering or eliminate it completely while potentially transforming a situation that was once draining and negative into one of empowerment, strength, fulfillment, and growth. We have this ability, should we choose to see it.

When you read the news of the day, you are placing yourself in a reactive state of being through your consumption of the information, which may only be riddled with the bias and subjectivity of the platform via which you receive such news. Furthermore, the news of the day is almost certainly triggering and anxiety-inducing.

10 Killed in Fiery Car Crash.
An Epic Twitter Feud Between a Teenage Popstar and Lead Politician.
New Law Increases Taxes on Everyone but the Rich.

When we read devastating headlines, we become stressed, anxious, frustrated, sad, or outright angry, which is the result of our interpretation of the external stimuli that we are choosing to allow into our awareness, ultimately causing various chemicals within our bodies to be released, as we continue living in a reactive state of being. Would you rather be stressed or relaxed? Reactive in your experience of life, or proactive? We could instead engage in activities that bring us joy by choosing the stimuli that we allow into our lives. Alternatively, we can alter our perception of the world around us and the headlines that we read so that they may not be interpreted negatively within our minds and bodies. The world in which we live is not good or bad, right or wrong, happy or sad. The world is all of these things and none of these things. For it is our interpretation and perception of the world that could ever make it any of these things. We provide the meaning of the world through our unique interpretations of it. If we cannot reasonably change our interpretation of it, we must consider removing that particular influence from our life, temporarily or permanently, by choosing to no longer give it domain over our physical state of being. We are the sole creators of our lives and of our experiences unless we grant others authority over our lives by providing them the access and the keys to our well-being through the surrendering of our power of choice. Some may suggest that by ignoring the news of the day, you are ignorant of the world around you. Regardless of what another suggests from their own subjective reality, you have a choice. Will you sacrifice your internal state of well-being, creativity, and happiness, for the information provided by the news sources? Or live and operate in a state of well-being, creativity, and happiness, by choosing the life you live and the external sources and influences you allow in your life, but otherwise unaware of the news of the day? Further, these questions are asked with the assumption that the information you are consuming and allowing to affect your being is wholly accurate, competent, and not intentionally deceptive, malicious, or controlling. There is a tradeoff. There is a cost for every choice that you make. Further, if a suggestion from another that you are ignorant of the world around you, according to their reality from which they reside, changes the way in which you live your life, are you the sunflower or the gardener?

When you are in a state of consumption, you are in a state of reactivity to others and the world. When you are watching a movie, the movie is creating your life through the emotions it intends to elicit within you as you engage with the content it provides. The movie controls your thoughts as it holds your attention firmly and creates the temporary world in which you reside, from the characters, the situations, and the protagonists, as well as the relationships, deaths, and obstacles faced as you live through the movie vicariously. In this way, are the influences of others, the news of the day, social media consumption, or your environment any different from watching a movie? The difference exists only in what you believe to be true or untrue, about the content you are consuming and how it impacts your life, thoughts, and well-being.

When you are creating your world from the depth of your being and from a place of passion, purpose, presence, and true desire, you are creating the world around you and your reality proactively. Though, even with a strong and positive chosen perception of the world, you are still to be impacted or created by it to some degree. For this reason, you must strive to create a life that aligns with your purposes and passions while bringing about peace, love, and satisfaction in your life. You may not yet know what this looks like for your own life, as you may unknowingly be the product of another's creation and have forgotten how to retain full control over your life, experience, emotions, and well-being. For this, consider cutting out distractions while becoming intentional with your life with everything that you do. Whenever you find yourself consciously aware of any present moment, stop what you are doing, and observe the thoughts currently in your brain. Observe your heart rate. Observe your state of being. Are you stressed or at peace? Are your thoughts positive or negative? Observe the very action you are taking part in and ask yourself why it is you are doing exactly that task or action in this exact moment. Are you enjoying the task that you are currently engaged with? Does this task bring about more peace and joy in your life? Are you taking part in this task to further a goal or desire of yours or fulfilling an obligatory commitment for another?

When various things and distractions in your life cannot be cut out, choosing a strong perception and interpretation of the events in your life can be leveraged to assist with your journey of self-growth and development. While you cannot control the environment, you can still control your perception. Detailing this perceptual shift as a "defense" might insinuate that you are operating out of a place of weakness; however, this is not the case.

If you are with another who has brought a seemingly negative impact to your present moment, their words, their presence, and their influence may change your state of being and physical form without your conscious control. Though you can always choose to interpret and perceive the negative stimuli differently in a way that minimizes their impact on your life and physical composition. We are all connected in such a way that even the greatest mental defense and perceptual shifts may not always prevent the unwanted influence and impact of others. While others may always have an impact on our lives, even if only through the momentary alteration of our chemistry and diversion of our conscious awareness, we never lose our ability to have a choice in our actions and our thoughts. With this, exercise caution with the influences you've allowed into your life and the level at which they may impact your well-being. Additionally, be careful of what you allow into your mind. Barring any potential situation of physical enslavement where you may not be able to escape your particular situation, you always have a choice to decide the influences around you. These influences alter your chemistry and require a constant defense and perceptual shift to maintain your independence. When practiced, this can be viewed as positive and empowering rather than detrimental.

Like the sunflower that could change the color of another, despite utilizing a filtered oxygen supply and different nutrients, there is not a singular way of being that allows us to affect others or for them to affect us. This impact and influence on others are not just the words we use, but also our tone of voice, our body language, our behaviors, and our actions. With this, do not discredit your impact in the world and the ripple effect you create, as you continually and invariably create one. This is why we must live every single day with passion and living out with authenticity to our truest selves. As in, when living out of love and purpose for your life, you will inevitably impact others in the same way, in proportion to this internalized state of being, and to the degree to which you feel and express it, even when done so unknowingly or subconsciously. You may never be president of a country, but the cashier at the local grocery store might be. Your kindness, love, and freedom that you demonstrate in your own life may be exactly what this individual needed to experience in your brief 45-second encounter with them to jostle something loose in their awareness that sets them on the path to realizing their own greatness, value, and potential. As you always influence others, independent of your choice to do so, the choice remains yours in regard to your ability to choose the ripple effect that you propagate. Your color impacts the color of another, which then impacts the color of many others. Knowing this, even when you aren't intentionally applying effort, how will you choose to live your life? Will it be one of love, compassion, and respect? Or anger, frustration, stress, judgment, and anxiety? Of significant importance, the colors you turn when nobody is watching still affect others, as the colors you choose impact your physical matter, which impacts your mood and the future colors that you turn.

You *are the point of all creation.*

What will you choose to create in this world for yourself, and inevitably, for others? Will you create others or allow others to create you?

2. THE FACE WITHOUT

We can know ourselves because we know others. We see ourselves only because we see the world. Without a contrary belief, opinion, or feeling, there would be no individuality to distinguish yourself from anything else, including your own internal emotions, thoughts, and dialog. Everything that you believe to exist in your reality exists only to the degree that you are able to distinguish it from something else. As in, you can only identify with being a kind person due to the cruelty you may see or interpret around you. You can only identify as being religious due to others choosing atheism or taking another spiritual path. You can only identify with being lazy due to others being motivated and self-disciplined. Each of the traits or beliefs we identify with exists as a result of the subjective reality we have all chosen for ourselves where it is impossible to consider one subjective reality being more superior to another. Rather than disparage the traits or beliefs of another, should they not instead be celebrated? For without them, there could not be you, nor could there ever be them, without you. Without these differences, we would lack the ability to form our own identities and would be wholly unable to define ourselves uniquely from any other thing in the universe. If everyone held your beliefs, you would no longer be identifiable for possessing your otherwise unique characteristics and convictions. If everyone was nothing but kind, the sweet and caring kindness you bring into the world on a regular basis would not be appreciated *or even recognized.* You see, it is precisely these differences that allow us to begin defining and differentiating ourselves from others and our environment. All too commonly, we dread and discredit people that oppose various elements of what we consider to be our core beliefs. Sure, we may not care all too much that someone else doesn't also like chocolate ice cream, but should they have an opposing belief to you about something deeper, such as the ideas involving life after death or political-party preferences, it all too frequently becomes a bloodbath, both literally and metaphorically. Yet, it is the very existence of these differences that allows us to define ourselves and form an identity in this world.

Everything you see around you is a direct result of who and what you choose to be. Both the perceived good and bad that you see are merely pieces of you scattered in every corner of the universe, from nature to animals, life situations, and other people. In this way, everything you perceive in this world as separate exists as a mirrored image of pieces that reside inside you. If you don't like what you see in the world and wish to change it, you must first change yourself, as the result of what you see can only ever be a direct reflection of yourself. Therefore, the world around you cannot be changed directly by forcing it to change to your selfish whims and desires. All the while, any of your attempts at such will be futile. Any perceived successes you find will be met with contempt from yourself and others and are most certainly temporary. To change others, you must not proceed with that intent, but rather the focus must only be on changing yourself. When your intent is set steadfastly in this manner, the world and others around you are changed and transformed purely as a symptom of your own internal change. Along those lines, to hold a personal goal to change or fix the world requires the prerequisite assumption based on your own subjective reality that there is even *something to fix*. This also implies that your assumption of how the world ought to work and operate is relatively superior to the subjective viewpoints and realities of the ones you seek to change.

The reflective reality in which you live is one of the greatest resources available to you, should you choose to use it and see it as such. However, the image seen that has been mirrored back to you isn't always pleasant or desirable. When we see something or someone we do not like, we attempt to change them, we despise them, or we blame the mirror. We divert responsibility for the reflection we are shown onto others, but like everything seen in a mirror, we are seeing our reality reversed, and a different approach must be taken to affect substantial and meaningful change. For example, if you feel frustrated or impatient, you may simply be an impatient person, at least in the particular context of a specific situation. When we are impatient towards another, we much prefer to blame the other person for making us feel this way. But instead, the mirror is only showing you an uncomfortable part of your own being—impatience. If you can find it within yourself to take responsibility and ownership for the feeling of impatience, you can proceed to the next step by asking yourself the question: "Do I strive to be a more patient person?"

If your answer is "yes," try first to understand your motivations for selecting this response and why you chose it. Did you choose it because society tells you that you *should* be more patient? Was it your religious convictions and associated doctrine that makes you feel like you *should* choose to be more patient? Are you afraid of how others will perceive you and your ego-identity *should* you not openly choose to be more patient?

While there is not necessarily a "good" or "bad" reason for choosing to be more patient, it is important to understand your motivations for choosing that path. If it is not a choice made out of a deep internal conviction as something that you truly desire for yourself and your life, the efforts to grow your patience in this situation and other trying events may lack substance, and the effects of choosing to develop patience may be only temporary. In this case, patience would not be part of the deep you, but only your fabricated ego-identity. Though you can make whatever choice you like and for whatever reason you'd like, take some time to truly understand your motivations behind any choice that you ever make. Are you choosing it for you, or choosing it because it is what you think you should do based on the preconditioning, pressures, and influences of your external world?

Once you understand your personal motivation for choosing to become a more patient person, you can choose to no longer be frustrated or impatient in this situation. Instead, you can laud and appreciate it for the wonderful opportunity to learn more about yourself and grow into what you strive to become. You can only grow your patience and become a patient person by choosing patience and actively demonstrating it in the very situation where it is challenged. Therefore, rather than detest and curse the frustrating situation or person you believed was responsible for your feeling, you can leverage it and allow yourself to be developed through it. Making a choice for growth is seldom easy and is regularly uncomfortable, though when we shift our perspective and align it with our true desires of who we believe ourselves to be in this world, the challenge presented turns itself into an exquisite, one-of-a-kind opportunity. You may never feel ready to make the choice to choose patience, or you'll formulate excuses as to why this situation is somehow different and doesn't apply, or the person you've assigned blame to is outside of the scope of your willingness to develop patience within yourself. If you instead choose not to grow your patience in this opportunity, that is always your choice to make, and there is nothing wrong with it; however, by not choosing patience, you are also indirectly choosing to remain frustrated and annoyed with the situation at hand by surrendering your power to another. With this, you must also accept full ownership of the situation and your feelings, as they are a direct product of the choice you have made. There is nothing outside of yourself responsible for the way you are feeling or the lack of patience shown to you by the mirror of reality. Furthermore, situations that test your patience will reappear in your life in countless ways until you make the choice to challenge yourself and change the source of the reflected image you see. You will only see the change in the world that you wish to see when you realize that the pain, suffering, disappointment, and impatience you experience exist only inside of you.

Remember, you always have a choice. Dependent on the situation, you may be able to physically walk away from it. You may be able to scream and yell at this individual. You may choose to engage in a physical altercation with them. Or, you may choose to reframe your belief about them and the situation. From a purely selfish standpoint, you can view this as an opportunity for self-development and growth, as previously discussed. Alternatively, you can reframe your mindset and belief system and choose to see this person as someone who is struggling internally and is in deep emotional pain, which is the ultimate cause of their actions that presently disturb or trigger you. Perhaps, you speculate, they haven't been able to make their mortgage payment this month and are set to be evicted tomorrow, or their mother is in the hospital with a terminal illness, and they have hardly slept as they have been tending to her care for the past several months. While this isn't to advocate that you change your perspective of this situation on pure speculation and fictional stories to make your experience of others in your life more palatable, it is utilized here to refocus the awareness inside of you in the present moment that you yourself are living in a subjective reality, one that you've created for yourself. As the sole member of your subjective reality, you've adopted various belief systems and assumptions about others and the world. The perfect combination of your assumptions, blind spots, core beliefs, and perception of the world, all viewed through your own subjective reality, have allowed you to find frustration in this situation. Your choices have created your subjective reality, which has given birth to the very way you have perceived this situation and how you feel about it. Understanding this, you are never trapped, nor are you ever forced to feel a certain way or act out in any way. This is always your choice, and no one has the power or influence to change this. If you continue to defer responsibility and assign blame to things outside you, you must realize that you are only trapping yourself within your own mind through your conscious or subconscious choices. Until this is fully actualized and implemented, you will continue to experience pain, discomfort, and disappointment at the hand of others and your experience of the world that you call "reality." If you ever desire to evolve beyond this perspective, you must take responsibility for your feelings and make another choice for yourself. It's **always** your choice. There are **no** exceptions.

Use the mirror of reality to see yourself more clearly from the flawless reflection it provides, which often is shown through encounters with other people. This mirror does not only exist in the world you observe around you externally but inside of you as well through your thoughts, feelings, and ideas. When you gaze carefully enough, you will find this mirror, as well as the reflection and guidance it provides, in every shred of your internal and external existence. The mirror can be seen as you lie in bed with your eyes closed. The mirror can be seen in your dreams, both awake and asleep. The mirror can be seen in your internal dialog and self-talk. The mirror can be seen in your fears, self-doubt, and the limitations you perceive. The mirror can be seen by observing your current state of life, your income, your relationships, and your quality of life in this very moment. It accurately reflects every element of who you believe yourself to be. This includes your very own emotions, every thought, and every feeling that you experience in every single moment. With this, you should **never deny** your version of reality, nor should you deny any feelings or emotions you are experiencing, no matter what others have told you or what you might have told yourself. Do not condemn yourself for anything you see, think, or feel, as this would be the ultimate denial of your deepest and most profound truths. Before anything can be fully realized for what it truly is, it must first be seen and accepted exactly as it has presented itself to you. Let these emotions, thoughts, and experiences flow through you as you fully embrace them. Once embraced and acknowledged, you can begin the journey of understanding them and why you feel the way that you do in that moment. Though it may take some time, you'll soon realize that the very way in which you are feeling or thinking, whether pleasant or unpleasant, is a direct result of a previous choice to select your subjective reality and a choice you've made in this moment.

This mirrored reality has the ability to serve you as an oracle, or all-seeing eye, that provides a continual and unrelenting opportunity to see the deepest parts of yourself with the utmost clarity while operating outside of traditional timeline constraints and the perceptive realities you've accepted for yourself. The mirror will show you the beauty and love present in this world, or it will show you the pain, suffering, and hate. If you dislike, despise, or hate what you see in this omniscient mirror, don't despair. **Be grateful** for the opportunity to see yourself *exactly* as you are. Be gentle, kind, and patient with yourself. Do not take your frustration out on the mirror or seek to destroy the mirror; it is here to serve and guide you, should you allow it. Celebrate the mirror and welcome it into your life as a tool for growth and development. It is never the mirror's fault for the reflection it serves back to you, as it is only reflecting what you have decided to be and what you have chosen for yourself inside of your subjective reality, nothing more and nothing less. The mirror can never deceive you, for it is only you that can ever deceive yourself. Do not kill the reflective messenger for the unwanted news it may deliver, but instead, thank the messenger for its generous service to you and for you. From there, it's up to you and your choice to decide what steps to take and what decisions to make with the message you receive. If you wish to see, feel, or experience something different in this world, you must seek to change the very image that the mirror is reflecting, yourself and your perception.

3. THE EVASIVE TRUTH

Even as we analyze the same objective world, we interpret it differently. We can stare truth right in the eyes, with our greatest focus and purest intent, yet receive anything but. Anyone who claims to know the truth does not know, nor can they ever. For the very manner in which they have arrived at the "truth" would first demand the requisite adoption of such a perceptual bias that they indeed can see the truth and know the truth when they see it. We are each the gatekeepers of our own truth. We can believe something to be as true as we wish it to be, independent of its grounding in any objective or material reality, and it will always be true to us, but never to another in the same way. Any "truth" anyone may arrive at can only be interpreted and accepted as truth by their own self, through their decisions and choices, as we individually command our own gates of acceptance.

Deception, on the other hand, is the intentional effort to persuade another from an honest interpretation of their truth, through manipulation and murky-making, so that the victim's subjective interpretation of events is covertly encouraged to maneuver further away from the objective truth that already hides beneath their existing biases. To intentionally deceive or manipulate another further from a truth for one's personal gain is not a gain at all. Dishonesty towards others may *appear* to yield temporary "gain," but only in ways that are not eternal, permanent, or otherwise meaningful, which can only fade or falter from you. This intentional dishonesty and externally broadcasted deception can only ever aid and magnify your own **internal deception** within than what you may have imposed upon others without. While we may never individually know truth, we further distance ourselves from it through dishonest and malicious intent to interfere with another's judgment. But in this way, our own interpretations of truth are subjective due to the presence of our own internal deceptions and biases, which cloud our own judgment. **Honesty is not synonymous with truth** and ought to not be improperly conflated. Honest and sincere communication of a personally held truth to others may intend to convey one's own subjective interpretation of reality sincerely, but it does not define objective truth in itself, as it is wholly unable to do so. Should we consider otherwise, we are only deceiving ourselves as a way to preemptively form incomplete conclusions or forcefully classify the world and events around us, to obtain a sense of knowing and peace, even if objectively false.

We seek truth, we desire truth, and we find peace in the sincere belief that we know, even if the knowing isn't true knowing, and the truth isn't true truth. To become closer to the truth, we must go within and seek it within ourselves honestly while battling our own assumptions, blind spots, and sophisticated internal deceptions that we are **all** equally subjected and vulnerable to. We must acutely challenge everything we believe and identify all of the assumptions we may be making unknowingly. This individualized journey, though difficult, is necessary to become closer to the ultimate truths in life. Though we may never fully arrive, we must strive to draw ever nearer to the truth, desiring to be in the constant presence of it while pursuing it with relentless passion, grace, patience, love, an open heart, and an open mind. Truth isn't always easy to consume as it reveals itself to you; therefore, we may deny the very truth that we seek when found or retranslate it to something more palatable that better aligns with our preferred reality. With this, we adopt a truth that is not the truth at all, providing the faux peace we desire in knowing it while deceiving ourselves to the contrary. Truth can sometimes be painful to hear or see, especially when it reveals things about ourselves that make known our stubbornness, internal deceptions, and the games we play with ourselves and others, often unknowingly, as a protection mechanism from the discomfort of facing such truths about ourselves. Therefore, to mask the distressing or uncomfortable truths, we tell ourselves instead that our truths are more valid or more accurate than another's, effectively, if not only for the moment, deferring responsibility and attention outward. We tell ourselves that the problem is with another or the world, which we blame as the cause for our unhappiness, pain, and suffering. We attempt to change others and the world around us through force and blame assignment, rather than look within, where the true truth may only ever reside. The truth can never be outside us, but only within, which is often the last place we look. When we do look, we do not look for long, or we look casually from a place of bias and defense. Even if we tell ourselves that we are looking with an open mind, this is often a strategy employed as part of our deceptive mindset to avoid, or overlook, the uncomfortable truths residing within.

With the stated desire for truth, we ought to dedicate ourselves to the relentless pursuit of it, to become intimately involved with it, and progress consistently towards it through every thought, action, and present moment. Truth only seems evasive in nature, but truth never changes, nor does it move, evolve, or actively work to evade our gaze. Our misconceptions of truth stem solely from our inherently subjective interpretations of it and reality. To bring the truth about more expeditiously in our lives, we must be willing to be honest with ourselves, as well as honest with others. This will encourage others to find their own truths as well, in their own ways unique to them, thereby drawing you nearer to your own. Through the sincere application of humility in this pursuit, knowing that we can never know truth wholly and completely, we can step ever closer to it. The degree to which we express humility and honesty with ourselves about truth and our unknowingness of it determines the degree to which we may become more familiar to it and with it. The closer we get to the truth, the closer others get to their truths. The closer others get to their truths, the closer we get to ours. This becomes a reinforcing cycle, but it begins and ends, within you alone. To cast blame upon another for the lack of your internal truth, regardless of their action, perceived dishonesty, or unfair treatment, is only a misdirection and internal deception, as it distracts from the journey within yourself, a journey only you can quest. Truth always brings clarity to our perception of an otherwise murky, cloudy, or confusing world. Though, the world itself is not actually murky or cloudy; it only appears as such due to our inability to interpret it accurately. As we reign in truth within ourselves, we also reign in clarity. As we reign in clarity, we reign in peace. As we reign in peace, we reign in love and gratitude, which can only ever yield additional and deeper truths in other aspects of our minds, lives, and souls, providing exponentially compounding effects each and every time this cycle repeats.

Truth is constant.

Truth is absolute.

Truth is immutable.

Truth never changes, for it is only our incomplete interpretation and individualized perception of it that can ever change. A truth that changes cannot be a truth at all. A truth to one may not be a truth to another, but "truth" in this context is not the enduring and inviolable truth, only an internally held permutation of it. For one to regard themselves as the holder of supreme truth only serves one of the greatest deceits to themselves. If one believes they hold the truth, they will cease their pursuit of it while condemning or judging others for not holding or arriving at the same definitive "truth." We may only hold versions of the truth, filtered through many layers of subjective abstraction, but never the inviolable truth as it stands. To further deceive ourselves, for reasons of comfort or to establish relative superiority to another, we may feign humility by admitting we don't know the full truth but claim to be relatively closer to it than another. When this occurs, we have only stepped further away from it, as one who claims to know the truth or to be closer to it than another can only be deceiving themselves.

If one can never know the truth and our version of truth can only be internalized in our subjective realities, does the real, objective, immutable, and constant truth matter? If it's only true in each's subjective reality, which affects our perception of the self and others, altering our very thoughts, actions, and behaviors, does the actual truth matter?

If not, why not?

If so, why so?

If not, what will you choose to believe and accept as your truth, which is always your choice, based on your subjective interpretation?

If so, at what lengths will you go to align more closely with the ultimate and immutable truths of your perceived being and perceived existence?

How will you treat your version of truth within yourself?

How will you treat the truth held by others that does not align with your truth?

Will you exert effort to protest the truth of others, or accept their truth as their truth, and your truth as your truth, without the employment of a fabricated superiority or validity ranking system in the attempt to compare and contrast that which cannot ever be measured?

Do you want your truth to be demeaned, or respected by others, when among those who don't agree with your truth, as they hold their own? The very behavior from others you desire towards your internalized version of the truth, consider embodying the active practice of that same desired behavior towards others regarding the truths they hold.

What is truth?

The choice is yours, as it can only ever be.

4. UNDERSTANDING CORE BELIEFS

The story and truth we provide ourselves are a product of the choices we have made to perceive and interpret our life and its happenings, which stem from our core beliefs. But where do our core beliefs come from?

Are they something we receive as an intrinsic part of our very being?

Or are core beliefs buckets of intellectual knowledge that we have chosen to intellectually apply to ourselves through our subjective interpretation of life experiences?

Are we even consciously aware of our deepest core beliefs, or have they become a seemingly automatic part of how we perceive "reality"?

Do we ever revisit our core beliefs? Can core beliefs be changed?

First, let's define the word **belief** as it appears in many English dictionaries:

- an **acceptance** that a statement is true or that something exists
- **trust**, **faith**, or **confidence** in someone or something
- an **opinion** or **conviction**
- an **attitude** that something is the case

There is a common theme between each of these definitions, which involves the element of **choice**. Though core beliefs often feel locked in, unchangeable, or objectively factual, our deepest-held beliefs are still the result of the **intellectual choices** we have decided to make for ourselves. We may have made these choices so early on in our lives that certain beliefs seem to be a concrete part of who and what we are, but nonetheless, we still chose them into our existence. Once fully accepted and integrated into our subconscious habitual mind and our constructs of thinking, we seldom revisit them. Further, everything we say, do, perceive, interpret, or think stems out of and from our chosen core beliefs. Every choice we make after we fully integrate a core belief builds and stacks upon all previously accepted core beliefs, creating what often becomes an unstable tower of incredible assumptions that we incorrectly internalize and classify as unquestionable truth. Like a skyscraper, the base and foundation tend to be broader, but as the tower ascends upwards, its width and scope do not expand, and instead, it begins to narrow and shrink the taller it climbs. This tower cannot become consistently wider than the base or foundation it is set upon without causing massive instability. We tend to lean on our core beliefs so significantly that we will endure much pain, suffering, confusion, and disappointment in life instead of revisiting the very core belief structure responsible for these experiences, impacting every element of our own perception.

More often than not, we have become unaware of the depths and significance of our core beliefs, and perhaps worse, that it was ever our choice to make. Until we allow ourselves to see that it was and always has been our choice to make in the establishment of our deepest-held truths and beliefs, we will continually blame others and the world around us for unpleasant things that are ultimately a result of our own perceptive flaws and misunderstandings, all while continuing to build an increasingly unstable tower of assumptions inside of ourselves. Core beliefs are not just reserved for the "big" beliefs; they also modify the way you view yourself, others, and your relationship with them and to them. If your core belief is that we are all part of the human race, that we are all hurting, and we ought just to spread love in this world, everything that happens to you in this world will be viewed through that particular lens. For example, what if you got cut off in traffic? Or someone stole your purse? Or a customer at work was very rude and aggressive towards you for what seemed like no reason at all? For each of these, you may be more inclined to demonstrate patience, see the pain in others, and choose to be a light and love for them rather than retaliate with anger and rage. If, instead, you held a differing core belief that everyone is selfish and it's a dog-eat-dog world out there, you may view and react to the same situations very differently, seemingly automatically and without realizing why you are feeling the way you are feeling. Regardless of the situation, pleasant or unpleasant, you will interpret all of the events and happenings of your life through the perception caused directly by your core beliefs, which are always products of **your choices**. Feel free to swap the beliefs and scenarios with anything you may believe about yourself, the world, or your relationship to others and evaluate how altering even a single core belief may very well change your perception about the world you find yourself living in.

Before we go any further, this next section of the book may be particularly triggering, upsetting, or difficult to accept. With this, the intent of this section is not to push a certain viewpoint as superior or diminish and shame any other viewpoint. It also is not intended to aimlessly peddle what some may consider to be tin-hat conspiracy theories. Quite simply, the examples used here are intentionally controversial in nature, but if you are open and willing to set your own biases and beliefs aside as you continue reading, you can actively dissect the essential building blocks of your own belief system. This may be uncomfortable, but it is your choice alone to proceed, as well as the depth in which you choose to allow yourself to engage ultimately. When you understand your beliefs and see them in a new light, you may also indirectly obtain a better understanding, appreciation, and respect for others who may not adhere to your preferred belief system. You may find some of your deepest-held beliefs challenged as you understand the assumptions and choices you've unknowingly made throughout your life to construct them. In some cases, this may be destabilizing, though, with persistence and compassion for yourself, you'll step away from this far more assured and confident in your selected belief systems. Either way, the purpose is to explore your core beliefs, the assumptions you've accepted to make them your reality, and understand the motivations for choosing to associate with your particular beliefs. If you find yourself triggered, frustrated, annoyed, irritated, destabilized, or offended in any way, take note of this feeling. Take a moment to allow yourself to feel what it is you are feeling and why you may be feeling this way. If you experience any negative emotions, be gentle and patient with yourself; these emotions do not indicate a failure of any kind. In actuality, any emotions or feelings you experience at this time are **always positive** if you choose to listen to them. They will inevitably guide you to your deeper truths, even if the exact origin or reason of your feelings is presently unknown or misunderstood. Use them as your guide and take the time that you need. Lastly, on this note, this warning is not so that you enter into the subsequent sections with your guard up and on edge, but instead to make you aware of any feelings that come up. If you find that you have already risen your guard in preparation for whatever you anticipate may be forthcoming, sit with that and feel it, as it is indicative of early progress towards the desired internal work you desire.

ASSUMPTIVELY CONCOCTED "TRUTHS"

To begin the exploration of this idea, we will first take a dive into something that the overwhelming majority of us consider as a fundamentally undeniable truth, something so certain for most of us that we may never think to revisit or question: **Is the earth flat or round?**

Straight away, this may already sound a bit preposterous to you to be used as an example, or you may even be thinking something along the lines of, "Okay... here we go with the conspiracy theories." Whatever it was that you might have felt at the mere mention of challenging and revisiting this often-mocked flat earth debate, **simply watch** your feelings as we continue forward while remembering how useful any of the emotions and reactions you catch yourself feeling are for your internal growth and development. There are no right and wrong feelings, so long as you can catch them and notice them. Let's take a moment to understand how you may have arrived at what seems to be a solid, unquestionable conclusion about the allegedly round planet you believe yourself to be living on. How have you arrived at this conclusion?

Here are some of the most likely ways you've adopted this belief as pure fact:

- You were taught this by your teachers and schoolbooks as a young and imaginative child.
- You've seen a round earth represented in countless posters, pictures, documentaries, and movies.
- You've read incredibly complex scientific literature about it, published by the world's greatest minds, detailing how it rotates, the precise gravitational pull it produces as a result of its imperfect spherical shape, and the mathematical algorithms that can be applied in rocket science and other studies to prove it to be true.
- Your parents have **accepted** it and **confirmed** it to be true.
- Your peers have **accepted** it and **confirmed** it to be true.
- Society and the mainstream media have **accepted** it and **confirmed** it to be true.
- The "flat earthers" movement that *somehow* still exist are publicly shamed and ridiculed for their alleged ignorance of the facts, labeled outcasts of society, and mocked for their continued conferences and documentaries. This social mockery of an opposing belief system serves as an effective deterrent for you, or others, to even consider it.

In addition to these points, try to think of any other reasons not listed here for why you believe the earth is quite certainly round and not flat. Express caution with any other reasons you may contrive and take note of the justifications you assign to each of these reasons.

Most of the reasons listed here and any of the ones you've thought of likely serve as excellent "evidence" that provides you with great confidence that the earth is undoubtedly round. The goal here is not to discredit any opinion, belief, or information source or to convince you that the earth is flat. Further, this isn't at all to insinuate that you've somehow been misled. Instead, we must simply seek to understand the **assumptions** we make when **accepting** a **belief** as an objective fact inside of our **subjective** realities. We were not born with the inherent knowledge that the earth was round, and the seemingly first historical reference alluding to the assumption that the earth might be round came as early as 500 B.C. by the Greek philosopher Pythagoras. This implies that our belief about a round earth was something that had to be taught or shown to us intellectually, rather than knowledge that everyone knew instinctively upon being aware of their own consciousness and existence. Therefore, how can you, or anyone, know with absolute certainty if the earth is round? The short answer is, you don't, and you can't, even if you *think* you do. You are only ever capable of making an educated guess based on the data, as it has been made available to you, and through your subjective interpretation of your relevant life experiences. Let's take a look at some of the assumptions you would have to make to claim with one-hundred percent certainty that the earth is round. Again, any claim to complete certainty is only your own internal deception of certainty. In actuality, your belief is exclusively based on a series of **educated guesses** and **assumptions**, **not** objective truths.

At this point, many of you may be triggered and disagree with what has been shared thus far. Rest assured, it's incredibly common and expected that you might have extreme resistance to this idea and the concepts referred to. Oftentimes, people have already sharply rebutted with something along the lines of:

"Yea, I guess I kind of see your point conceptually, **but** there's just no way it could be flat. I mean, it's all over history and in science books. We've known that it is round for so long. If it were flat, wouldn't we hear about it from an observer or scientist somewhere in the world by now? It's just not possible or likely at this point to be any other way."

Do you see what has happened with the response? Anything after the "but" and subsequent justifications and reasoning in the response is purely intellectually regurgitated rhetoric, serving as a defense to one's own chosen belief for something they cannot ever truly know. No one is trying to convince them that the world has been flat all along; in fact, not a single argument or shred of evidence has even been provided in an attempt to convince them that we live on a flat planet, yet a defensive position has been established. We have only asked them to analyze and observe how they might have arrived at this belief. Much like the gentle wiggling of a low-level Jenga block located near the base of the structure, the simple challenge to something that they have adopted as unquestionable truth in life has caused significant reaction and defense. The mere questioning of this core belief caused frustration and resistance, in which they **quickly step back** into **their ideal reality** and then begin making statements **from** the **comfort zone** of their familiar **core belief**. They will also blame the questioner, or in this case, the author of this book, for the reaction they have triggered. Remember, we are only asking you to explore the origins of your belief about the shape of the earth, which really doesn't affect your day-to-day reality, relationships, or experience of life, yet it may still provoke a notable emotional reaction and resistance. If this has all occurred as a result of questioning the shape of our planet, how much more profound could this reaction be if we questioned beliefs that most tend to be far more passionate about, such as religion, political views, or something of especially controversial significance, like abortion?

Below are some additional assumptions you've made, unconscionable or not, to arrive at your **subjective conclusion** that the earth is round. You can simply respond to these assumptions listed here internally with "true" or "false." For this, it doesn't matter how ridiculous, certain, or commonplace any of these points are, even if you feel that any reasonable person would agree or disagree with them. Simply acknowledge the assumptions you've made, which you cannot ever prove for yourself, without first having to make additional assumptions to support any prior assumptions:

- You **trust** the education system and teachers, **believing** that they would not intentionally mislead you or deceive you.

- You **trust** the **accuracy** of the science textbooks you've been provided with that allegedly share an objective and conclusive reality.

- You **trust** the **beliefs and opinions** of your parents, peers, and the greater society.
  - If they themselves are **certain** of this alleged truth, you ought to be as well; after all, who are **you** to question it? Though **how** can they be **certain** of this **truth**? They have **formed** their **opinion** and classified it as a **certainty** in precisely the same manner that you have become certain of your opinion. Opinions are inherently subjective. **Opinions**, by definition, are **belief-based** and cannot become fact on their own. Even the strongest and most compelling opinions are incapable of becoming fact.
  - If one other person has an opposing opinion, it may

seem inconsequential. But if one million people share an opinion, we view it as significant and commonly mistake it for truth. Yet, they have made their own assumptions in their own subjective realities to form their own beliefs and opinions. Even if a substantial number of individuals shared the same collective **opinion**, it could **only ever be** your **acceptance** of their **opinion** that would allow it to root inside of you as your own opinion or belief while masquerading as truth.

- o How many of the aforementioned one million people formed their **opinion** based on the high number of others who appeared to share the same **opinion** collectively? Even if unintentionally communicated by the masses, this is a form of peer pressure, which clouds our ability to make our own free choice out of fear of isolation or ridicule for holding an unpopular decision. We are more likely to accept the opinion held by the masses as fact than to challenge or explore it for ourselves completely untethered. Aside from this, the education system in the United States does not allow untethered exploration in this manner. As in, should a student actively question or challenge the materials presented to them in school and choose not to regurgitate and propagate something they do not choose to believe for themselves, this will result in a failing grade, as well as ridicule, judgment, and isolation from others.

- o What if the significant masses did not share this particular **opinion**? Would you still have arrived at this conclusion regardless? And if it wasn't shared collectively, would it even appear in academic literature to the degree that it does, **as objective fact**?

- When reading about a round earth from the greatest scientific minds and the tremendous research they've conducted throughout their dedicated and passionate lives, you are assuming that their research is wholly competent and error-free. Remember, we **all** live in a subjective reality, which places even the world's greatest scientists in a subjective reality of their own interpretations. Assuming no malintent whatsoever, they've made various assumptions themselves along the way in their research that they have presented to you, and the world, as factual.

- Imagine for a moment you built your own rocket to fly yourself successfully into orbit, then once in outer space, you looked down on earth, and it appeared round. You may state confidently at this point that you can now conclusively affirm that the earth is round after all; however, **even in this scenario,** you would be making an **assumption**. You would be **assuming** that what you believe to be seeing with your own eyes is what is truly there in front of you as you interpret it to be. You would **assume** that even with all of the remaining mysterious unknowns of space and the very origins of life, consciousness, and this human experience, that it is **absolutely impossible** for the combination of the atmosphere's particles, bending light waves in an oxygen-free environment, and other visual phenomena to form an incredible optical illusion that has led the way to your perceptual visualization of a round planet, that may otherwise truly be flat, or another shape entirely.

Regardless of how much intellectual evidence appears to point to a certain objective truth, we must be **willing** to acknowledge **the assumptions** we've made along the way towards our core belief. The very moment you've accepted something as an absolute fact, you've undoubtedly created an associated assumption, which, when not honestly acknowledged, yields a blind spot. The more strongly held your particular belief is, the more you view it as absolute truth. In turn, the deeper held a particular belief is, the more difficult it will be to see beyond your self-concocted blind spot. For clarity of intent, this isn't to suggest that deeply held beliefs of any kind are discouraged; in many cases, beliefs are necessary through various moments and periods of our lives and for the expansion of our own knowledge and interpretations. **Beliefs**, and the associated **assumptions**, are a **requirement** for discovery and exploration. We may hold certain beliefs for our entire lives without changing or altering them; this is completely acceptable. It is only your lack of awareness of your **choice** to **accept** various **assumptions** as reality without question that brings about a dangerously limited pattern of thinking. Some patterns may never be broken, even with what appears to be sincere intent and willpower to overcome them. This is precisely why we must use the mirror of reality as our guide to help understand ourselves better as we listen to each of our feelings, never denying or outright rejecting our current version of reality and using our imagination to challenge the status quos that we have chosen for our life. Even with what we consider to be our deepest-held core beliefs, they cannot ever be more than **choices** that we have made for ourselves inside of our subjective realities, riddled with assumptions, and vulnerable to our own perceptual biases.

There is nothing wrong with leveraging assumptions to create beliefs, so long as we are aware that they exist inside of us. When we are unaware or fail to honestly acknowledge the assumptions that we have **chosen** inside of us, they become true blind spots and tether our ability to think clearly, openly, and freely. This is precisely where our beliefs begin to turn into the skyscraper that becomes increasingly narrow the taller it grows. When we fill in the gaps with assumptions in order to arrive at a particular conclusion, we seldomly revisit them or sincerely challenge them, especially as the tower representative of our belief system becomes sky high. Like the Jenga tower, should we begin to wiggle and nudge one of the lower blocks closer to the base of the tower, we subconsciously fear that the entire thing may collapse. Even if the lower block appears loose to the touch, we ignore it to keep the greater tower erect out of our need for comfort, stability, and predictability. Everything that we say, do, or think from the position of a seemingly objective conclusion inside of us keeps those assumptions alive as the unstable tower continues to climb ever taller.

As core beliefs reside among the deepest layers of ourselves, they completely alter our resulting perception of life, usually without us even realizing it. Should we realize that our beliefs alter our perceptions of life, we may still be unaware of the degree to which they truly affect us. In this way, our core beliefs give way to a rudimentary perceptual filter that highlights what we do, and do not, pay attention to in this world. It changes our interpretation of the already selective things allowed through the initial filter. Essentially, most of what we *think* we consciously observe in this world is a result of **multiple stages of perceptual filtration**, and it all begins with our chosen core beliefs. Long before you get to observe and make "informed" and "educated" decisions about the world around you, your subconscious mind and internal filtration processes have already translated and autocorrected much of the information ultimately presented to your conscious mind to align with your biases. When we are unaware of this process as well as the core beliefs and triggers inside us, we observe our lives through a peephole. Much like actual peepholes used in common doorways, this peephole not only limits the entirety of what we see but also warps the already-narrow image coming through. We are effectively operating from this limited viewpoint with every decision we make and every feeling we experience in every moment. When we apply this understanding to the prior scenario, we understand that **people will see what they choose to see**. Those who have decided that a flat earth is their reality will find every piece of evidence that proves or validates their point while ignoring or discrediting any equally valid evidence presented by the opposing side. They will view life through this lens, filtering out anything that discredits their viewpoint while disproportionately amplifying anything that validates it. Regardless of which belief you may hold or which side of any belief you may be on, the perceptual filters active on **each and every one of us** operate in the **same exact way**. We seem to understand this concept when in opposition with someone else and in regard to them specifically, but very rarely, if ever, see it operating to the same degree within ourselves from where we might stand.

When we become frustrated that something or someone does not align with a core belief that we hold, we will blame the world or the actions and opinions of others long before we use our own emotions and our own reactions as a guide to look within. Our own reactions and feelings are beautiful tools that, should we choose to use them as such, provide incredible clarity to our inner world that we do not pay much attention to otherwise. There are seemingly infinite things that we may do before looking inwards, if at all. We will defend our position gratuitously, make excuses, deny evidence or proof that opposes it, and openly judge others for their ignorance. Pair this with an opinion or belief that contradicts the mainstream narrative of society or of a group of people, and we will intensify our criticisms in an effort to belittle their unpopular and "outlandish" opinion by using peer pressure in our favor. Many will go as far as to lie to others, and themselves, even to the extent of censoring or subconsciously suppressing their own memories and experiences. We do all of this to protect and defend our core beliefs, many of which we may not even consciously be aware that we hold, or the reason why we hold them.

5. CONFLICTING CORE BELIEFS

We initially explored the idea of core beliefs, assumptions, blind spots, and how they work in shifting our perceptions of life, using a flat earth as an example. While this scenario doesn't have an immediate impact on the day-to-day lives of most individuals, it was *still* triggering in some way. As a reminder, be as attentive to your feelings as you are able throughout not only the next example but the entire book as we prepare to dive into a topic that may be more contentious than the former. We use varying examples throughout the book in an attempt to produce the desired outcome of understanding the principles of core beliefs. The examples used are no more than placeholders to help us achieve this purpose. As with all of the example scenarios provided within this book, the concepts they express can be applied to many other situations as well once understood in greater depth. If the examples shared in the book do not necessarily apply to you, attempt to understand the concepts and fundamentals of what is being discussed, then apply it to other more relevant situations present in your personal life. Therefore, we mustn't place excessive focus or attention on the examples or the issues discussed themselves, but rather, the principles of core beliefs they seek to highlight.

For this next example, we explore the same fundamentals of core beliefs outlined in the previous chapter and apply them to perhaps a more applicable and common scenario: the opposing core beliefs of Christianity and atheism.

Like believers of a greater God or religion like Christianity, atheists have arrived at this conclusion by choice, based on their subjective perceptions and interpretation of the life they have experienced. Even if they were initially raised religiously by their family, their experience and interpretation of life have placed the perspective in their mind that God does not exist. **This is their reality**. Everything that they perceive in life upon acceptance of this belief will only further validate and solidify their beliefs within themselves. **We see only what we choose to see**, and we typically only see the things that align with our core beliefs as they provide us stability, comfort, validation, and security, regardless of any underlying truths or objective reality that may be present. We treat our own views, beliefs, and opinions as factual and absolute for ourselves. For those who believe in God and religion, the concept of atheism may be seen as ignorant or simply as someone who is greatly lost or misguided. They may also suggest that the atheist is refusing to acknowledge a greater power out of their own fear to address and turn away from the "sinful life," as dictated by their own religious doctrine and convictions, thereby imposing their beliefs on the atheist, who holds a differing belief set.

Whether we are willing or able to admit this to ourselves, we tend to default into the mindset that what we choose to believe is objectively more factual than any other viewpoint that opposes our own. When we feel this way, we have forgotten that our own subjective version of reality is completely unique to another's subjective view. During these lapses, we often impose the structures, limitations, and ideals of our own chosen beliefs onto others that don't share the same belief, effectively rendering any efforts to engage in any meaningful or respectful communication not only a fruitless endeavor but one that is likely to create resentment, offense, and frustration for all parties involved. For example, if an atheist shares with a Christian that they do not believe in God or the words of the Holy Bible, what meaningful impact might this Christian have by responding with something that does not align with the atheist's chosen belief set? We must be willing to meet one another where the other stands. Should we only speak from within the confines of our own belief system, while expecting others to see the fallibility in their beliefs using the subjective measurements residing within our own, we may as well be speaking different and incompatible languages entirely.

A Christian might attempt to coerce an atheist into

accepting their belief through a scriptural reference such as, "For the wages of sin is death, but the gift of God is eternal life in Christ Jesus our Lord" (Romans 6:23, NIV) or perhaps the even more widely known passage of love, "For God so loved the world that He gave his one and only Son, that whoever believes in Him shall not perish, but have everlasting life" (John 3:16, NIV). For the Christian, John 3:16 is a beautifully elegant and reassuring passage that demonstrates the loving and caring God that they experience as part of their Christian faith and belief. To the atheist, who had just stated to the Christian that they do not believe in God or what is written in the Holy Bible, these verses are devoid of all meaning. We must realize that when our chosen belief differs from one held by another, the rules, confines, and ideals that seem to exist concretely within our subjective reality do not apply to someone who has not accepted it, as we have, inside their own subjective reality. If we are ever to find peace within our own chosen beliefs or to understand the belief of another, we must first accept our own subjectivity completely and respect the other's right to their subjectivity. For any meaningful dialog ever to occur, we must also respect them and their internal process for arriving at their chosen belief, as their process for doing so is conceptually identical to our own. Remember that **both** views, beliefs, and realities are **equally subjective**, regardless of how strongly you hold to your personal beliefs. Consider taking a moment before moving onto the next paragraph to think of someone, or a group, that holds a differing belief that is difficult for you to understand, and perhaps, one that you may consider to be ignorant, blind, or deplorable. With this in mind, attempt to apply the idea that no one viewpoint can ever be superior or a more accurate version of reality than another, with both being equally subjective within each other's own reality. Additionally, reflect on the principles shared within the "The Evasive Truth" chapter, as each chapter is intended to build on the prior elements and examples.

With subjective realities and beliefs, it doesn't matter how much more educated, researched, experienced, or informed you believe yourself to be, as these serve only as internal deceptions and justifications to validate oneself. Even from this place, your belief is still inherently subjective and can only ever be subjective due to the foundational choices required. You, of course, are free to maintain your own opinion about what you think about your belief or their belief, or even their perceived credibility. Though, any opinion, no matter how strongly held, can ever truly dictate or define the reality of another, for another. This is often a triggering realization for many, and if you find yourself feeling triggered, violated, offended, or in blatant disagreement with this concept, consider taking a moment to rest and observe anything that you are feeling before continuing. It isn't necessarily important at this time to resolve and fully understand these feelings before continuing, but simply making a conscious note of it and recognizing its existence within you is sufficient. It is important to realize that anything that you may be feeling at this moment can only ever be a direct result of your perception, which is the product of a choice you've made from within your belief structures and chosen interpretation of your world in this present moment. Consider setting your intentions and manner of approach moving forward to understand yourself, your chosen beliefs, your triggers, and your own assumptions on a much deeper level. This is for you, not against you, only should you choose to recognize it as such. It is in the moments of challenge or confliction that realization and growth occur. Leading from that position, you will see yourself and the world around you with far more clarity, understanding, compassion, and peace. Place your focus solely within yourself and not with the intent of changing others.

If everyone's reality is subjectively interpreted and core beliefs are chosen by us individually through an internal processing of the life we've experienced, could anybody ever truly stake a claim that their belief or perception is superior to another, regardless of background, education, experience, or mainstream and popular opinions? To expand upon the brief challenge shared earlier in this chapter whereby you thought of an individual or group with an opposing belief to your own, assume that they, just like you, desire to be respected and they believe they are capable of making free and competent choices based on their unique interpretation of life as they've lived it. Also, assume that, like you, they are a well-meaning person with a good heart and are not intentionally malicious or inherently rude. Further, assume that they attempt to do their best in life not only for themselves but for those around them and the ones that they truly care for and that they have selected their path and associated choices from their own subjective interpretation of reality and unique experiences. You may not see this other in this light, but that is only when viewed through your currently applied perceptual bias. For now, employ your imagination and apply the recommended assumptions. With this individual or group in mind, along with the recommended assumptions, how can someone who believes themselves to be kind, well-intentioned, and good-natured, arrive at a completely opposing and unsatisfactory viewpoint to what you hold as true for yourself? We desperately wish others understood and agreed with our opinion, as we label them ignorant or blind, yet when the perspective is flipped and viewed through the eyes of the other, are they not likely viewing you, your subjective interpretation of reality, and your beliefs in a similar manner in which you view theirs? Do they not wish to be understood and respected for their opinions also? Even if the other maintains what appears to be a brazen superiority complex, does this require you to treat them in the same undesirable way in which they currently might be treating you? Is it not possible that they are not overtly disrespectful, but it is only your own improperly initiated defense mechanisms and perceptual lens that have made it so within the confines of your subjective reality? Or perhaps, could they be acting out in defense to the disrespect they have interpreted to be coming from you, whether or not you have intentionally subjected them to such treatment? Remember, it is the differences and variances in life, opinions, and opposing forces that provide us the opportunity to define ourselves in this world. Without one side, belief, ideal, or opinion, we quite simply cannot have the other. In this way, do we not require one another to hold and maintain the very viewpoint, ideals, traits, and characteristics we identify with so intimately? Without darkness, there could be no concept of light. We believe that we are always on the side of light and the other on the side of darkness, but the only true darkness is what resides within us when we do not free ourselves from the blind spots and assumptions we've made through our choices while continuing to operate within our preferred fabrication of reality. This is among the greatest of darkness and internal deceptions.

When we inadvertently view our core beliefs and ideals as an objective reality and assume that others who do not think, act, feel, or believe the same as we do are ignorant or misinformed, we are only blinding ourselves. To be very clear, there is **nothing** wrong with holding a belief so strongly that you would live, fight, and die for it; this is always your free choice to make. The sole intention here is to expose the choices **you** have made and the assumptions you have created through the formulation of your chosen belief system and the associated reality you've produced from it. Regardless of what your belief is or what another's may be, it is **your choice** to allow the opposing belief of another to strip you of your internal peace and contentment. When we feel violated, offended, or robbed of our own internal peace based on the actions or words of another, we must realize that we have chosen this internalized turmoil and outcome for ourselves by viewing this situation in the very way we are choosing to view it. Take for example, a Christian that holds their belief so strongly that their genuine and loving heart hurts and pains for the atheist in a very pure, kind, and honest way. They are saddened that this beautiful and lost soul will end up burning in hell for eternity if they aren't saved by accepting Christ into their life. With this scenario, they must realize that they've **chosen** this very narrative on how to view the situation by believing into the structures about sin, hell, and their own God-given purpose in life to bring others to Christ. Again, there is nothing wrong with this narrative, as many Christians that find themselves in these situations are acting out of place of true kindness and love and are well-intentioned. However, it is of critical importance that we understand that, at the deepest level, the way in which we see the world is directly a **product** of **our choice** to see it in the way we have **chosen** to see it. Remember, if any other person has the ability to view the world in an altered way than how you may presently experience and assert it to be, no matter how real it seems to you, it affirms categorically that subjectivity is at play. Subjectivity, by definition, can **never** be applied in only one direction.

6. FEAR TO UNRAVEL

Through the various examples explored, we can see how difficult it may be for most to see beyond the core beliefs that we've all accepted into our lives. In addition, the challenge, or even the mere existence of an opposing force, to one's chosen belief causes much discomfort and frustration, often producing a deferment of responsibility for the unpleasant feelings onto something or someone external rather than looking within. Though we understand that unraveling the origins of our core beliefs can be triggering, we also understand the necessity of doing so through the further exploration of them. In doing so, we must sincerely and wholeheartedly desire to discover our own blind spots and internal deceptions that keep our minds artificially tethered from seeing reality. In this chapter, we take the exploration into our core beliefs a step further to determine a few more of the underlying elements that cause this strong resistance to occur.

Much of what we feel and experience in life is temporary. Moods come and go. Emotions come and go. Possessions come and go. Even relationships come and go. But our core beliefs? These are among the most stable elements about us, and in many cases, are more stable and constant than what we perceive to be our own personalities. The word "stable" in this context should not be confused with factual, as we are still dealing with subjective realities. Instead, "stable" in that it does not often vary or change and is not generally prone to fly-by-night or whimsical alterations. Core beliefs that are adopted and integrated by one need not be rooted in any type of objective reality to exist within us. For example, if you were raised in a religious home to believe in God for your entire life, including up to the present, this core belief has outlasted even personality. You've become bolder, stronger, more courageous, or perhaps have become more fearful or guarded as a result of some painful life circumstances over the years. You've grown taller, you've gained and lost weight, you've switched jobs, you've graduated, you've moved to another country and have a new social circle, and beyond. Yet, among all of these life transitions and changes, some of your deepest-held core beliefs have remained. When we have held onto our core beliefs as long as we have, especially any lower-level blocks residing at the base of the skyscraper that consist of our many assumptions, we have learned to identify with them intimately, as if they were an undetachable part of us. We improperly associate with them as if they were our own true identity. This realization is where we begin to dwell deeper than before. Additionally, this is a primary factor as to why we become easily triggered or offended, as it feels like a direct attack on the very essence of not only what we think we are, but who.

With certain beliefs, we also tend to become easily triggered not only because we may perceive any challenge to our belief as an attack, but because the **contents and themes** of the belief may be very dire and a matter of life or death, according to the value system **contained within the belief**. We may not see the opposing person as ignorant, but we may see them as actively harmful, physically or otherwise, to another person or group of people or actively contrary to the furtherment of our own ideology. It may also be viewed undoubtedly as outright dangerous, within the context of that particular belief system, in the sense of spreading disinformation and propaganda that may harm the agenda or underlying mission statement of your belief. In this way, for every move the opposing party makes, you may "lose ground" with the mission intrinsic to your own beliefs. If we take core beliefs out of the equation and settle on any topic where there is direct competition for the same target audience, this has already become a frustrating situation to deal with. If even this relatively standard competition feels like a battle or a war of sorts, when core beliefs are added to the mix, it becomes exponentially more personal to the degree and depth that the belief is held.

Another factor in our hesitance to unravel our core beliefs and assumptions stems from our own insecurities. When we entrench ourselves so deeply inside our core beliefs and identify with them as ourselves and the building blocks start showing potential signs of wiggling loose, this can be terrifying. Though, we seldom admit this to ourselves or others as the source of our frustration or discontent, as we may be unaware of it consciously. Not only can it be very destabilizing to have a single core belief challenged, but should it be found that it wasn't at all what you originally thought and perhaps you were even "proved" wrong to some meaningful degree through this journey of internal exploration, this holds the potential to shake, disrupt, and jostle a person, and their perceived identity, to their core. Furthermore, if core beliefs and the assumptions made with each are stacked on top of one another, this might entail that if one core belief falls, it may immediately introduce a challenge to another held belief that required acceptance of the recently disintegrated one. In some cases, if one core belief falls, any of the beliefs that were accepted as a result of the deeper core belief must all be reconsidered through a new perspective. But even for the core beliefs that were not directly affected by the crumbling of this one, it may still cause you to question all others that you hold and believe to be objectively true. After all, you may have held a particular core belief so deeply and personally that you never thought it was possible that it could not be true. In this way, you may start exploring other "objective truths" and core beliefs inside of you, wondering what others may be built on assumptions, blind spots, ignorance, disinformation, or influences from society, friends, or family that you previously never called into question.

For anything that you believe, it may be a good time to reflect and ask yourself some honest questions. If you choose not to proceed and are not ready to explore your own assumptions and blind spots sincerely, that's perfectly acceptable, as it is your choice. It must be something that you are willing and ready to do, and even with genuine willingness, desire, and commitment, your own internal defenses and deceptions are not always easy to identify. It may be simpler to begin this practice by challenging other beliefs you hold that might be a bit easier to conceptualize in these earlier phases of exploration. By challenging relatively less important beliefs, you can begin to understand the assumptions you have made to arrive at your particular conclusion. Then, by analyzing and observing another, who might have arrived at an opposing opinion despite viewing the same objective world and information, this allows us to begin breaking down the process and awareness required. Though challenging the beliefs sitting closer to the top of your tower might be easier to conceptualize in these earlier phases, you must understand and be acutely aware that you are still inherently bound by the assumptions of the beliefs that reside beneath it in which this belief relies upon.

To continue our understanding of the assumptions we make, we will use a simple example that may feel a bit obtuse or out of place for some; however, this example was chosen carefully for a specific purpose due to its simplicity and ability to identify common assumptions that we make without realizing we have made them, even if seemingly grounded in what many might consider "common sense." The intellectual justifications you apply, or classification of absurdness, to the various assumptions, matters not. We must strive to identify **all assumptions**, many of which we unintentionally brush over, leaving smears and smudges in their wake as they create blind spots in our perceptual gaze. For this next example, perhaps you see on the news broadcast camera footage showcasing fire and smoke on a faraway mountaintop. The news reports this "live and breaking" coverage, as they state a small plane has appeared to crash onto this mountaintop, causing the smoke, fire, and debris seen in the footage. They have one witness on the scene that details their account of the story. The witness states:

> *"I was riding my bike, and I heard the loud engine whirring of an airplane, followed by an explosion, then I turned my head and saw all of this fire and smoke on the top of the mountain."*

From this, the headline on the news coverage says, "Small Plane Crashes and Explodes on Local Mountaintop." They report that a recovery effort is underway. At this point, you have likely accepted everything that you have viewed on your television screen or mobile device. You may have even shared this on social media and with others who might live nearby while hoping that anyone on board the airplane was able to either eject safely prior to the crash or manage to break free from the debris unscathed. Further, you anxiously await to hear back from your local friends that you have shared the article with to ensure that they have not been injured or harmed in any way.

Now, take a moment to think about all of the assumptions you have made to accept this information and story into your reality as factual.

Here are a few ideas to get you started:

- You trust the accuracy and competency of the news report.
- You trust the integrity of the news station that covered it.
- You assume that no one involved in the reporting of this situation intends to deceive or manipulate anyone for any reason.
- You trust the witness' account of the story, whom you've never met or seen before, which seems to be the lead basis for how this story has unfolded and the claims it has made.

Did anyone actually see a small plane flying, then crash into the side of a mountain?

Even if someone claimed to have seen it, could you completely trust the stranger's eyewitness account **and** their subjective interpretation of it? How do you know that this eyewitness didn't actually witness the event at all, but upon the news crew asking him, "Did you see anything? Do you know anything about the fire?" he realized his opportunity to be on a news broadcast as a prank, or to finally be on TV, crossing out an item off his bucket list?

Let's assume that, in the context of this story, the news crew began broadcasting footage of the plane crashing, allegedly captured by someone who witnessed it. But who is this person, or group, that uploaded the footage? Where did it come from?

Why was this individual video recording the plane prior to the crash?

With the advancements in photorealistic special effects and digital imagery, including the ease and access to it in the form of mobile apps, how can we trust the authenticity of the footage?

Now, all of this isn't to suggest that **everything** is a lie or that you shouldn't trust anything; however, the point is to simply realize the **assumptions** you make when **accepting** something into your **reality**. At some point, the assumptions may not *feel* like assumptions at all. As with the sample questions posed in response to this plane crash, you might say:

"Oh, come on now. Who would go through all the effort to create special-effect imagery of a plane crashing, upload that footage to the news station, then even go as far as to create a real fiery explosion on the mountaintop for everyone local to see, just as a prank?"

Sure, it does sound a bit nonsensical, absurd, highly improbable, and unlikely, but that is **hardly the point**. Should you attempt to discredit this exercise with logic, analysis, and reason, while labeling it as nonsensical, you will remain lost inside your own mind as you continue to riddle your perception with blind spots that only you can create within yourself. No matter the strength of conviction towards the educated guess you have made or how certain you may be of a particular idea or concept, you must realize that at some level, there are assumptions that you have. There is no "conclusion" or belief that can ever be arrived upon and integrated without **accepting** assumptions into your **reality**, as it was **presented to you** and **interpreted by you**. As stated previously, there is nothing wrong with making assumptions that you feel are reasonable and acceptable to guide you towards a particular conclusion or belief. The primary objective is merely to understand the very assumptions that you **chose** to **accept** prior to the integration of any of your beliefs into your perception and reality. In essence, the assumptions of which you are not aware can only ever become blind spots, which, by nature of definition, you cannot be aware of and are unable to see clearly within yourself.

For when you blindly accept assumptions and do not acknowledge them, you limit your ability to think freely. In addition, and perhaps more concerning, your reality may be vulnerable to incredible misinterpretations, and even intentional deception, by another party who seeks to leverage these common assumptions and blind spots knowingly.

Place one of your deepest truths in the forefront of your mind, one that you consider to be so objectively true to you that it would seem unreasonable to question. Then, consider asking yourself the following questions sincerely:

- Why do you believe what you believe so strongly? How have you arrived at this belief so strongly when other opposing opinions exist?

- What are your earliest memories of the establishment of this particular belief? What began your journey to and through the acceptance of this belief? What if the acceptance of this belief precedes your conscious memory, as it may have occurred early on in childhood? Were you truly responsible for this choice or another?

- Are you hesitant to dig deep and question this belief? Why or why not?

- If this belief seems so objectively true, what could ever cause you to feel hesitation or fear to challenge it as you seek to discover its root origins inside your being? Would this indirectly suggest that you might be afraid of what you might see or uncover as you begin the internal poking, prodding, and questioning process? How else can offense from another with an opposing belief occur if what you believe is objectively true, and you believe it to be so with the utmost and sincerest certainty?

- o Any hesitation in this regard may suggest a subconscious acknowledgment of the assumptions you've made to accept this belief that has not yet been consciously acknowledged, challenged, or revisited.

- o Is the questioning of this belief against the rules of the belief itself? Oftentimes, many within a particular belief will state that they are indeed allowed to question it, but generally, only to the degree that this quest seeks to further cement their own position within it or to bring another into the eventual adoption and acceptance of it. Only the "right" questions must be asked and phrased appropriately, with other questions avoided entirely, though they may not be willing or able to admit this inherent limitation as it relates to the challenging of their belief.

- o This also suggests that you may have personally attached yourself to this belief and have associated it with part of your deepest and truest identity. However, the rules of certain beliefs require the follower of the belief system to consider it undetachable from their real identity, which may cause confusion for the holder of such beliefs. As in, to even begin the challenge of this belief system requires the rules existing within it to be broken, or at least temporarily set aside, which this in itself breaks the foundational core of the belief system. By its very nature, a belief has to **first** be **accepted** before the rules of the belief apply to the individual. Of course, those within a particular belief system may immediately disagree with this sentiment, stating that the rules of their belief apply to everyone, whether or not it is accepted by others. Though, is this not a demonstration in an effort to assert superiority to validate your belief above others while standing from within the comfort zone of your own belief to make such assertions to those who, at least logistically and intellectually, exist outside of it? If you are fearful of detaching this belief from your identity or refuse to do so, you are operating within the bounds of the belief and have not stepped outside of it fully and can only make statements, observations, and assertions from within it. This realization is of **critical importance** to your ability to understand yourself, others, and the world. This particular point is a common stumbling block of substantial difficulty for most to transcend beyond.

- Would being honest to your friends, family, society, culture, or community about questioning, challenging, or even doubting this belief result in them judging or criticizing you in any way?
  - If they would help guide you through this exploration, would they only do this so long as you end up back in the comforts of this shared belief system?
  - Would this criticism or judgment from others within your community prevent you from being honest with your feelings as you journey through this challenge, not only to them but to yourself?
  - Do you feel guilty, wrong, or ashamed for challenging the origins of this particular belief? Why, or why not? And if so, where does this guilt originate? Is the guilt a result of the belief system indicating that you should feel guilty, serving as a self-validating loop within the belief system itself?
  - Would you risk losing friends, family, or your community if you ultimately arrived at a different belief than them? If so, does this known risk prevent you from digging deeper within yourself, out of fear that you may

lose those who are important to you?

- o Have you known others who were once inside this belief system but moved on to another belief? How were they treated by those who once shared a community with them?
- Close your eyes for a moment and try to vividly imagine a scenario where you somehow, someway, ultimately find that you can no longer hold to this belief due to the conflicting information you uncovered or upon discovering assumptions you previously made but are unwilling to continue making.
  - o What would you do next? How would you feel?
  - o Were you even able to imagine **conceptually** a scenario where your belief could be untrue? If not, you may not be ready to truly challenge this core belief. If another can arrive at a different belief, then other viewpoints and perspectives do indeed exist, with the only limitation existing within your inability to imagine it. Whether you classify those viewpoints as "right" or "wrong" is wholly irrelevant for the purpose of this exercise.
  - o If you could not imagine how anyone else could possibly arrive at the opposing belief or opinion, would this not place you within the category of **genius**? As in, has your individually assigned and profoundly supreme intelligence allowed you to arrive at a very specific

conclusion and belief system that most others in the entire world, for one reason or another, are simply not intelligent or experienced enough to arrive at on their own? Who has made this definitive determination that you hold the most accurate representations of truth and reality, if not only you yourself, as you validate your position using the very truths present **within the belief system** that you've **adopted** and others have not?

If this process was difficult, be patient with yourself and do not force it. It may take longer than a quick session to understand each and every assumption you've made to **accept** your **chosen** belief. However, should you be willing to continue your exploration into how you've elegantly bound this belief to your very perception of reality, hold these questions in your mind as you consider the various assumptions you've made to fully accept every aspect of this belief into your life. At varying times in this ongoing journey, it may be helpful to take breaks from your personal exploration and think of someone who holds a conflicting belief. Try to imagine all of the assumptions that they have likely made to arrive at the opposite conclusion that you have. By flipping the roles, you may be able to uncover more of your own assumptions by understanding the assumptions they've made by reversing the relevant details to apply to your acceptance of the belief. The assumptions that they've made to reject your belief are often the same assumptions you've made to accept the same belief. Lastly, if you can do so peacefully and respectfully with the other party, it may be worth having an open conversation with someone who holds a completely opposing view to your own. This conversation's purpose would not be to persuade or convince either side but would serve as an engaging opportunity for your own exploration, assumptions, and triggers. Internally, you may approach this conversation with a relatively detached mindset, such as imagining that you are writing a research paper that explores both plausible sides of this belief while attempting to remain as unbiased and untriggered as possible. You must also approach this conversation with love and respect for the other person and their beliefs; otherwise, you will not be capable of hearing the words they are communicating to you without filtering them through your internal autocorrect. You may ask them questions like:

- How certain are you that the belief you hold is objectively true?

- What life experience or research have you considered to arrive at this conclusion? Books, articles, relationships, life experience, educational material, etc.

- Is there anything that anyone could present you with that could possibly change your mind? If so, what kind of evidence or proof would you need for it to change your current stance?

- Regardless of the answer to the question immediately

preceding this one, can you imagine a scenario where your belief has been proved untrue, and the belief or position that presently opposes your own is instead true? If so, what would you do upon discovering this? If not, why do you believe you are unable to do so?

You may also consider leading with elements of your belief that are inseparable from the core belief itself. If they answer "no" to any of the questions, always inquire why and simply take note of the reasons and evidence they reference to arrive at their current position. With every challenge, follow the thread and chain of events as deeply as you can, or rather, as deeply as they are able to. answer. Most commonly, many are unable to dig that deeply into themselves, even with another gently guiding them through it. In this case, do not push beyond what they are currently capable of sharing or verbalizing with you. This will help you reveal not only their assumptions but your own that you've accepted for yourself as well. Replace the sample questions for ones that are relevant to your particular challenge by solely focusing on the core elements of the belief until you can get to the deepest and most fundamental reasons responsible for the differing opinions.

For example:

- I believe the Holy Bible is the true, unaltered Word of God. Do you?
- I believe Jesus died on the cross for our sins. Do you?

- I believe the scientific literature provided in schools is wholly accurate and not intentionally deceptive. Do you?
- I believe that no one would go through so much effort to stage a plane crash on the news. Do you?
- I believe that news reporting is reputable and can be taken at its word. Do you?

Through deeper questions such as these, we begin to boil down the most fundamental areas in which disagreements about reality occur. Should we only debate from within the higher **layers of abstraction** on the content itself, any potential progress towards better understanding one another will seldom be made. However, when drilling down to the core issues where beliefs differ, we may have more impactful and meaningful discussions with others. As in, what purpose would a discussion regarding the details about the alleged plane crash serve if one party did not trust the news as a valid information source? Perhaps a new discussion can involve why this individual is skeptical towards trusting the news, which does not have anything to do with the original topic at hand, but begins to highlight the more significant reason behind the opposing opinion. Then, in the same way, you must continue expanding the conversation to the most fundamental elements where opinions differ.

SUSCEPTIBILITY TO BELIEF ALTERATION

We know now that, should we hold a belief of any kind, we have **accepted** some **assumptions** along the way. We understand that any assumption we choose not to honestly acknowledge becomes a blind spot, which affects our ability to see ourselves and the world around us with the clarity we deeply desire. We also understand that assumptions are a necessary part of establishing a belief about ourselves, others, life situations, and our perception of our subjective reality.

Should we be more open-minded and susceptible to alteration when it comes to the things we believe, knowing that we have undoubtedly made assumptions along the way through the formation of this belief?

Or should we stick to our beliefs wholeheartedly and without compromise, living them out with every thought, action, and word that comes forth from our bodies and being while failing to entertain an altering or opposing belief?

The answer to these questions isn't quite as binary as it may initially seem, choosing between a diehard approach versus a more open-minded one. By assuming there's only a binary choice on how to manage our beliefs and assumptions, we have falsely bought into the premise that only one must be chosen. We assume that if we have an open mind, we are not wholeheartedly committed to our beliefs, and if we are wholeheartedly committed to our beliefs, we cannot be open-minded. At its core, this assumption implies that we are so attached to our beliefs that we have identified with them. When we learn to truly separate ourselves and our being from our beliefs as the observer and ultimate chooser of the belief, in the consciousness that we are, we achieve greater visibility into the choices that we have in front of us. If we can successfully separate our being and truest essence from even our deepest-rooted beliefs, we can simultaneously choose to commit wholeheartedly to our chosen belief while fully acknowledging all of the assumptions that we've made. To **identify** and **acknowledge** assumptions **does not require** doubting the structures or elements of the belief system. When we see the assumptions, while accepting our role in consciously and willfully choosing them, we obtain a greater understanding of our true identity and our chosen belief system. When we are in this place, the opposing and conflicting opinions from others **cannot disturb us**. From here, we no longer identify with the belief and realize that we exist separately from it, as it was something that we made a decision to choose, adopt, and integrate. Therefore, we no longer feel directly attacked when opposed or at the mere existence of a differing position. We can then choose to adjust our gaze and perception of the opposing belief in a way that suits us and our own purpose in a greater way. If we catch ourselves ever becoming offended and frustrated, we can notice when this occurs and **look**

within. Once we are aware of these feelings, we can then choose to perceive the situation differently by becoming the outside observer rather than interconnected and entangled with the emotions, feelings, and situation at hand. We can choose to view the challenging situation however we wish in a way that aligns with our chosen belief set, and when we genuinely understand the assumptions we've made with our core beliefs, we understand that any frustration, anger, pain, happiness, ecstasy, or purpose that we feel in any of these moments is a direct result of our chosen beliefs and assumptions, **for better or for worse**. We realize that no one can cause us frustration or impose it on us unless we allow this to occur. We realize that all feelings and emotions, regardless of what someone else does or believes in the world that appears external to us, can only ever be a result of a choice that we have made within ourselves to perceive the situation exactly as it is being perceived by us, in this very moment.

When we realize that we need not choose between two binary approaches to our beliefs, we experience true freedom as we separate our true identity from the **intellectually chosen** belief system. Some belief systems dictate how you ought to view the real you, which may make this separation process difficult. For this, think about some of your earliest memories, whether as a child or perhaps an infant. What is the earliest memory you can recall? With this memory, do you remember experiencing it first-hand as you view life through your curious eyes? Who, or what, was the observer of this experience? As in, this observer or experiencer of this particular memory is part of the incredibly deep version of you, prior to attachments, baggage, or any beliefs you may not have been capable of intellectually choosing and adopting for yourself at this early phase of life. This version of you, as briefly recalled and relived from your own memory, has always been there as you have grown, developed, and continued to experience life in all of its varying phases, ultimately leading you right here, right now, as you read this book in the present moment. Is the observer reading these words the same observer present from your earliest memories? It was only later in life that you were intellectually taught or shown "what" your real self was and gleaned from something or someone external to you. This intellectual moment required you to make a choice to accept the classification this influence provided for the deep you. None of this is to suggest that whatever you chose as your core belief or how you choose to identify your true self with is incorrect; merely, it's only to demonstrate the separation from an intellectually accepted and chosen belief and the version of you that you have always known to exist even prior to being shown it by another, for it has always only ever been you as the observer, independent of any core belief or classification. This version of you had always existed for as long as you can remember, even before you had a label, purpose, rhyme or reason, assigned to it. This is the true you that has, and always will, exist separately from any belief you can ever choose for your life.

In a moment of reflection, ask yourself if your beliefs bring you true happiness, purpose, and contentment. If not, it might be time to adjust your perception of life, situations, and others, even if staying within the overarching framework provided by your chosen belief system. If modifying your perception is not something you are willing to do, then simply consider acknowledging and accepting that any unhappiness or suffering you are experiencing is a direct result of your chosen belief. There is not a single person or resource in this world that can, or should, convince you to make another choice. The choice is yours. Own it, and accept all that it brings to you, both the pleasant and unpleasant. These experiences, the costs, and the outcomes are the very fruits representative of your choices.

With this, be encouraged and emboldened to trudge forward with whatever belief you choose to hold. Continue to challenge it. Accept it. As you embrace it, understand it is your subjective view of the world that you've chosen to live in. Be honest about your assumptions to the best of your ability to prevent blind spots that only cloud your visibility and assessment of your life and the world. When you implement this perspective, approach, and understanding into your life, your **chosen belief**, whatever it may be, will be **empowering**, as you become even prouder than before to wield it. You'll become braver in expressing your beliefs and opinions to yourself and others without the stagnant fear of rejection, criticism, or opposition. You'll demonstrate more respect for others and their chosen beliefs without needing to feel like you must persistently defend your own within yourself. Your confidence in your belief, and your expression of it, will increase exponentially, all without the unwanted arrogance or judgment. When you understand the process you have utilized for adopting a belief and arriving at a particular conclusion, you can now begin to understand the process that others have adopted as well. Though in some cases you may never understand or agree with the merits of an opposing viewpoint, you will no longer be threatened or disturbed by it. With this, you'll make a greater impact in this world, and it all began **inside of you**.

7. COLLIDING REALITIES

We understand now that each of our realities are incredibly subjective and products of our perception. These stem from our chosen core beliefs that originate from a choice we've made or continue to make. With this perspective, we may not only better understand our beliefs and our chosen realities, but we also glean a deeper understanding and respect for others and their chosen realities. However, what happens when two or more subjective realities collide in a seemingly unavoidable way?

We will lead this chapter using a simple example of colliding realities prior to moving on to a more complex scenario in order better to establish the context and understanding of this principle. With some subjective realities and beliefs, they can peacefully coexist, and we can shape our perception to interpret the situation and conflict in a number of different ways that may bring peace and clarity, especially when we maintain respect for one another even when we may not agree. However, there are moments where two or more subjective realities collide in a way that cannot typically be resolved through even the most respectful dialog. In the first example, we explore a commonplace scenario involving two people having a discussion. In this scenario, both individuals remember the same exact conversation very differently. They disagree not only over the intent or meaning of the original conversation but on the very substance and words used in it. For example, you might remember specifically asking another person to watch your dog while you are out of town over this coming weekend and recall your friend's response being an enthusiastic, "Yea, of course!" You might even remember discussing logistics such as what time you'd like them to arrive each day, where the treats and dog leash are located, and more. Yet, when the weekend comes up, your friend never arrives to watch your dog, and to your absolute shock, they deny that you even asked them to do it. They allegedly possess no recollection of the conversation involving your dog at all, or perhaps alternatively, they remember you asking about it, but distinctly remember replying with, "I'm so sorry, but I have other plans this weekend, so I will not be able to do this for you." Assuming you and your friend both truly respect and cherish one another and there is no malintent or intentional dishonesty at play, how can this situation be resolved when you cannot even agree on the actual events that unfolded? Short of having a video or audio recording of the entire interaction, how the actual conversation played out may never be known. But to be clear, an objective reality detailing the authentic unfolding of events in this scenario does indeed exist, regardless of the subjective interpretations and realities each person has personally subscribed to. Though a real truth does exist, it's possible that neither party holds it. As in, you or your friend may both be wrong, and the real truth is something else entirely. Or perhaps you each hold pieces of the truth but have filled in the perceptive gaps with assumptions unknowingly. It's possible that your friend replied while their mind was preoccupied with another mental task, or daydream, meaning the words were actually spoken and a reply was given in alignment with your version of the story, but it is something they may never accurately recall. It's also possible that you never asked them, or you misinterpreted their reply. This is an extremely difficult scenario to dissect. Just as sure as you are that you most certainly asked them, heard their reply, and remember it so vividly, they quite simply do not remember it in the same way. What happens now? No matter how many discussions you have with your friend about this, you may never manage to get to the bottom of what actually unfolded during that mysterious interaction. Meaning, the truth of what occurred will be **forever unknown**, despite its existence in an objective reality. With both parties firmly grasping to their own versions of reality, what could the possible truth be? In a scenario like this, it may cause some contention and frustration in the friendship, but it won't likely be the end of an otherwise healthy and happy relationship. They'll simply choose to move on from it and chalk it up as a misunderstanding. With this, they'll set aside their different versions of the story and will stop debating whose recollection of the story is superior or more accurate.

Though, what if this colliding reality was something that occurred on a regular basis with this friend? At some point, it may not be enough to set it aside and call it a misunderstanding if it has become a pattern and must be addressed.

When addressed, there are only a few possible outcomes:

- You convince your friend that **your version** of the event is true.
    - And they truly believe it, with no hard feelings.
    - Your account of events, in reality, is actually true, or they are not representative of what actually occurred **but** have been accepted and adopted by both parties.
    - Each party now holds the **same** version of events within this particular segment of a shared reality, **regardless of the validity** in any objective reality.
- Your friend convinces you that **their version** of the event is true.
    - And you truly believe it, with no hard feelings.
    - Their account of events, in reality, is actually true, or they are not representative of what actually occurred **but** have been accepted and adopted by both parties.

- o Each party now holds the same version of events within this particular segment of a shared reality, **regardless of the validity** in any objective reality.

- Both you and your friend dig your heels in deeper and resent one another, as you are unable to persuade the other.
  - o This creates **two new realities** based on the **same colliding instance**, with each reality **existing separately** within the person who created it.
  - o One, both, or neither version may be based on actual truth, but each person has committed completely to their interpretation of events as factual.

In the case where you or your friend can convince the other that the events happened a certain way and this version of events is accepted by both parties, this outcome may be preferred. However, something far more unsettling may be occurring instead—the **creation of unsubstantiated realities** that are accepted as wholly objective realities.

Consider for a moment that you convinced your friend that your version of the story is true, and you both truly believed it to be true, with no resentment or hard feelings. Let's also assume that your recollection of the events was **actually flawed**, but due to your insistence on it being true and your friend's willingness to accept the story as you presented it, a reality that had never actually existed on any plane of **true reality** has now been accepted as an objective reality for both of the parties that were present during the interaction. From the moment both parties agreed on this shared version of reality, a new reality has sprung into existence that was **not** based on facts or absolute truth. What had only previously existed in fragmented memories, flawed perceptions, assumptions, and theories has now come into existence as an unquestionable and objective truth that has been mutually agreed upon by all parties involved. When a reality, especially one that is mutually agreed upon and shared among others, is considered an objectively true reality, it may never be called into question or challenged. Quite literally, a new and **unsubstantiated reality** has been **spoken into existence** and **accepted**. Essentially, this is not only creating just something, but an **entire reality**, out of nothing but perception and mutual acceptance.

Alternatively, should both parties completely disagree and only trust their personal recollections of the story, **two realities** have sprung to life based on the **same objective event**. This means that both you and your friend have a different version of the same event, and each person has accepted their own recollection as absolute truth in their own subjective realities, **making it appear** objectively true, which cannot be questioned within each other's own reality. Everything from that moment forward will be seen and interpreted through this **artificial extension of reality** belonging to each person. One person may be right, both may be right, or it's possible that neither could be right. When operating from varying and artificial extensions of realities, how many additional realities may be created over time as you and your friend continue to interpret events differently, using previous experiences and subjectively held realities as the basis for the fabrication and interpretation of another reality? Regardless, we can begin to see how **entire realities**, whether objectively true in an objective world or not, are created based on our perceptions and choices alone.

Up until this point, we have not assumed any maleficence on behalf of either party. Even without this element, it is entirely possible to create new, seemingly objective realities from mere perception alone. Should we decide to consider the potential involvement of manipulation or deception tactics, such as intentional gaslighting, a new reality and version of the "truth" can be created in the mind and world of another. When we add deceptive elements, the extent to which new realities can be created for varying reasons becomes boundless. Perhaps you feel like your friend hasn't been treating you well or hasn't been giving you enough of the attention you expect from them, so you deceive them into thinking they really dropped the ball for not watching your dog when you know truly that you didn't even ask them to begin with. Let's assume that, in this instance, your friend accepted your intentionally corrupt and misleading version of the story, though they are not privy to the deception utilized. Not only have you artificially altered their subjective reality into one that you prefer for their life and yours, but you may also possess a certain degree of control over them by using guilt, all of which has been completely manufactured and did not exist in true reality, until now. Once these alternative realities are accepted, does it matter what the real and factual truth is? If our unique versions of reality are as **real as anything could ever be** to each of us individually, it might as well have actually happened, as we now experience the outcome, consequences, perceptions, and emotions that would have unfolded should this situation have occurred in actual reality. Our actions, thoughts, and feelings now respond to life in alignment as if this version of reality occurred in the objective world. Quite simply, it's as real as anything can ever be to those that accept this reality. Any conscious decisions that we make for our lives will be made in direct accordance with the realities we have accepted, regardless of any true validity, facts, or truth residing in an objective world. In this way, should your friend believe that they really dropped the ball with their listening skills and watching your dog, despite your injection of intentionally deceptive information, they will now respond to you differently moving forward in this relationship. They may also be more vulnerable to future manipulation, as you may be able to gently remind them of their previous patterns and memory issues with a statement such as, "Well, I know you remember things differently, but this isn't the first time I've told you something and you didn't remember, and you ended up recalling the situation incorrectly." You may solidify this with a pointed jab, disguised as humor, by bringing up "that one time you didn't show up to watch my dog" as you both casually laugh it off, as a way to continue feeding into the manufactured reality that you have created for them to live within.

Perhaps you feel that you could never fall victim to the manufactured reality of another, whether intentionally intended to deceive you or simply a product of their own misinterpreted and misunderstood reality and fragmented memories. Regardless, this is a natural and expected occurrence of life. In many ways, it's unavoidable due to every person living solely within their own subjective realities, which are inherently flawed and do not have the ability to perceive the entire story accurately. We like to think that the version of reality we have accepted is the "best" one, or the most accurate, especially when we look at others and the seemingly ridiculous or ignorant realities that they have accepted for their lives. We might even look at them and how out of touch they seem to be with reality and ask ourselves, "What planet are they living on?" Oddly enough, it's the same planet that you live on. They may also be wondering which planet you are living on. In their reality, you stand out and are different, but in your reality, they stand out and are different. We often get confused with this concept when the reality that we have chosen seems to align more with popular opinions or the reality accepted by the greater society. When the reality that we hold aligns with the more populous side, we tend to believe that this somehow validates our own reality. We ought not to mistakenly conflate a populous version of reality as more valid than any individual version of reality. At the very core, we can only hold our individual subjective versions of reality, which should always be internally interpreted and accepted, while acknowledging all of the assumptions we've made along the way to accept this particular belief and associated reality. When choosing to align with the general consensus version of a mainstream reality, you must acknowledge the assumptions that come with this choice while also understanding that just because the masses appear to believe something, it **does not** make it any more true or false than any **reality** held by any other.

REALITY INTEGRITY

Now that we hold a stronger understanding of core beliefs, perceptions, and now colliding realities, we can apply these principles to a more meaningful scenario. The following real-world example serves as an intricate case study that has been experienced by many of us on this planet, the highly contentious 2020 United States presidential election between the incumbent President Donald Trump and former Vice President Joe Biden. Unlike most of the prior United States elections, the 2020 election was particularly controversial as it occurred during an unprecedented pandemic (COVID-19) and involved substantial allegations of voting irregularities. For this case study, it doesn't matter which opinion you hold, nor will any opinion be pushed on you. This example is purely to highlight the impact of colliding realities in a greater context than the previous example, as this singular event disrupted the subjective realities of billions of people around the world.

There is a lot of conflicting information about the real voting numbers of the election, which greatly differ based on which sources of information you trust and retrieve the data from. So, for this example, we will intentionally stick with generalities as this will be sufficient for the purpose of our analysis into colliding realities. Each of the two candidates received roughly half of the votes in the country. Generally speaking, the voters that cast votes for Joe Biden believe that this was the most secure election in the nation's history. These voters believe the generally accepted narrative that the mainstream media reports on regarding this as a highly secure election. Whereas the voters that had cast a vote for incumbent Donald Trump allege incredible amounts of voter fraud that effectively denied Donald Trump his reelection. They also generally deny the mainstream media's reporting about the integrity of the election. Prior to the inauguration day for Joe Biden on January 20th, 2021, many social media platforms began prohibiting the sharing of data and posts that continued to allege election fraud, as they felt it was dangerous for the United States' democratic process to spread what was deemed as blatant misinformation. The users that attempted to share information involving voter fraud perceived this as censorship, as it effectively limited the sharing of information involving the alleged and perceived voter fraud. This action ultimately all but silenced this narrative in the mainstream's eye as users began resorting to underground resources to share information and connect with one another, though many of these alternative avenues were also actively pursued and squashed. Even after the inauguration of Joe Biden, some do not regard him as a duly elected president due to their perception that voter fraud unfairly swayed the election. In this way, we have **two mainstream subjective realities** colliding that have an incredible effect of altering history and our perception of the events that unfolded.

Regardless of what your opinion might be on this particular topic, consider the example used earlier in this chapter and all the possible scenarios that could occur as a result of colliding realities. Though millions continue to contest the election results, with Joe Biden being sworn in as the president, the history books will be written according to the generally accepted, and more populous, mainstream consensus. This consensus currently stands as, "Most secure election in United States history, President Joe Biden received a historic number of votes." This narrative and representation of history will be taught to your children, your grandchildren, and beyond as the objective and unquestionable reality.

There have been certain pieces of "evidence," signed affidavits, and even video footage that have been released and shared that seek to prove the existence of voter fraud. But remember, our core beliefs alter our perception, and **this is key** to grasping what had occurred during this turbulent process. If your belief is that the media is generally trustworthy and the election wasn't stolen, **this alters your perception**. As you view the available evidence with this perception, you'll view it with a perceptual bias that aligns with your belief. This "evidence" will be seen as baseless, irrelevant, or manufactured while discrediting those that consider it to be true in their subjective realities. But for those who believe that it was a stolen election, this same "evidence" is seen as the "smoking gun" that "proves" unprecedented election fraud. Furthermore, by this same group, the silencing of this information from the mainstream media and social media companies that prohibited the sharing of this content is seen as blatant censorship and a systemic cover-up attempt. This is an extremely frightening reality for those that have accepted this as their subjective reality. With these examples, it becomes increasingly clear that we can all look at the **same exact** information and **infer varying conclusions** from it based on our chosen beliefs and perceptions, then align it to our idealistic and preferred version of our own subjective realities. As covered previously in the core beliefs section, we consider the other side to be ignorant or blind while affirming to ourselves through the use of our own perceptual bias that we ourselves hold the more accurate and reasonable truth.

However, what is the actual and objective truth in this situation? What really happened on November 3rd, 2020? Whatever you believe and think, take a moment to acknowledge the assumptions you've made to arrive at the belief you hold. To dive in deeper, let's assume for a moment that, at some point in the future, additional "evidence" gets released that provides seemingly irrefutable proof that there was indeed enough election fraud to sway the election. Think of what evidence might be required to coerce one who believes it to be the most secure election in history to align themselves with the side they once opposed. Perhaps this "evidence" would appear as email conversations "proving" collusion to commit fraud from high-level individuals in the government and technology sector, or video recordings, network packet captures, or any other pieces of irrefutable, relevant, and convincing "evidence." Even in the case that **all that existed** and became **revealed**, this would be seen through the perceptual biases and filters belonging to each side and would unlikely be enough to sway the chosen reality for those that already hold their chosen realities as objective truth. Once a reality is firmly decided on, especially one of a highly contentious or controversial nature, it is unlikely to be swayed or reconsidered, even in light of new and potentially damning evidence. This is akin to the prior example of wiggling the lower-level block on the Jenga tower but in the context of a mutually shared reality spanning billions of people. One side may see it as fabricated, unverifiable, irrelevant, staged, or planted, or perhaps would declare that illegal entrapment techniques were used or deceptive editing of various conversations to point to a particular narrative favoring one side over the other, especially if the **information sources** that they **trust** declare and classify it as such. In this way, the individual holding such a reality may not feel the need to view the "evidence" or data for themselves, as they have trusted the media as an authoritative, integrous, and accurate information source. Whereas the other side would see this additional information as more irrefutable evidence, further validating their own accepted reality from within their reality. As you see, both sides continue to operate within their preferred realities and make decisions and judgments exclusively from within it, while using the same objective data only to validate their existing positions further.

Like the prior example when asking your friend to watch your dog, a true and objective reality did indeed exist, though there was no way to verify or validate it when fragments and incomplete interpretations of it existed within each other's subjectively held reality. In the same way, does the **real truth** matter, whatever that might be, should it ever be revealed definitively in its entirety if

most people stay within their subjective realities, regardless of whatever alleged evidence or proof gets revealed or shared? Would this alleged evidence be broadcast on mainstream media or social media, or would it be prohibited for peddling more of an "already-debunked" conspiracy theory? We all believe we seek and desire the truth, though we seldom allow ourselves to see it.

Going a bit further, let's assume for a moment that this alleged evidence was real, but the mainstream media did not report on it. Would people who might have actually changed their minds after viewing the available data in its entirety continue instead to dispute election fraud evidence as more conspiracy theories based on the following assumption, "Well, if it were real and valid, wouldn't it be all over the news?"

As we continue exploring the various subjective realities, let's assume no intentional deception in the delivery or withholding of information regarding the election and potential fraud. With this, we also assume that any irregularities in perception among the different groups are simply a different, but otherwise honest, perception of an otherwise objective series of events. Let's take a moment to explore some possible scenarios that are based on the subjective realities and interpretations presently held:

- Joe Biden, in reality, received the most votes in United States history and is a duly elected president.

- Donald Trump, in reality, received the most votes in United States history, but due to unprecedented voter fraud, this election was stolen from him and his supporters.

Let's assume that Joe Biden, in a true reality, actually did win the United States election fairly, and there wasn't enough voter fraud to sway or otherwise steal the election from Donald Trump. The current mainstream and global consensus would align with this particular scenario. History books would be written about this unique election and pandemic, labeling it the most secure election in history. Additionally, anyone that continued to baselessly rant and propagate conspiracy theories about a stolen election would be regarded as a social outcast, out of touch with reality, and they'd be banned and blocked from spreading these harmful conspiracy theories on social media. At that rate, it would not be until we cycled through an entire generation or two of humans that there may still be some that continue to believe the election of 2020 was stolen, though the numbers of these individuals would greatly diminish over time as the **accepted reality** becomes more and more prevalent. For a time, this will be turbulent until those that believe the election was stolen become the insignificant minority. This process is effectively accelerated, as those who hold this opinion are not able to easily gather or share information across the major social platforms. Those that believe the election was stolen will be living in a depressing version of their subjective reality, believing that the very freedom and democracy of the United

States is forever lost. Whereas those that believe it was the most secure election in history are at peace with the results, even if their preferred candidate didn't get voted in. They also are frustrated at the ones that still live in a reality where the election was stolen for not facing the "reality" of what "actually" occurred. We have **two realities** that stemmed from the same objective series of events, with one reality ultimately overpowering the other until the other reality becomes obsolete or forgotten. Anyone that questions the prominently accepted reality, either now or in the future, will be seen as a conspiracy theorist in the same way that the flat earthers are viewed now. At some point, most everyone will accept Joe Biden as a legitimate president of the United States, as this will be taught to children in school through academic books and by their parents, society, and peers, reducing the possibility of conspiracy theories arising without intense criticism for **questioning the validity of documented history**. This is not at all unlike a child who challenges the shape of planet earth, or anything else presented to them as factual, during their early school years, as they receive criticism, judgment, and a failing grade for refusing to accept a reality that is imposed upon them by another. If in true reality, no voter fraud occurred and the election wasn't stolen, many **still** have a subjective reality created in their minds, to the tune of potentially millions of individuals, that is not based on any **objective fact**, but **only** their **perception** that stemmed ultimately from their various supporting **core beliefs**. Also, in this case, the reality that they have created has been completely fabricated, but it's **very real to them, as real as anything could ever be to anyone**, just like any of our own subjective realities are to us individually. No matter the side on which you stand on any issue, belief, or opinion, this point is of **critical importance** to understand the validity and realness of one's feelings, perceptions, and actions inside of their chosen reality.

Now imagine for a moment that the inverse was **actually true**, that the election was stolen, and there was unprecedented voter fraud that swayed the election unfairly. Let's assume the perspective, perception, and point of view of those who live inside this subjective reality of the election events. For this to be true, it would entail that there were actual evidence and proof of this in true reality, but it was being actively censored and blocked by the media and technology companies. Also, in this case, the rejected court cases would have been a coordinated effort to prohibit the truth from being exposed about this massive theft. Regardless of whether this was the actual truth, the mainstream reality and narrative still demonstrated and actively voiced a victory for Joe Biden. In this way, the ones who believe this was the most secure election in history have subscribed to and fully accepted a reality that was not based on any actual truth, but it has become truth to them inside their own subjective realities based on their perceptual biases and the information sources they have chosen to trust. Then, as this unsubstantiated reality became an unquestionable and objective reality for those that accepted it, it would be documented in history books, and nearly the entire globe would accept this as reality. If this scenario played out as stated here, we would have the actual, objective, and **substantiated reality** being phased out with an **unsubstantiated reality**. Once entirely phased out, the **fabricated reality** becomes **just as real** as any reality could ever be to anyone, despite it not being based on any real truths. For clarity, this possible collision of subjective realities, regardless of the context or specific examples utilized, could occur in **either direction,** whereby an unsubstantiated reality becomes the unquestionable and objective reality.

COLLISION COURSE

When two or more realities collide in such a way, whether something of significant importance like the presidential election in the United States or anything else, we are presented with a choice. We get to choose which reality we accept as our own. As we make a choice, we analyze the "facts" and the information at hand as they appear and are presented to us through the information sources we trust. Though we may analyze the information of any situation very carefully, we do so through our existing core beliefs, assumptions, and perceptual biases. In this way, are we really making informed decisions at all, or are our core beliefs and perceptions filtering the data in such a way, as we force it to align with what we choose for ourselves within our ideal realities? If we ever desire truth for ourselves, it is of the utmost importance to understand the assumptions we've made with each and every one of our beliefs, as this alters our very perception of the world around us, giving it a story and a narrative to align with our chosen belief. Without being aware of the assumptions you've made for your beliefs, they become blind spots to any objective truth that may be directly in front of you. Even if the real truth is presented to you, you will fail to see it and will not be capable of interpreting it for what it truly is. Remember, it's irrelevant whether you've conveniently validated your assumptions as being "reasonable" or "common knowledge" or from within the sphere of rules, guidelines, and beliefs where you presently stand. It must only be acknowledged that an assumption was made and what assumptions they might be, which **does not require** doubting your chosen ideology.

What if the truth of any reality you've accepted for yourself was completely turned on its head, upside down, and the evidence was right in front of you? Do you think you would see the truth as it was revealed and presented to you? Most of us like to think we would indeed see, acknowledge, and accept it, but under the same light, do we not each think that we are **already** living our personal lives in **the most accurate** version of reality? If we each feel this way, certainly some of us must be incorrect or off-base. We might perceive or remember things very differently from one another, but in certain situations, there are objective truths of what actually occurred and unfolded. As with the initial example used when asking your friend to watch your dog while you are out of town, unless there was a video recording of the entire conversation, the actual truth of how the series of events unfolded may never be known or uncovered. The "truth" or objective reality, in this case, only exists inside the individual or shared subjective realities of those present at the moment the objective events occurred. Perhaps there was a video of this conversation, and you discover that you never actually did ask your friend to watch your dog during that interaction. Would that be enough proof that you didn't actually ask your friend after all, even though you still vividly remember it? Or would you stand by your story and double down by suggesting that you must have asked your friend in a different room of the house where a camera was not present, or maybe you claim that you must have discussed it on a phone call with them instead? How many excuses or justifications would you make before allowing yourself to sincerely question your own perceptions, assumptions, and subjective reality?

Imagine for a moment that the world was shaken by the announcement that earth was actually flat after all, after a new discovery that was previously unknown due to a breakthrough in quantum science. How would this make you feel? Would you latch onto this new information, despite the previously shared information that was propagated and imposed on you being inaccurate? What if you had previously challenged the shape of the planet and received ridicule and social blacklisting as a result of your challenge?

With some questions, the answer you ultimately receive may depend on **when** you ask the question, along with which information sources you have **decided** to trust.

THREADING THE NEEDLE

For the following questions, you may hold in your mind any colliding reality of your choosing that you have personally experienced, no matter how big or small. Remember, even if it may not seem like a colliding reality, any situation where there were two or more opposing views of what should have otherwise been an objective situation is considered a case of colliding realities.

- How much does the actual truth of any situation matter to you?
  - Would you rather become devastated and have to reconstruct your core beliefs and perceptions, but in turn, know an **actual truth**? Or would you prefer to stick with your idealistic and subjective reality, potentially subscribing to a reality that **only exists in your perception**?

- o How sure can you ever be that your subjective reality is superior or more accurate than any other?
- Would you be able to see the real truth if shown to you, should it conflict with your core beliefs and current subjective reality?
  - o If so, how will you be uniquely capable of seeing the truth in such a situation if we believe others that are in their own subjective realities seem to be unable to accept any truth that seems to be staring right at them?
  - o When it comes to core beliefs or colliding realities, how would you define ignorance as it applies to yourself? How would you anticipate others on the opposing side define ignorance if they pointed their finger at you?
  - o How are you less ignorant or blind than a peer on the opposing side? Do you think they would agree with the self-analysis you provide for yourself? Would you agree with the assessment they provide for themselves, of themselves?
- In cases where subjective realities collide, and only one may be accepted in a society, how will you ultimately select the one you choose?
  - o Will you revisit your core beliefs and associated assumptions?
  - o Will you stick to your already-established beliefs and perceive everything under the established processes

you've identified for yourself?

o   Will popular opinion influence your choice if your preferred subjective reality is in the numerical minority?

In any case, whatever reality you accept into your world, **you've chosen** to accept it. You've chosen to accept the assumptions, as well as any pain, suffering, joy, or ecstasy, that you experience as a result of your belief and choice. These choices, along with the realities we accept for ourselves, align with our core beliefs one way or another, which ultimately provides us with a story and narrative. There is no prerequisite for deception to occur for one to accept a reality that does not exist in any substantiated reality, as our perception and acceptance of such a reality make it become just as real as any objective reality we ever could believe or experience for ourselves. We are all capable of misinterpreting and misrepresenting things, as we each observe the world through our own subjectivity and personal beliefs.

The most important point to take away from this section is to remember that you have a choice, one that only you can make. With every choice, you've made assumptions. Everything you interpret in this world is viewed through your unique lens and gives way to your own subjective reality in which you live. **This subjective reality is truly the only real reality that will ever exist to you.** Everyone exists within their own subjective realities.

We must fully understand this. Additionally, how they've arrived inside their subjectively held reality is conceptually identical to how we've arrived inside our own. We must continually reassess ourselves, our assumptions, our feelings, our triggers, and our beliefs. We must remember to **use the mirror** of our subjective reality as our personal guide to reveal our assumptions, choices, and beliefs we've accepted for ourselves within our lives.

8. GATEKEEPER OF TRUTH

What is **truth**? Does **truth** matter?

Most people reading this, or if asked separately in a different context, would declare that truth does indeed matter for themselves. On the surface, this sounds like a good concept that many would agree on; however, in true reality, this is not commonly the case. One of the more dangerous internal deceptions occurs when we believe ourselves to be **infallible truth-seekers** that claim to value objective facts and absolutes over mere conspiracies or speculation. Those that seek truth through the exploration of conspiracies and speculation have denied the information presented to them by a society in search of something else, even if not obtained through standard pipelines and **pre-approved** means. How can some people consider various things as **truth**, whereas another in their own subjective reality wholeheartedly disagrees with the same information while passionately pursuing another truth for themselves? Through the attachments that we have to our core beliefs, we more often than not cannot see the truth, or reality, for what it really is or isn't. We align ourselves and our perceptual filters with what we've **already accepted** inside our subjective realities as concrete truth and absolutes in our own lives, along with an ego-constructed persona and belief that we cannot be easily fooled by mistruths or inaccuracies. This, perhaps, is one of the greatest internal deceptions of all, whereby we believe our reality to be the truest version and that we cannot easily be fooled, manipulated, or hijacked by false information. Whether the false information referred to here is intentionally deceptive or not is not relevant to the greater context. On the same token, what might be deemed as irrefutably false information to one, may be an unbreakable truth to another. To that end, what information can ever be false or true when the fact-checking point of demarcation resides exclusively inside each of us individually, which can only be subjected to our pre-existing biases? For this reason, **we are the gatekeepers and arbiters of our own truth.** We accept the truths and perceptions that align with our pre-existing ideals, core beliefs, and general understanding of the world in which we live, while denying, rejecting, and criticizing anything that contradicts our preferred version of reality. Conversely, the most dangerously fallible person is the one who believes to be the most infallible among us.

The self-proclaimed infallible hold onto their core beliefs more firmly than others, believing that what they hold is truer than what others hold. We all do this to a degree, which has been expressed throughout this book; however, the ones who believe they are supremely infallible, which exists in most of us one way or another in different areas and aspects of our lives, are the most susceptible to manipulation, deception, and fallibility. Though they may be generally more infallible than others, their fallibility becomes especially dangerous. This comes as they may never know that they have been fooled since they hold themselves, and their perceived inability to absorb anything that is not true, with the highest regard. Therefore, if one tells himself that he cannot be fooled and he ultimately does indeed become fooled, how could he ever know he has been fooled or has subscribed to an untrue, inaccurate, incomplete, or even deceptive version of reality or facts when he doesn't believe that he is capable of being fooled? We may occasionally exhibit curiosity and venture outside of our realms of comfortability, predictability, and **reality**. Though, more often than not, this exploration and the questions asked as a result of it occur from the very perspective in which we originate, thereby perceptually skewing the information we receive in accordance with our pre-existing biases, expectations, and desires.

Take a moment and consider the following questions:

- Do you think you are open-minded to other people's ideas, opinions, and beliefs?
- What does it mean to you personally to be open-minded?

Think of some people you've met, dealt with, or spoken to on various matters that you have considered not to be very open-minded at all, and to the contrary, you found them to be quite guarded, defensive, and blatantly close-minded. With this person or group of people in mind, if they were asked separately from your interaction with them if they believed themselves to be an open-minded person and could view **all information without bias** and make informed and educated decisions based on the information available, all without allowing their beliefs or predispositions to stand in the way, how do you think they would answer?

Like most of us, they would likely answer that they believe themselves to be very open-minded, yet your experience with them made you feel otherwise, effectively conflicting with the assessment they have provided for themselves, of themselves. How do you think they viewed you as a result of the interaction: open-minded or close-minded?

Who's right, and who's wrong?

Why, or why not?

Though we like to believe that we hold a solid understanding of not only "reality," but of our own selves and inner workings, how can we know if we are truly open-minded if the very belief of such is prone to our own internal deception, blindness, and bias? Whatever we believe of ourselves becomes true to us.

Is it possible that you are indeed open-minded but that others are not, so they are only projecting their own close-mindedness onto you? But if that were the case involving the use of projection from another, would that also suggest the possibility that you have projected your own close-mindedness onto them?

Why strive for open-mindedness?

What is the goal or intent of the interaction?

To decide who is "right" or "wrong?"

To determine who is more open-minded?

Or perhaps we can decide to use the interaction or conflict for what it really is: a skill-building opportunity to learn more about the world by learning more about ourselves. If you find yourself becoming frustrated while engaging with someone you deem to be close-minded, this can either continue to add frustration to your life as you externalize the blame and the frustration you feel, or you can decide to use it as an opportunity for self-exploration and self-improvement. You may decide to ask yourself:

- Why exactly did I become so frustrated?
- Was the frustration that I experienced truly the fault of the ignorance and general rudeness I perceived from them or was it the result of **my inability** to process the information apart from my own biases and preconceived notions, which ultimately clouded my vision and perception of this situation?

If you were truly open-minded, would you have become as frustrated in this scenario? Would you be able to manage the situation and your emotions with calm and ease, as you stand firm in your position while detaching from your own beliefs to listen and hear the other person and their unique viewpoint, without becoming emotionally triggered?

We must remember that the primary goal of any interaction should not be to change the mind of another to your biasedly more superior way. Proceeding with this intent will only be reflected by the other and back towards you, leading to internal frustration and disappointment caused by you alone. Any interaction must be first based on love, admiration, and respect for yourself, as well as equal love, admiration, and respect for the other. From this position, we may use all of our experiences and interactions with others to learn more about ourselves, what makes us tick, what triggers us, and then use that information for self-improvement and growth.

ARBITER OF TRUTH

Compared to yesterday, you are an evolved individual. The experiences, thoughts, and actions of your yesterday impact your perception of yourself in the present moment. Our subjective realities are built from our chosen core beliefs, as well as from our perception of events that have happened to us during our experience of life. These experiences mold us and change us, but only in the way we perceive and ultimately desire them to. We believe that we learn more about the world around us and ourselves every day, but in reality, **there is nothing that we can learn about the world that we do not already believe or understand within ourselves.** Any attempt to extract or otherwise obtain knowledge from others or the world can only ever satiate this curiosity by **confirming what we already know** to be true. For this reason, we are the arbiters and gatekeepers of our own truth. Through this, nothing outside us can ever teach or show us anything that we do not already know or believe for ourselves to be already true.

To illustrate this point, we will explore several examples over this next section. Imagine you meet a professional within your network for the first time over coffee. As you begin to get to know one another, the other individual begins to share with you their personally held views on globalization. They express that globalization is a great thing for the world, as it allows resources and goods to be freely traded while working to improve relationships across various regions and countries through this co-opted interdependency. For this, let's assume that you agree with their assessment, personal opinion, and research, in which case, you nod in agreement and have an **internal resonance** with the material you are presented. Perhaps you even learn a few new things from them that you had not previously considered or understood, as you proudly add this to your existing body of knowledge on this particular topic. Afterwards, the conversation pivots to that of global warming and climate change. This individual suggests that global warming is caused by the pollution and poor treatment of our planet and its resources, which not only erodes our ozone layer but is indirectly responsible for other natural disasters that could have otherwise been avoided entirely. On this point, you happen to disagree vehemently, but you listen to the other, and the interaction itself remains respectful. Through the other's explanation and passion regarding the dangers and causes of global warming, you were again presented with things you hadn't considered or knew about prior to this conversation, but it didn't necessarily matter, as you **already held your opinion** on this particular topic. In fact, the more evidence they presented to you, including the previously unknown or unheard evidence, only made you **more certain** in your own personal belief and opinion on this matter. What was the point of this interaction with the other if each party only brought in with them their own concepts and ideas, with no intention ever to accept or consider the opinion of another by changing their own? You nodded at one another when in agreement, then shook your heads in disagreement on the topics in which you were not aligned. What did you learn? Were any opinions changed? What was the goal of the conversation? Perhaps to change the mind of the other or to defend your own position?

As the gatekeepers of our own truth, **we hold the ultimate authority** of what we allow to process within us as factual. This is often what we **determine** to be in alignment with our existing beliefs, as well as what we reject, which typically contradicts our **existing beliefs**. We might have the opportunity to intellectually learn more about a topic from another, such as globalization, but only as long as we **deem it worthy** of being added to our knowledge bank. When referencing the prior globalization example, you, as the gatekeeper of your own truth, first confirmed that the information about globalization aligned with your existing belief system; therefore, you allowed yourself to consider it. Second, you quickly established a rapport with the source material, which in this case is the individual at the coffee shop sharing this information with you. Though they were previously just a stranger, rapport was established quickly as we tend to favor those people who share a similar opinion or stance on something that is important to us. With globalization being among the first topics discussed during this interaction, rapport and favor were built quickly, ultimately allowing the information this source shared with you to take a stake within your existing intellectual understanding of this topic. Though once the conversation pivoted to global warming, you held onto your existing belief structure, regardless of the bountiful information provided by this other. Previously, you found this source to be reliable and likable, as they aligned with an area of passion for you, but after discussing global warming, you, as the gatekeeper, **shut down the well-researched points** of the individual whom you previously trusted as an information source. Only now have you begun to question this individual and the research they conducted, as it conflicts greatly with your own research efforts. You've perceived their contrarian opinion and the data they presented as insulting or challenging to your own intelligence, understanding, and subjective reality. You may even begin to renege your favor and rapport with this individual, as you provide reasons why the information they present is invalid. You may begin discrediting their research or their intellect on this topic. You may still trust them as an information source, but on the topic of globalization, because **their research and conclusions align with your own**. Whereas anything related to the conflicting topic of global warming will be immediately **disregarded by your internal gatekeeper**.

You've effectively stepped into this interaction primed with your existing beliefs and biases, hoping that others will present points that collate with your own. All this to **confirm** and **validate** what you **already know** to be **true**. Should their opinions and research align with yours, you will allow the information to take root inside your mind as you stack it confidently within your own internal body of knowledge. Even if the information source was previously unknown, you'd make exceptions for this individual. You believe they **must** know what they are speaking of since they have arrived at the same or a similar conclusion as you did in the research you have conducted. Effectively, you've **confirmed and validated** their intellect on this topic by measuring it against your own. In this case, you've selectively engaged the intellect of the stranger and have used them to **confirm** your **existing** body of knowledge while using them to **validate** your own intelligence, so long as it was a topic you were in alignment with; therefore, you'll allow the information in, even if from an otherwise unknown source. They've passed the test of your internal gatekeeper by sharing with you what you **already know** to be true.

As previously discussed, many people believe that they have an open mind while determining most others to be close-minded, even to the point of accusing the other of arrogance and raw stubbornness. When considering the prior example, it becomes clear that **we cannot learn anything new that we do not validate as truth internally**. If it fails to fit our existing narrative and belief structure, we will not accept it, as it contradicts what we already believe to be true for ourselves. Returning to the question that opened this chapter, "Does truth matter?", we begin to create the picture of how our subjective interpretation of the alleged truth shapes our internal processing of applied truth, as we are the **ultimate authority** above all else for what we perceive as truth. We regard no authority greater than ourselves to serve as the gatekeeper of truth, even if we do not consciously realize or are willing to admit this to ourselves. Are we this arrogant and stubborn, or perhaps just immensely fragile and insecure? For those who may not agree that they trust their gatekeeping ability more than anything else in the outer world, how might you have arrived at this particular opposing opinion, should you hold it for yourself? Did something external to you already invalidate the information contained within this book, or have you **chosen** to reject or question it? What vast library of intellect exists inside you that has the real-time ability to choose what is or isn't truth, then subsequently apply that **decided version of reality**, truth, and the associated filtration inherent to it, to the information you continue to process?

To expand a bit further, let's explore the global warming concept discussed earlier, but in the greater context of the issue itself rather than within the confines of the conversation with the stranger. Let's first assume that you believe global warming is indeed a real issue and that it is caused by humans' mistreatment and disregard for the planet and its resources. Furthermore, the consequences of this have caused and will continue to cause additional climate-related issues that could otherwise be avoided if proper precautions were employed around the world. In coherence with the "Understanding Core Beliefs" chapter, to accept any belief into your reality, assumptions must always be made. In this case, some of the assumptions you would have likely made are:

- The research I've been provided to support this belief is **accurate**.

- The research I've been provided to support this belief is **honest**.

- The scientists and researchers that have conducted research on this topic are competent and have fully accounted for their own assumptions.

- There is no ulterior motive to skew the results to promote the creation of new technologies or transfer wealth from one industry to another. If such a motive exists, it is irrelevant to the fact that global warming is, in fact, occurring as otherwise stated.

- There is no incentive by private companies, academic institutions, or researchers to provide inaccurate results as a means to receive government funding for additional research on this topic and others.

- Though history and science seem to indicate that the planet has undergone major climate transitionary periods, such as several glacial periods known as "ice ages," the current movement towards a warmer planet earth is not the result of a naturally occurring climate rotational pattern that would have occurred regardless of destructive human actions and pollution.

- News reports, news articles, and other literature about global warming are true and accurate.

- Anyone who suggests global warming is not real or that it is a hoax is a denier of science, perhaps less intelligent or simply ignorant, and dangerous.

Some of these assumptions may not apply, and many others may be utilized that were not included above. Though to believe in the concept of global warming, it takes the assumption to trust a resource outside of yourself. To trust a resource, scientific study, report, or literature, you must **first make the choice that such a source is reliable**, accurate, and honest. But where does even this choice come from, if not from the **assumption to trust** a resource that you've already accepted prior to this one? It matters not if it seems to be "common knowledge." It matters not if the research is conducted by the world's greatest minds and peer-reviewed by the top scientists from each country of the world. The only thing that matters is that you've made an educated guess, or assumption, based on your interpretation, faith, and trust in the data made available to you. When we sidestep and start discussing any topic by its **alleged** merit, its scientific backing, or historical references, we lose the greater point by conversing within these higher layers of intellectual abstraction. We must go deeper, **much deeper**, to the point where the **original choice** was made to accept or reject various elements, such as our trust for academic literature, scientists, the honesty of the participants, and the accuracy of the information itself. **These are all choices that only we are capable of making.** From this deeper place, all of our subsequent decisions are made. This details why some of the sharpest minds in the world can debate in circles with one another while failing to agree on the conclusion or "facts" of global warming, as they are **only discussing within these higher layers of abstraction**. Whereas the **real discussion** ought to speak to the assumptions they have each made, not on the research, but for themselves, which has influenced and formed their gatekeepers. To this end, each party may still end the conversation or debate on opposite ends, though at least they'd understand the reasoning of the other, as well as take into account their own subjectivity, assumptions, and core beliefs they themselves hold. To debate the issue on the alleged science alone may not yield the desired results for either party, as they leap to discredit one another while lifting up and encouraging any resource or individual that aligns with their opinion and intellect. Furthermore, when discussing such a topic on the world stage, both sets of incredibly talented scientists and researchers have their credibility, reputation, and egos on the line regarding an issue of potentially grave importance and severe ramifications, for those that believe it to be such.

For this reason, let's say your decision to trust a world-renowned scientist or collective of scientists on this matter supersedes and predates the material that they ultimately present and that we choose to accept and allow into our intellect.

How do we **really** know what's best for ourselves?

How do we **really** know what's accurate, what's true, and what's complete?

How can we ever know, if we alone are the gatekeepers of our truth, as we only accept what we have chosen to accept and while denying only what we choose to deny?

Do we suppose that we hold all of the intelligence and foresight required to make such bold assertions for global truth, as we execute a trust-fall exercise into the hands, opinions, research, and beliefs of others, who are just as prone to accepting unsubstantiated realities and misinterpretations as we are?

Regardless of the reasoning anyone might have for making the root-level choice to trust the source material, it becomes clear that we do not allow anything into our intellectual minds without the decision to first accept the source information as true, accurate, and reliable. **This is a decision that only we can make.** No one can ever make this decision for us, though many try directly, or indirectly, through various societal frameworks, structures, and peer pressures to convince us to accept various bodies of data or information, while receiving condemnation or judgment should we not comply with the template laid out before us. **We are the arbiters of our own truth.** Though we might make the decision to trust source material and information based on educated guesses and the available data, even the available data itself that we are considering as part of our "educated guess" must first involve the decision to accept this data for consideration in this process. All the data used during the research and educated guessing phase must be accepted as true and reliable by **you** as the **gatekeeper**, or even, as inaccurate or unworthy of consideration. Throughout this entire process, **you** are the gatekeeper for what you trust and what **you** allow to add to your intellectual body of knowledge. Any reference to an overwhelming body of knowledge, or "common sense" only deters from the responsibility and authority within yourself to make the decision to trust the body of knowledge and allow it to be considered and applied within your life, future research, and opinions on the topic. With this, **there cannot be a single thing** that you believe or know that you didn't **first** determine as true or valid within your world and subjective reality, before ultimately applying it to your knowledge and experience of life.

9. THE SPINNING ARROW

If one were to strive to be a "better" or more "noble" person, what might that look like? For the most part, it would depend on who you ask, the core beliefs they hold, and the context of the situation. What one might think is the "right" thing may be seen as "wrong" or irresponsible from another's perspective. For some, it may be as simple as following the laws of your country and using that as your morality guide. Meaning that so long as you aren't breaking the laws, you are doing the "right" thing. For others, they may hold to their religious beliefs as the ultimate authority of what is "right" and what is "wrong," as their belief system dictates. This can quickly become a difficult situation when your personal or religious belief system of morality conflicts with the local laws or the popular opinion of the masses and your peers. But even then, were laws not written by **other humans** with their own **subjective opinions**? Did they not use their personal moral compasses to create these laws? If each human interprets reality through the lens of their own biases, beliefs, and morality, and no human's reality is any more superior or valid than another's, is this no more than a case of the **blind leading the blind**? Or at the very least, the visually impaired leading the visually impaired? Perhaps they have based these laws heavily on their chosen religious or spiritual belief system. In doing so, they have interlaced the morality of their preferred doctrine into enforceable laws that others must follow or face the legal consequences, all for not honoring the laws written from the context of another human's preferred reality for how other humans must live their own lives. Additionally, these laws are enforceable even when those who are subjected to such laws, through the distinct verbiage placed by the law creators, may not share the personal convictions and morality of the originator of said laws. This also makes the **assumption** that laws written by humans of the past and present were not intentionally written to control or manipulate the masses or with the sole intent to keep themselves in power over others. This only suggests the forced behavior and compliance of others through the preferred ideals of the subjective realities of others. The subjectivity of morality and its inevitable influence in law creation makes clear why certain behaviors or possessions are dangerous and illegal in one country, while another country may actively encourage the same behavior or possessions among its citizens.

More often than not, citizens do not decide the laws or the structure they reside in, as they are only born into a pre-existing system. The system, depending on where it is located, may suggest that citizens have a right to change or modify it through legal means, such as voting or running for political office. However, these "paths" on their own are inherently flawed, as the path to modify the system is based on the rules of the system they intend to alter, all without possessing the immediate option to make the desired changes outside of the rules of the existing system. Furthermore, should the individual who wishes to change the laws forge their own path for doing so outside of the pre-existing system, it will be classified as illegal. It may even be labeled as a coup attempt to "overthrow" the existing system and government, but it may only be classified as such when viewed through the lens of this particular system. If this individual believes the laws of the land are unethical and wishes to change them, would it be the "right" thing to violate the existing laws for the purpose of implementing more "ethical" ones if they truly interpret the existing ones as unfair, suppressive, or immoral? But to whom would these proposed new laws or systems appear more ethical or moral? Would it be more immoral to break the laws and risk the manufactured consequences that only exist within the system itself, or to stand by and allow the existing unethical laws to prevail without challenge? If one's belief system suggested they must follow the laws of the land but determined the existing laws to contradict their own belief system, would the moral "ends" justify the immoral "means" if the ultimate goal was to align the laws more acutely with their own subjective morality and beliefs? With various influences, ranging from cultures, religious backgrounds, family values learned from one's upbringing, and personally held convictions, people everywhere interpret situations differently based on their own perceptions, core beliefs, and subjective realities. They also decide "how" to act and "how" to feel based on these moral convictions. With that, some may be willing to set their own convictions aside and follow the convictions of another in observance of the local laws to avoid punishment.

The comparison between greater groups, such as the laws of an entire country or a centralized religious group, may be easier to compare, contrast, and generally grasp. However, the variances of morality and ethics of what might be considered "good" or "bad" exist even within sub-groups of belief systems, which are already sub-groups of society within themselves. This creates a trickle-down and nested form of personally accepted morality. Of note, a morality that is "personally accepted" is not the same as one that aligns personally as a result of convictions within oneself. For example, some within the Christian faith believe that obtaining a tattoo on one's body is a sin, declaring that the body is a temple of God (1 Corinthians 6:19), whereas other Christians do not interpret the particular references in scripture to apply to restrictions for tattooing one's body. In this example, both sides of this morality coin come from the same religious doctrine and belief system but have been interpreted differently, as each holds their personal convictions on the matter. Though, do our personal convictions matter? Do we have the intrinsic right to follow and adhere to our own personally held convictions of morality if they are in conflict with laws, a group, or others, or must we submit to the personally held convictions of another? On this particular topic, the internet is filled with Christians asking in forums and within social media posts, "Is it okay to get a tattoo if my body is considered a temple of the Holy Spirit?" This suggests that when it comes to one's own moral compass, they may not only defer to local laws but also to their religion and interpretation of the doctrine **over their personally held convictions**. As in, if the Christian desiring a tattoo did not personally believe getting a tattoo conflicted with their convictions, but another Christian within their church, social circle, or elsewhere on the internet warned against receiving a tattoo, the other with opposing interpretations and convictions states that receiving a tattoo would effectively be abusing the temple of the Holy Spirit. Ultimately, the one desiring the tattoo may not proceed with the tattoo, fearing that they would be straying from the **expected behavior** as they, or others, have interpreted from the same religious doctrine source. Meanwhile, many Christians do not interpret the same scripture in the same way, nor do they have personal convictions against tattoos and have obtained one for themselves without any embedded fear, guilt, or shame. Therefore, even within the same country, religion, or other sub-groups of core beliefs and morality, what is determined "good" or "bad" continues to **vary greatly**. This suggests that ethics and morality cannot be defined or bound by even the strictest of belief systems or laws, even if only adhered to out of fear of consequence or punishment by the individual. As every person lives within their own subjective reality, this "reality" also carries with it its own moral compass that **is completely unique to the individual**. Even if they are influenced by external factors, such as fear, **it's still their choice** of what moral compass they will follow through their own perception of the world. In this way, do we not choose our morality? We believe morality to be mostly static, especially those who have adopted a strict belief and are unable to see outside of it. They believe that the morals they hold dictate the ultimate authority and moral compass that everyone else ought to follow. They will see the thoughts, actions, and behaviors of others through the morality they have accepted for themselves as they judge, criticize, and demean. Through this, we begin to see that even morality is vulnerable to intense subjectivity. The subjectively interpreted morals that we have accepted for ourselves **reside within** our subjectively held realities. Therefore, knowing that one subjective version of reality cannot be more superior to another, this includes everything within this reality, including the accepted morals.

THE SOUTHWEST-POINTING COMPASS

As we continue to compound the various concepts covered within this book, we have demonstrated the subjective nature of each person's unique perception of the world they believe themself to live in. From being the arbiter and ultimate authority of the truth that you allow into your life to accept or reject information to the core belief you select for yourself that alters your perceptions and modifies the reality presented to your conscious mind, we can see that it **all begins with a choice**, your choice. As discussed in this chapter, we have started to break down the subjectivity of morality based on the subjectivity of one's own chosen reality. This next section may be particularly triggering for some, but it is a necessary example to detail the depths of subjective morality and the layers of individual choices that precede it. When approaching this section, consider all of the sections, examples, and principles that have preceded this one, as well as the strategies, mindsets, and perspectives employed to navigate through each. The relative placement of this example in this book is intentional, as it stacks on the concepts that have come before. As with the prior examples, evaluate your emotions and feelings should you find yourself triggered at any point and use those as your internal guide. Lastly, the essential goal of this section is to understand your own perspective more thoroughly. With this, you may begin to understand how it could be possible for another to arrive at an opposing opinion that is so deeply against your subjective version of morality. There is no intention to change your existing belief system, only to understand it better, the choices you've made, and the perceptual bias inherent to any belief system. Then, you may leverage this deeper understanding of yourself and apply it to another that holds a seemingly immoral, or even evil, opposing ideology.

For this example, we will explore the events that took place on September 11th, 2001, in the United States of America, also known as "9/11". Before we continue, we must first state the assumptions taken to ensure clarity and uniformity as we proceed. The first assumption that we will make as we explore this is to assume that the events of 9/11 took place, more or less, how the general American mainstream consensus perceives the events to have taken place, based on the history books and the media coverage at the time, leading into the present. For American readers, this assumption might seem odd or even unnecessary to declare, but as stated all throughout this book, any assumptions that are not acknowledged and accepted become blind spots in our ability to perceive the world.

From the mainstream American perspective, the events that occurred on 9/11 were undeniably vile, as the al-Qaeda terrorist group hijacked four commercial airplanes, crashing two of them into the Twin Towers in New York City, ultimately killing around 3,000 people. These actions created a war in Afghanistan where many more military men and women died. For Americans, this was tragic and has left many around the world with heavy hearts for all those innocent people who had lost their lives, as well as the greater impact it had on the United States and the global war on terrorism. In the context of subjective realities and subjective morality, is it possible that even an event as historically destructive as 9/11 could be interpreted in a different way? The answer is, of course, a resounding and undeniable "yes." After all, there are two sides to this story, with each side believing they have taken the **moral high ground**. One of these sides involves the followers of al-Qaeda who chose to hijack the planes, ultimately causing tremendous damage and taking many American lives. What else did these terrorists choose prior to hijacking the planes? They chose their core belief, even if through an extremist form of Islamism, which involves efforts to restore God's law through bringing Jihad. Jihad, in this context, refers to the struggle between **good and evil** through bringing "strife or struggle" with the ultimate goal of **setting things right** in the Muslim world. For this reason, we can derive the mindset and perspective possessed by the al-Qaeda terrorists that ultimately led them to plot and execute one of the largest terrorist attacks in the history of America. For a moment, think of the American population's collective reaction to the Twin Towers collapsing; they were confused, devastated, and scared. For the members of al-Qaeda, in that same moment, as they watched the same live broadcast seen by all Americans, they were cheering, celebrating, filled with glee and ecstasy at the remarkable deed they had come to accomplish. They had executed their mission successfully according to their desired plans, perhaps except for the airplane that crashed in Pennsylvania. How could they possibly be celebrating the excessive loss of innocent American lives? How could anyone ever see this act as anything other than absolute evil?

Like many prior examples involving core beliefs, perception, subjective realities, and subjective morality, we cannot understand or grasp opposing or conflicting opinions from **the current position in which we originate**. To reiterate a previous example that involves Christians discussing God with atheists, whereby a Christian essentially shares their personally held belief that, "Anyone who doesn't accept God as their savior will go to hell" means nothing to the atheist, since the atheist **has not subscribed** to the same belief system as the Christian. In the same way, the Christian has not subscribed to the same belief system as the atheist and therefore may not understand how the atheist may be interpreting the words through the lens of their subjective core belief and reality. Without the ability to set aside our preconceived ideas, core beliefs, and perceptions, we will always debate at length from the very positions from which we originate, seldom making progress or obtaining a resolution or mutual understanding of one another. To be clear, none of this is to suggest that you ought to change your mindset regarding the events of 9/11, or even, that you ought to find a mutual understanding or respect for the terrorists. This example, and the questions asked within, are used only for demonstration purposes to highlight the subjective realities and subjective moralities of individuals, as well as how **each side effectively justifies their own belief system and actions**, while confidently self-labeling as "good" and the other as "bad." We mustn't need to agree with another's conflicting opinion, as we have the freedom to select and choose our own. Though, there is significant value in understanding the mindsets, perspectives, and assumptions that the opposing party has made to arrive at their particular conclusion. As we see here, to simply "do the right thing" is subjective, as the very essence of "right" and "wrong," "good" and "bad," can only ever be subjectively interpreted within the individual realities held by each. Even in the case of a mass loss of human lives through intentional acts to cause this, groups of people exist whereby this action is not only justifiable but honorable, good, and moral. Does this make those who think this way crazy? Unjust? Disgusting? Despicable? This answer depends on whom you pose this question to and the core belief system they've adopted for themselves inside their subjective reality.

Suppose you are on the American side of this opinion. You likely feel incredible disgust at these horrendous acts of violence. Many Americans who had not previously considered joining the military decided to enlist following the events of 9/11. The **conviction**, the **passion**, and the **motivation** to **serve a cause greater than themselves** inspired them to not only place their personal lives on hold but to **risk their lives** entirely, leaving behind their significant others, families, and children. These **brave** men and women seek **justice and vengeance** against those responsible for these attacks that took **innocent** American lives. America stands for justice, what is moral, and does not take innocent lives. Many Americans of western faith, such as Christians, Catholics, Baptists, and others, also felt threatened by the Islamic extremism religion, and therefore, fight to protect the religious freedoms available to all in the United States of America. Americans also seek to destroy, **through force and violence**, the al-Qaeda group and any others involved with these **acts of terrorism** so that no further harm or attacks can take place against us **by crippling their nation and organization**. Furthermore, the American CIA and other intelligence organizations **surveil** al-Qaeda and any other linked entities through the placement of spies, technology, drones, and underground agents to **infiltrate the organization** in order to destroy it, while also **working with allies** who may assist and aid in these efforts to do the same. America's surveillance and infiltration of these organizations, even if done preemptively, would be **justified as necessary** for the protection of the American people. If surveillance and infiltration were only done reactively, it would also be justified to prevent future attacks from occurring again. When interpreted through the mainstream American perspective, most if not all of the actions stated in this paragraph are completely justified, honorable, and undoubtedly the "right" thing to do to scrub this **dangerous evil** from this planet.

Lastly, the general American perspective on the events surrounding 9/11 regards the media's broadcast and depiction of the events to be true, honest, and accurate.

With this and with our deeper understanding of how core beliefs, perceptions, assumptions, and subjective realities are established, how might the al-Qaeda terrorists view America as a country and as its citizens to **justify** their actions? Not only this, but how have they become so **passionate** about their mission that they will live, fight, and die for their cause, which has caused the Americans so much pain and suffering as a result of 9/11? As we've identified previously, objective truth is **not required** for a core belief to be accepted and adopted during the creation of one's subjective reality. We are all the gatekeepers of our own truths, and **what we choose to believe is a choice** based on our unique interpretations of life, influenced by our culture, religion, upbringing, peers, and much more. The assumptions stated below are not intended to be a comprehensive or exhaustive list but allow us to begin the exploration into how such core beliefs and perceptions could be formed by another with opposing interpretations of life and reality, even when contradictory and immoral to our own. Let's take for a moment some of the assumptions the terrorists might have made to believe in their subjective reality to take the actions that they did:

Assumption: "America is evil and immoral."

When considering the extremists' belief system, they consider, among other things, gambling and homosexuality as **greatly immoral** and an **evil** that must be **destroyed**, as it disrupts the natural order of things and inhibits God's plan.

This belief system also suggests it is the believer's personal responsibility to **right these wrongs** with the exertion of their effort, through strife and struggle, even at the expense of their own life. It's their **righteous duty** and their assigned **purpose**. To **fight and die** for this righting of wrongs is **honorable** to them, their family, and the eyes of their God as they see it. For them, it takes **bravery and courage** to execute their purpose according to their adopted beliefs. In this way, they are passionate about serving **a moral and spiritual cause** that is **greater than themselves** and their own lives.

Assumption: "America struck first and started the war through pre-existing acts of foreign interference, or through taking part in sinful and destructive acts. 9/11 was only retaliation."

They believe that America had **already meddled** in their affairs and the affairs of their allies, **committing acts of war**. This can occur in many forms, such as foreign election interference, disputes with trade, or the placement of seemingly unfair sanctions on them or their allies, believing **America is spying on them** via technology or underground agents. Therefore, 9/11 was **justifiable retaliation** and **vengeance** for **terroristic acts perpetrated by**

America against them, according to them. Whether or not any or all of these occurred in true and objective reality is irrelevant, so long as it is adopted to be true by the chooser of this belief.

If based in reality, would the American military report these actions? **No.**

Would the American media broadcast these actions? **No.**

If another country's government or media reported such actions, would America deny it and simply call the reports lies and not based in reality? Would they not claim it to be psychological or information warfare by enemies of America in an attempt to "protect" the American people from accepting this information, whether true or not? America also currently puts forth great efforts to discredit information coming in from countries that they are not in a current alliance with, such as China or Russia. Therefore, any reports coming from these countries are quickly discredited, which has led to American citizens themselves not to trust the information since they do not believe the **information source**. They have been conditioned to accept the information presented by their own government while rejecting information from governments that their own government has discredited. In this way, the decision to reject the information coming from a foreign nation first came from the decision to trust the information coming from America directly. Therefore, once the initial information source is trusted, this information source sets the pace, tone, terms, and desired acceptance and tolerance for any other information sources while promoting itself as a reputable, reliable, authoritative, and unquestionable source. Americans maintain the general belief system that their government, military, and media are generally truthful and honest, which also claims that reports from other countries are entirely fabricated.

For this reason, Americans do not trust media sources outside of their own government or domestic media organizations while actively discrediting reports from foreign nations. This is due to the influence of their own trusted media sources and governments relaying that particular message, belief, and perspective for them to adopt. With al-Qaeda possessing the directly opposing view, America to them is an **evil and hostile** foreign nation that **cannot be trusted**, while their own internal reporting from their country or their personal and cultural opinions about America can be trusted instead as a more reliable source. They believe America is already utilizing technology, drones, and undercover spies to infiltrate the al-Qaeda organization and other foreign governments for intelligence purposes. Therefore, for al-Qaeda to place "sleepers" inside of America that can be activated for intelligence-gathering purposes or future terrorist attacks, it's no different than the general strategy already implemented by America towards them. Even if America was "first to strike" only in regard to the sins they commit as a nation by allowing immoral acts inside American borders, they believe that America is an evil that must be destroyed to **balance good and evil** in this world.

Assumption: "Most Americans are not innocent and are directly contributing to the evil agenda America holds, as most partake in immoral acts against God's will. For those that might be deemed innocent, sometimes collateral damage is necessary to achieve the greater purpose."

The destruction of the Twin Towers and all the other lives lost as a result of these events occurred for the greater good by damaging the evil and ungodly country that is America and its citizens. If those within the al-Qaeda belief system deemed any Americans innocent that perished as a result of 9/11, it would be seen as necessary and acceptable collateral damage.

During the American military's hunt for terrorists or other high-profile figures in times of war, has America ever caused collateral damage and murdered innocent people otherwise unaffiliated with the greater war or mission, if it meant destroying a powerful general in the enemy's army? In the al-Qaeda belief system, they would perceive this as true, regardless of its validity or invalidity in objective reality.

They believe that America has already murdered innocent lives all around the world, as America denies this "reality" publicly through the media. Therefore, they see America as no stranger to taking innocent lives.

Assumption: "American military and intelligence organizations are terrorists."

According to America's own definition of terrorism taken from the FBI's official website, terrorism is a "violent, criminal act committed by individuals and/or groups who are inspired by, or associated with, designated foreign terrorist organizations or nations."

If the al-Qaeda belief system adopts a similar definition of terrorism but directed towards their own nation and interests while interpreting the acts of Americans on their soil to be in alignment with this definition, Americans and their military are labeled as terrorists by the very people America labels as terrorists. By definition, are both parties terrorists to the other in their own regard?

SELF-VALIDATING LOOPS

Americans will, nearly unanimously, consider the events of 9/11 to not only be "bad" but among the greatest of "evil" acts ever done to America and the world. This chapter does not intend to change one's beliefs but only to revisit the structure of how core beliefs are created in each individual's subjective reality using an example that most are intimately familiar with. Through the explorations and analyses conducted in this chapter by compounding previously covered concepts and elements, we demonstrate how others with beliefs and ideals that greatly conflict with our own are built, created, and adopted. We see that the **fundamental structure** in which humans **concoct** their core beliefs, perceptions, assumptions, subjective reality, and subjective morality is **universally applied** across every single person, and it all begins with a choice. **The choice you have is the same choice your opponent has.** It's the same choice that we all have. In this very way, we are all responsible for **choosing our own morality**, on an individual basis. For you may view al-Qaeda's choices as evil, corrupt, and immoral, but according to them, your choice is just as destructive and evil, if not more so. If one were to suggest that, unlike their opponent's core belief system, their own beliefs do not involve recklessly murdering others, they would be missing the point entirely. This is due to the opposing core belief simply not classifying the actions they take as immoral or murderous, but only as good and righteous. For the suggestion that taking lives is evil requires first the choice to adopt a core belief determining this as such, as well as the choice to classify and define the word "evil" in itself. This word has been shaped by one's culture, government, religion, and other external influences, subjectively accepted through one's choice, then subsequently applied to their own internal reality and morality. As is the case with most belief systems, religious or otherwise, they often become self-validating loops and circles of subjective truth misidentified as objective truth, whereby the believer of such a system steers the interpretation of their beliefs and perceptions in the very way they see themselves, their actions, and the world. After an American makes a choice to trust the American media then assuming the media claims that reports from Russia cannot be trusted and only domestic reports can be trusted, this is a self-validating loop.

What other assumptions do we make in our lives, especially with things that we consider objectively "good" or "bad?"

If any other person could justify their behavior, thoughts, or actions as "good," where you see the same as undeniably "bad," who could possibly be more right when morality itself is subjective and based on the subjective choice of the individual?

If not bound by religious or other convictions, would we defer to the greater public opinion on the matter to achieve greater clarity into who might be more moral than another? What would be considered the "greater" public opinion in this case? 90%? 75%? Or perhaps 51%?

Would we establish our morality by the opinion that carries the loudest voice, with the most prominent advertising campaigns, tweets, or media coverage?

Would this opinion vary across cultures, nations, governments, or religions?

Does our morality come from our chosen religion?

Where did religion, of any kind, come from, along with its associated doctrine? Some forms of religion originate from a supernatural event experienced by an individual, or individuals, then written into an understandable language by man. For the religions that believe it was inspired or even written directly by God, the One, or any other supernatural being, the alleged source of the religion as believed is precisely that, a belief, which like all beliefs, first requires a choice to accept the belief and everything it entails within while accepting all of the associated assumptions. Any failure to honestly accept and acknowledge the assumptions and instead consider them as objective truths can only become a blind spot.

Do we derive our version of "good" or "bad" from our upbringing and values that our families, friends, and peers have influenced us with, who are all experiencing subjective versions of their own realities, vulnerable to the same influences from their outer world?

Do we receive our interpretations of morals from the local laws we are subjected to? Where do laws come from, if not from other humans with their own subjective interpretations of realities, forming laws based on their subjectivity moralities, influences, experiences, religions, or originating nations and cultures?

THE MAGNETIC NORTH POLE

If we choose to inherit our own morality from anything created by another, such as local laws, religion, or the opinion of someone else, **it can only ever be subjective**, which in turn, is vulnerable to reinterpretation or destruction. For example, consider for a moment you receive your moral guidance from the local laws. Laws can vary from city to city, state to state, and country to country. In this way, your morality will be influenced by the place you were born, raised, and perhaps where you presently reside. Additionally, laws are often changed and modified, and always created by means of another through their own subjective reality and respective morality. We allow laws to influence our morality, as failure to comply with the laws results in consequences, similar to how those who raised us **taught** us the difference between what's "good" and "bad." Though, "good" and "bad" in this context may be more accurately referred to as what is acceptable and pleasing to the life of another, and what is unacceptable and unpleasing. To avoid punishment, pain, or unnecessary suffering, we comply with those who have a **manufactured authority** over us. We determine those who find themselves behind the bars of a jail cell to be troubled individuals who are lost, misguided, or otherwise lack the discipline and morality necessary to quite simply do the "right" thing. When they get released from confinement, it becomes difficult for them to get a job and become employable, as they are classified by the manufactured society in which we live as an ex-convict through the very same laws that labeled the behavior they exhibited as illegal. In our society, they are often judged or even feared, as they are criminals by the definition of the law. Many citizens are fine with this concept, using the justification that laws are there to protect us—but to protect us from what? To protect society from those exhibiting "bad" behaviors? Or from the possession of "bad" substances? The crafters of the laws, who are humans with subjective interpretations of reality and riddled with their personal biases, utilized their own subjective moral compasses to determine what is "good" and "bad" for the general public, many of whom may have different morals and convictions for themselves.

Consider for a moment the War on Drugs in the United States, enacted in 1971. This declaration made the sale, distribution, and use of many substances illegal, such as N,N-dimethyltryptamine (DMT), commonly found in Ayahuasca, while also banning psilocybin, present in magic mushrooms. The substances referred to here are considered Schedule One (Schedule I) drugs, which the United States defines as "the most dangerous drugs," with a "high potential for abuse," and "no accepted medical use." For reference, other drugs in this category are the likes of heroin and methaqualone (meth). The highly illegal nature of these substances has greatly discouraged research and possession while also effectively influencing the perceived "good" and "bad" nature of the substances through the significant enforcement efforts and punishments associated with them. Though in recent years, illegal drugs like marijuana, psilocybin, and DMT have resurged, as they begin to show promise in the treatment of various mental illnesses and helping those recover from crippling disorders like post-traumatic stress disorder (PTSD). Marijuana is actively being used as an alternative to prescription-strength opioids, of which there is presently an epidemic, with many well-intentioned and responsible individuals accidentally becoming **addicted** to the substance despite it being legally prescribed by a doctor. Legally prescribed opioids that have caused many to become addicted are **deemed moral and ethical** for many, yet substances like marijuana carry a negative moral stigma, with possession penalties placing those in confinement for years. With the latest research indicating these substances to be viable and non-addictive alternatives to their prescription-strength counterparts, have we invertedly based our own morality on the laws of the land, which change each day with new research and legislation? Additionally, preliminary data indicates that psilocybin is anti-addictive, has a greater success rate in treating patients, including those who have been unable to be successfully treated in the past using conventional and legal methods. Further, treatment with psilocybin does not require regular or daily use, like selective serotonin reuptake inhibitors (SSRIs), while seemingly carrying fewer side effects. In some cases, a single high dose and therapeutic session of psilocybin can result in positive effects lasting for months, if not longer, as it possesses the ability to completely heal the patient's trauma rather than simply managing it.

Perhaps during the War on Drugs, there was simply not enough data out about these substances to determine the dangers that might be associated with the unmonitored consumption of them. Therefore, the government banned them to protect American citizens. Now that updated research is available, and the ban is starting to show signs of being lifted across many states, the tone and stigma are beginning to shift. If all states ultimately decide that these natural substances are safe to use and are viable alternatives to prescription-strength drugs, would this alter your pre-existing core beliefs and morality stigmas about these substances? It is likely that you were raised to stay away from drugs like marijuana by your parents, as well as through your schooling, employer, and the risk of life-altering imprisonment?

- With that, how easily can your own morality and opinion be swayed?
- Who, or what, have you **given power** over your ability to determine your own ethics?
- What would it take for you to modify your stance on these substances and become equally accepting of their use as the

legal pharmaceuticals you've already accepted as safe and moral?

- Does your religion or personal convictions refrain you from revisiting this moral, or, like the tattoo example, is this susceptible to varying interpretations of the associated doctrine and principles?

- Where have you derived your morals and ethics from? There are often more than one originating source.

- What hypothetical situation would need to occur for you to revisit some of your deepest-held morals?

- What information might you need to be presented to question your morals? With that, which information sources have you chosen to trust to provide you with such information? And, should such morality-altering information exist, would your core beliefs and existing perceptual biases allow you to see and process the information at hand?

10. STRINGS OF REALITY

As we begin to understand the implications of subjective realities and apply this to our own perceptions of life, it may become destabilizing to the foundations of our being and consciousness. Further, it may also introduce extreme uncertainty in the perceptual models, chosen core beliefs, and ultimate version of reality that we select for ourselves. After all, if truth, morality, reality, beliefs, interpretations, and perceptions are all subjective products of our choice, then how can we ever be certain that the reality we have selected for ourselves is the "right" one, "moral" one, "best" one, or most "accurate" one? When we break down the fabricated and illusory structures of our own perceptions and biases, we can identify the many options available to us regarding our incredible power to choose the reality in which we most desire to live. In some ways, this can be absolutely freeing, especially if you have most recently escaped from a perceptual model that you had been subconsciously trapped in that brought about a seemingly sad, depressive, or otherwise victimhood view of your existence and reality. If you recently arrived from a perception of reality that engendered much anxiety, fear, and insecurity, while appropriately identifying this version of existence as a series of choices that you've made, you've begun to set yourself free. As you continue to make new choices to perceive life in a way that is pleasurable, freeing, exciting, and filled with optimism, you'll likely be thrilled at the rediscovery of the power that you hold and have always held. However, even in the case that one chooses a perception of reality and the associated core beliefs that are more pleasant to experience, one cannot escape the realization that, precisely like the previous unpleasant experience of life, this new experience is still the result of a subjective choice. In this way, you may wonder if the version of reality you've selected is a more accurate interpretation of reality, or one that causes you to live outside of reality in an ignorant, or even hallucinatory manner. Furthermore, when we are fully aware of the seemingly infinite array of choices we can make and the realities to subjectively live within, we may wonder if we are making the "right" choice, as we begin to experience what is known in behavioral economics as "Choice Overload" or "Overchoice" (Alvin Toffler, Future Shock, 1970). Whereby, the satisfaction related to the chooser's selection decreases when the number of known and available choices increases, as the chooser questions whether or not they've made the "right" or "best" choice for themselves. When fewer choices are present, the chooser's satisfaction with their choice is greater, even when the experience of their reality is relatively subpar to another choice that would yield a greater experience if the relatively superior choice was nested within a vast array of other options.

First, we explore the concern related to selecting a reality that may not be accurate or aligned with an objective reality. For this, we consider the proverbial phrase to generally classify one as being either an optimistic or pessimistic individual, "Is the glass half-empty or half-full?" Should you be unaware of the choice you have and instead identify intrinsically with your viewpoint, you may not experience any uncertainty or instability, as this "reality" is unquestionable since it is what it always has been for you. Though, when you realize you have the choice to alter your perception and core beliefs completely, you may begin to doubt if the reality you chose is the correct one. Assume that you begin in the reality that the glass is half-empty, but after self-reflection and analysis, you realize that this view causes you to operate in a state of fear, lack, or negativity. You instead decide to view the glass as half-full. With this view, you feel happier, generally more optimistic, while operating in a state of abundance rather than lack. This feels good and enjoyable until one of two things occurs:

- You recall that your renewed perception of the glass is a result of your subjective choice. You feel happier but begin to feel like you may be ignoring the other "reality" that the glass is also indeed half-empty. You feel that you may be unrealistically optimistic and living outside of "reality."

- Another individual, who happens to unequivocally view the glass as half-empty, questions your reality. They openly call you ignorant, unrealistically optimistic, or living out of touch with reality. They claim you are ignoring the lack and negativity present in this situation while also suggesting that your head is in the clouds.

When you firmly realize your power to alter your experience of life and perception based on your conscious ability to choose, you encounter a concern that was not present when you were unaware of the choice you always had. On the one hand, you feel empowered, realizing that your perception is a choice that only you can make; therefore, you make the choice that brings forth the more pleasant and enjoyable experience of life. This is truly a freeing realization for one to embody. Yet, on the other hand, and despite you feeling happier, you question your choice and its existence in actual reality, especially when challenged by another with an opposing or contradictory view. However, when we remember that, like us, others are also living in their subjective versions of reality whether or not they are consciously aware of it, **they cannot be more right or more wrong about any possible objective reality**, as their very perception of reality is based on a choice that they've made to perceive it as such. To rank your perception as superior to another's can only ever be ignorant, but similarly, to rank your perception as inferior to another's would be equally ignorant. With this understanding, which version of reality regarding the liquid volume of the glass is more accurate? Neither, and both. The realities exist concurrently, not only in the subjectively held realities and interpretations of each person but also within the objective world itself. The glass simultaneously exists both as half-full and half-empty in the objective world, but the individual has the power to decide which state to see and actively experience. You have the power to choose, as **neither choice could be wrong**. It is within your natural ability to choose the reality that you experience and live. Understanding that both states exist concurrently and that any contradiction you receive from another is only a result of their subjective choice and subjective interpretation that cannot be more or less complete than your own, you may choose your preferred perception confidently, knowing that it can only ever be your choice. It's your life, it's your perception, it's your experience, it's your choice. You are neither correct nor incorrect with whatever choice you make, as all variables in any perceptual model or belief exist concurrently.

The prior example involving the glass being half-full or half-empty was intentionally simplistic to outline the existence of both realities simultaneously. True reality was present in both subjective realities held by the individuals holding their chosen viewpoints. However, what about other situations and viewpoints that are far more complex than a physical glass holding unknown liquids? What about the subjectivity of morality in itself? Why are things "good" or "bad," and is there a universal standard for morality that humans from all walks and interpretations of life can agree upon? What if something is "good" or "pure" to one, but "bad" or "impure" to another? Which interpretation is more accurate or correct? Surely, the holder of a particular viewpoint will undoubtedly express that the reality they hold is the most accurate, along with all of the reasons why this is the case. All the while, they recruit their chosen core beliefs and perceptual model as the all-inclusive "evidence" required to support this particular viewpoint. This "evidence" only exists within their subjective reality but not in the subjective reality of another. For this reason, what makes something universally "good" or universally "bad" if the perception and classification of such occur solely within the subjective reality of the one experiencing it? In this way, **any situation** involving morals is **both good and bad**, as well as neither, all simultaneously within the objective world. For it is not the objective world that maintains these labels and classifications but only within the chosen interpretation of the relative observer. Meaning, all variables, forms, and possible perceptions, exist at once. It is the responsibility, duty, obligation, or freedom inherent to the consciousness of the individual to choose the existence and perspective that brings about the most joy, purpose, or meaning for them. Though, even purpose and joy are subjectively interpreted and experienced. Even if a perceptual model regarding a particular situation may bring about sadness, the individual may only need to re-evaluate their perception of sadness itself without altering the core choice that initially brought about the sadness. We choose the layers of perception in which we operate and can expand this influence without limits to encompass all elements of our being. Any perceived restriction or boundary to do so, to any particular degree, **exists artificially** within one's self-limiting belief system.

SYMPHONY OF PERCEPTION

Every choice you make that results in a perceptual shift is akin to playing a single string on a harp. In the case of a concert harp, there are 47 strings to choose from. Though you may choose one string that carries a pleasant tone for you, this does not mean the other 46 strings do not exist. All 47 strings exist simultaneously, but the only one you currently hear is the one you choose to play. At any point, **you can always choose any other string**. You, as the individual, have the power to choose the string you most desire to play. In one moment, a particular string may be soothing and relaxing, but in another moment, you may decide to play another string altogether. **No one can choose a string for you**, nor is any choice of string correct, incorrect, or tone-deaf. Furthermore, a string that sounds pleasant to you may not sound pleasant to another, as they are subjectively interpreting the sound of the string you chose to play through the lens of their subjective reality and personal preferences. Likewise, a string that another plays consistently may not resonate with your personal preferences due to your own subjective biases and interpretations. Realizing this, you may free yourself to play any string on this harp that you choose, completely independent of the opinions or preferences of another. Additionally, if you consistently play the same two or three strings, it does not mean that you cannot choose any other strings, as you are free to play them all at any time of your choosing. When aware and present in the current moment, you can feel the emotions, mindset, and perspective associated with the string you are playing, then change the string dynamically as you wish to best coincide with your present moment. Even when we are not aware that we are choosing a string, a string **is always being played**. We either make the conscious choice to select a string, or we choose a string subconsciously. When we choose a string subconsciously, we may complain about the sound we hear, we may blame the harp, or another; however, when we realize that it can only ever be us to play our harp, we can take full ownership and responsibility for the beautiful symphony it emits at our hand.

There are no strings that you "should" play, only the ones that you want to play. External influences, or even our own bounding boxes and core beliefs, may blind our vision into seeing only half of the strings. Some beliefs or influences may allow us to see all of the available strings but attach a consequence or judgment to a string that we would otherwise have the sole right to play. Should we not take full ownership of our natural right to play our own instrument freely, we allow our musical score to become hijacked through the pressure or expectation to play a sound that others would much prefer to hear. We cannot play a song for another and a song for ourselves at the same time; we must choose which song to play at any given moment. Should we allow our score to be hijacked, we may justify this as the resulting song we hear is "close enough" to what we originally envisioned or wish to hear ourselves. Oftentimes, one hijacked note turns into two, then three, then seven, until the emanating arrangement is unrecognizable. Your harp is yours alone, as well as your personal intuitions, feelings, and preferences in what you choose to play with it. If the sound you hear through your string selection is pleasant and enjoyable, do not allow the subjective judgments, opinions, or preferences of another to steer you towards a less-than-ideal string than what you would ultimately prefer for yourself. At all times, remember that the sound they hear emitting from your harp is subjectively heard and interpreted by them, through the musical resonances of the string that they themselves are choosing to play at that moment.

To expand on this further, the strings may relate to any particular belief you hold or perception you currently possess of yourself, another, or situation. For example, if you are personally going through the break-up of a serious relationship, you may choose to view the situation optimistically, understanding that the relationship wasn't ever quite what you were looking for, and by breaking it off, you are freeing yourself to focus on yourself, or find someone else who may be a better match for you. This doesn't necessarily insinuate that you don't feel any emotional pain over the ordeal, only that you are overall choosing to perceive the situation in a positive and empowering manner. Your inner circle, however, thinks that you are "moving on" too quickly and that you aren't being sensitive enough to your feelings. They claim you haven't spent enough time crying, binge-eating your favorite ice cream, and cursing at the "unrealistic" relationships demonstrated in the various romantic comedies you "should be" endlessly streaming. If people within your inner circle believe you are being too optimistic, or in other words, that you are playing the "wrong" string of perception for your life, **they are correct**. However, your choice to play the more pleasing and optimistic string is also **correct**, as both perceptions of reality exist concurrently. This suggestion of theirs is the equivalent of them playing one note of the many other available notes while insisting that you are playing the incorrect string. Strangely enough, they have exclusive control of their own harp, and to even make such a suggestion for you, they must be playing a string of their own. Yet, they question your ability and intrinsic right to play yours however you wish. Why must your harp become tuned to theirs? In reality, two or more harps must not be tuned in relation to one another, as they exist independently. Though, many will try and attempt to guilt or persuade you to not only tune yours to theirs but to play the string that they desire the most for their life. With this, they hope to add to their own symphony at the expense of the creative and unique expression of your own. If the tone you intend to play is optimistic and enjoyable, why would you change it for another? The other may attempt to guilt you and project their selfishness onto you; however, any unhappiness or discontent they may be feeling is only the result of their own perceptions and the string of their own harp that they are presently playing. Even when hijacked, it is still only you who can ever play your harp; no one can play it for you.

There will be people that walk around and play a sad or depressive note continually, but that doesn't mean that it should ever be the note that you choose for yourself, despite their persistence or the demands they place on you. Surely, that note does exist, as does the reality associated with it, but you are choosing to play another. If people around you play the same note over and over again that interferes with your symphony, you either must distance yourself from them or you must alter your perception regarding the notes that they are playing and why they might be choosing to play them for themselves. When you realize that no one but you can play a note on your harp, you effectively maintain control of your perceptual experience, even in the midst of an off-beat orchestra. You will maintain strength, resilience, and certainty in your chosen string despite others attempting to judge, criticize, or otherwise coerce you to play another note other than the one you intend to play. Regardless, responsibility for our perception is solely within our control, and nothing and no one can affect that unless we allow them to.

Relating to the world of music, let's assume the string you choose to play is equivalent to a "C" note, and another is also playing a "C." This is the same sound, resulting in coherence, alignment, and a pleasant experience for all. Alternatively, you play a "C" while another plays a "G." Though these notes are different, they harmonize together extremely well, with each note adding to the experience and enjoyment of the other. Further, you play a "C," another plays a "G," and a third chooses an "E." This is a synchronous chord; though different notes are being played, they work well with one another. Not only do they work well together, but they also enhance and supplement each of the individual symphonies in ways that cannot be achieved by a solo artist alone. On the other hand, should another insist on playing a note that does not align with the symphony that you and others are creating together, it does not necessarily mean that the note they play is "bad" or tone-deaf, but just that it does not currently match your current sheet of music. Just as well, their "bad" note that they play may very well be the missing note in a chord for a group of others playing a different symphony entirely. Therefore, we must recognize and appreciate the diversity in the notes we all choose to play. We all have our choice and mustn't actively work to hijack the musical arrangements of another, for we can only ever control our own. Throughout the journey, we may find some that enhance our own symphonies. Do not change your music for another, even if your intentions are pure. There are others who will appreciate the authentic music you share with the world. If you change your music for another, you will not only rob yourself of your own authenticity but rob others of the opportunity to find you and the missing piece they deeply desire to complete their own symphonies.

Though we are free to choose any string of perception that we desire, do not be ignorant and only see the string that you are playing. **All strings exist at once**. If one is being played, the others are still wholly present. Refrain from believing that the string or strings you most commonly play are all that there is or that the string played by another is incorrect or invalid, as this will prevent you and your ability to compassionately collaborate with others.

In terms of our choices and perceptions of reality, there are far more than 47 strings to select from. In reality, the options are undoubtedly infinite. Knowing this, there is always more than one way to view a situation, your life, and others. If you feel trapped, restricted, or pressured to play, or view the situation in a static way, you must have forgotten the infinite array of perceptual strings available to you. As all realities exist at once, our perception of the objective world is not objective at all, despite our willingness and determination to suggest otherwise.

The world is not "happy."

The world is not "sad."

The world is not "good."

The world is not "evil."

Instead, the world is formless and boundless. Much like playdoh or clay, we are the sculptors of the world through our chosen perceptions of it. In that, what we choose to perceive is what becomes created. Through our intention, perception, consciousness, interpretation, observation, and experience of the world, it takes form within our own subjective realities. We mold, craft, and design it to be exactly what we desire. Whether we are intentional and conscious in this process or not, **we are always creating our worlds.** What we see in our lives is the direct manifestation of our own creations, crafted from the otherwise boundless, infinite, and formless "reality" around us. Do not blame the clay for a disfigured or triggering sculpture, but instead, evaluate and understand the potter. For it can only be you, the potter, that is capable of creation. The clay is unbiased, nameless, while also existing independently without restrictions, classifications, or labels.

Whatever it is you are feeling is a direct result of the string you have decided to play for your life. Any deferment of responsibility to another person, situation, or event only further harms yourself. **All strings exist at once, and only you can play yours.**

No, you are not over-reacting.

No, you are not being too harsh.

No, you are not being too sensitive.

No, you are not being overbearing.

No, you don't cry too much.

No, you are not being overly optimistic.

You are perfect as you are and as you choose to be, so long as you are playing the strings that are authentic to your being. Your string selection has the capability to bring about the most pleasant experiences of life for you to journey through. Ideally, your string selection will encourage others to use their harps independently, as you help empower others to play what is most authentic to them. In this way, we celebrate diversity and unique creative expressions rather than demean them, knowing that others add to our symphonies as well. Even the others that do not align with the symphony we choose to play, we can only define ourselves through others and the variances in frequencies they provide. Each note, even the seemingly most unpleasant ones, must exist for us to experience the more pleasant notes of our own reality and perception.

The pleasant or unpleasant nature of your experience and existence is your choice, with no one and nothing able to decide this experience for you.

What defines pleasant? This is up to you.

What defines unpleasant? This is up to you.

What defines "good?" This is up to you.

What defines "bad?" This is up to you.

Remember **your power** and remember **your choice**.

You are in control.

You choose your string.

You choose your morality.

You choose your reality.

You choose your experience.

You choose your life.

11. YOU ARE YOUR PURPOSE

You are something exponentially deeper and more substantial than your beliefs. When we lose sight of this and begin identifying with our story, our narrative, our personality traits, and our accepted core beliefs as material parts of ourselves, we become afraid to challenge them, unsure what of us will remain. We easily become defensive or offended when a core belief of ours is challenged because we have intimately identified and chosen to believe it to be part of our real identity. When a core belief of ours is questioned, we interpret it as an attack on the essence of who we are due to a case of mistaken identity. Anything that can be taught or shown to you externally is not part of your true identity. Similarly, anything that you have artificially affixed to yourself as a result of a choice cannot ever become part of your true identity. In this sense, when we have defined ourselves and our identity as a result of things that are external to us, we have forgotten the deeper part of who we really are. Anything that we can ever add to ourselves can always be removed from ourselves. If a belief can be altered, changed, or modified, it cannot be your true identity. What is this part of ourselves that allows us to make these deep choices, change existing beliefs or perceptions, and provides us with the ability to analyze ourselves and the fundamental elements of our internal structure and concept of self? This is the part that can never be changed, altered, or stripped away, no matter your life circumstances. This is who you've always been, in your earliest of memories, and who you will always be. This is your infinite being, your essence, that supersedes even what you and others may consider to be "locked-in" traits such as your personality and likeness.

With that, who, or what, would we be if everything was taken away from us? What if all of your possessions, your chosen beliefs, your relationships, your children, your family, your spouse, your career, your titles, and your accomplishments were no longer yours, or the status of them changed? What of "you" would remain? To know this, we must dive deeper into what you aren't before we can define what you truly are. In essence, anything that can be changed, added, or removed from you is not part of you. This can only be a temporary and artificial attachment, much like baggage that you've chosen to carry with you, identify with, or even hide behind. There is nothing inherently wrong with attachments, only in your improper identification with them and your level of attachment to these attachments. Surely, one can identify with them as intimately as they'd like; however, this can only bring pain and suffering. In other cases, it may bring about an existential crisis if the elements of this illusory identity are challenged or fall apart completely.

Should you find your identity in being a parent and something were to happen to your children, then what happens to whom you've identified with using a manufactured bounding box, label, or status of being a "parent?" If you can become a parent, you can unbecome one.

Should you find your identity in your compassion, kindness, and patience for others, but through difficult challenges of life, you no longer exhibit and embody those traits, then what remains?

Who, or what is this deeper being that can attach and detach from things that we had assumed were part of us all along until these items were no longer present?

We can use a variety of labels to identify with and ultimately hide behind.

Are you attractive?

Are you kind?

Are you insecure?

Are you happy?

Are you an introvert?

Are you obese?

Are you successful?

Are you wealthy?

Are you smart?

Are you important?

Are you popular?

Are you selfish?

Are you a good spouse?

Not only can we never truly be any of these things, but most of these internalizations of the alleged external are subjective and relative interpretations that cannot be clearly defined. This is due to the variances in perception across the subjective interpretations of realities from yourself and others while also contrasting these against other fabricated structures such as religions and cultures, which ultimately originated from another's subjective reality.

If we create what we think to be our identity from external influences, then we become enormously threatened by other external influences that directly oppose or challenge the associated identity we've formed for ourselves. As in, if we have allowed external perceptions and influences to determine who we are, we fear that the external world can also take this identity away from us. By nature, anything that we add to ourselves in this manner can also be taken from us using the same source modality, thereby validating this fear. Inversely, when we have deep confidence about who we truly are, and our identity stems exclusively from our internal state of being and is not based on any external influence or definition, we realize that we can never be threatened by any external influence, as we know who and what we are and have always been.

MOTIVATION HALLUCINATION

We derive our sense of self through our sense of purpose, which further reinforces our sense of self. But, which comes first? Where does our story begin?

When we base our identity and sense of self upon the narratives, stories, labels, and titles that we have provided for ourselves, we also base our potential impact in this world, even our most ambitious dreams, off of these artificial attachments and chosen beliefs. In some cases, these stories and labels can be empowering, allowing you to take chances, risks, and seek out your deepest passions without hesitation or limitations. Though in most cases, the stories we accept for ourselves create limitations that only exist within the mental prison we've concocted for ourselves. We believe we are too shy to earn the management role. We believe we are not disciplined enough to start our own business. We believe we are not smart enough to move to a more lucrative career. Regardless of the self-limiting or self-empowering beliefs, these begin to shape what you believe to be your purpose.

We shape our purpose based on what we believe we are capable of achieving, not what we are actually capable of achieving, should we possess an empowering mindset that aligns with our truest self. Or in the case that we maintain our unaltered sense of purpose, we make excuses as to why we have not yet achieved it, typically blaming an external condition or asserting it to be out of our control. For this reason, what we may deem to be our purpose and potential in life can all too easily become subjective based on the beliefs we hold for ourselves.

If our idea of our purpose can be subjective or altered, how do we find it? To find it, we must first find ourselves. We do this by stripping everything that is not us away while analyzing our motivations and passions for the things we aspire to do in this moment. Though our passions and motivations can lead us towards our purpose, they can also be misinterpreted or channeled away from our truest self and truest purpose. This is precisely why all actions and motivations must be honestly analyzed in the present moment while visualizing the desired "end" goal. Furthermore, we must ask ourselves what our current condition and experience of life are as we pursue these passions.

To lead into this point, take, for instance, an individual who received excellent grades in school, relentlessly commits to his studies, and is currently powering through many years of college diligently to become a neurosurgeon. If one were to ask him what his purpose is, he would state that it is to become a neurosurgeon to help those in need. He may very well be stating this sincerely, though **genuinely communicated honesty does not guarantee truth.** He believes his purpose is to become a neurosurgeon so that he can deploy to foreign countries that do not have access to such specialty medical care in order to compassionately take care of others in a very meaningful and impactful way. Though his grades are excellent, he is stressed-out, his health is declining, he suffers from panic attacks, and he is taking antidepressants. He keeps his head high, with his eyes on the distant future, with many more years of rigorous academic studies to go before he can finally "achieve" his self-assigned purpose, find peace, contentment, and happiness. Where did this specific purpose come from? Why is he trading arguably the best years of his life and well-being to achieve it, if sick and miserable in the process? Where does this motivation or passion come from, and why has it only yielded suffering for what seems to be a noble and compassionate goal otherwise?

As a child in grade school, he didn't care too much about learning, and his grades reflected that, though he always cared so much for others while being attentive to their needs. When bringing home a report card to his father that revealed subpar grades, his father would punish him through restriction of possessions and privileges while also withholding affection and love. But when he applied himself in school and his grades went up, he not only got to keep his possessions and privileges, but his father would show him much affection and love while spending an abundance of time with him to encourage his improved performance in school. Through this experience, he learned that without achieving good grades consistently, he would not feel loved, desired, or valued by his father. Essentially, without good grades, he did not feel worthy of love or affection on the merits of his being alone, as it required additional effort, achievements, or accomplishments external to him to feel valued by others. For this reason, he learned that in order to reduce the frequency of punishments and the emotional pain of rejection from his father, he must apply himself in school. Given that he has always cared so much for others and their needs, he saw how upset his father became and wanted to be attentive to his father's needs to bring him joy. In this way, he obtained his value and purpose as a human being through achievements rather than something that was intrinsic to his own being. Throughout his life, he learned that not only did his father show love for him when he did well in school, but others also valued him as well, such as teachers, fellow students, and prospective colleges that offered him scholarships for his attendance. His entire sense of self and purpose had been based purely on his ability to demonstrate competence and intelligence through effort within an artificial structure, which over time, distanced him from who he really was and wanted to be. He did not find value in himself and continued to supplement his insecurities and lack of self-worth with achievements and external successes. Now in college, he continues to work aggressively towards his goal but is not receiving fulfillment in the same way. His father is still proud of him, but the dynamic, relationship, and dependency are different from when he was a child. He has become worn-down and unhappy, which he is unable to admit not only to others but to himself. Why can he not admit this to himself? Because to do so would destroy the value system he has built for himself to navigate this life. Furthermore, internal deceptions have been employed to protect him from such an existential crisis should this narrative be challenged or questioned. As we dig deeper into his story, we can now see that though he appears to be highly motivated and passionate, he is only driven by one thing: **fear.**

For if it was true motivation that drove him, would he not be happy with the opportunity to pursue his greatest passions relentlessly? Instead, he was driven by his fear of rejection, failure, and unworthiness, but under the guise of motivation, passion, purpose, and compassion for others. In an attempt to remedy this and align with his deepest desire to love and care for others, he chose an ambitious and high-paying career to please his father and others. He has subconsciously framed his ambitions in such a way, unbeknownst to even himself, that he could still pursue what brought him the greatest joy and satisfaction of all, helping and loving others. When he attempted to live a life authentic to his inner self and purpose, he felt rejected, abandoned, and unloved until he fit a particular mold that others had created for him. In an indirect way, he temporarily satiated his goal of serving and loving others by seeing them pleased and happy with his performance in school. This allowed him to justify his new direction and path as he doubted the motives and desires true to himself. For him to be himself, he perceived, meant rejection from others.

When revisiting the origin of these motivations and passions, he realizes why he has been so dissatisfied with life, on edge, and stressed for many years. He thought he had been true to himself and living out his purpose when this wasn't actually the case, as his present moments of life were anything but pleasant. He had been living his life according to the desires and preferences of another and had temporarily lost himself and his true passions along the way. Now that he has rediscovered who he is through the process of stripping away what he isn't, he obtained the opportunity to re-evaluate not only himself but his life, his intrinsic value, and his relationships as well.

PATH VERSUS PERCEPTION

We only have the present moment. The past does not belong to us and can only be shaped and experienced through this present moment. The future does not belong to anyone, as it only exists in our imaginations as uncertain anticipations of projected events and circumstances. With that, what condition are we waiting for to live pleasant and fulfilling lives? Are we enjoying the ride and our completely unique journey through life inside the present moment? If not, you must either adjust your perception or your path to align with your purpose and goals.

Revisiting the example story in this chapter, he realized that he had been chasing something out of fear. When operating from a place of fear, this inevitably leads to unnecessary pain, suffering, and inner turmoil. Through this realization, he received the opportunity to decide what he will do with his life from this moment forward. He determines that he desires to enjoy as many moments as possible through presence as he continues pursuing his passions and purpose. He decides he still wants to help people, but he also wants to ensure he is enjoying the ride of life as he pursues his goal of making the most significant impact on others that he can. Does he wish to continue pursuing his path through medical school? Or change his career path and life entirely? Our life is a gift. With this gift, we are given a choice. With our choice, **there is no wrong choice, only the choice that we make**. Therefore, no matter what he chooses, he cannot choose incorrectly, so long as he takes ownership for his choice and any associated consequences and costs.

One might wonder, would it make sense for him to continue his rigorous studies at medical school for many more years after discovering it to be the source of his suffering and depression for so long? This question is unfairly loaded, as it inaccurately suggests that his schooling was the source of his suffering, whereby, in reality, it was only his perception and interpretation of his life and circumstances that caused him pain. Therefore, should he consider remaining in school with the original goal of helping foreign nations in poverty with healthcare procedures, he must only alter his perception to make his present moment enjoyable, exciting, and a life worth living. For instance, rather than stressing out to achieve perfection out of his deep-rooted fear of rejection, unworthiness, and failure, he may now redirect his focus to that of a more empowering mindset. This could be something similar to:

"I am so grateful to be in this classroom learning the things that I am learning. I want to make the greatest impact on the world and become one of the leading doctors in this field. This way, when I am deployed to a foreign nation, I will have the knowledge, tools, skills, and resources to help anyone that trusts me with their care, as I will possess the necessary expertise. The general demands and stress that I experience as part of the packed school schedule serve as an opportunity to improve my time management and functional abilities. These stressors actively work on preparing me for the stressful environments I may face when deployed to foreign nations. Every class and every test presents me with the incredible opportunity to obtain more knowledge, which will only allow me to create the largest positive impact on those who are in true need and unable to take care of themselves."

Though nothing material in his path has changed, his perception, attitude, and behaviors would, enabling a state of happiness in his day-to-day life as he continues towards a goal, but without his happiness being conditional on an end objective, which would have never arrived regardless.

Should he instead decide that the medical school grind is not for him after all, but he still has a desire to help people in need, he realizes that he doesn't necessarily need to attend many years of mentally exhausting education to achieve the feeling that comes with helping others in the way he desires.

As you see, there is no incorrect decision for him to make, as the only thing that needed to change was the rediscovery of who he is. With this, he also rediscovered his value and has learned to obtain a state of unconditional well-being in the present moment, regardless of what the moment itself would look like. He also realized that it wasn't necessarily the specific goal of helping people in foreign nations that brought him the most joy; it was simply the feeling of what it would be like to be in a position whereby he was satisfied, living in synchronous unity with his deepest desires and purpose in each moment, and making a difference in people's lives.

FOLLOW THE FEELING

We don't have a single purpose, at least not in the way it has been defined by our societies and things external to us. There can be multiple purposes. We can find purpose in anything. We get to choose our purpose, which can be determined by our sense of self, life satisfaction, what we enjoy, what drives us. Society and others may want to pigeon-hole us into a singular purpose, but we can change our aim anytime we wish as we realize more about our true self through this journey into ourselves. When we realize that our purpose does not reside in material things or the external world that brings us joy, but in an inner state, we must only **follow that feeling.**

When we follow the feeling and live in the moment of what brings us the truest joy and passion while leveraging a self-empowering perceptive model, we create an abundance of energy. Rather than struggling to get out of bed and using sheer willpower to grind through each day with a sense of obligation and depression, we will instead operate from a place of passion. This is living with purpose and passion, which is **decided entirely by us.**

You begin to align with your purpose only upon discovering your true self, which reveals your truest passions and desires through the feeling they provide. When you engage with your purpose and deepest passions, you will not need only willpower to get through the day, the morning, your life. **Your passion will drive you** when the limited reserves of your willpower flounder. Your passion won't only accelerate and help you achieve your goals; it'll be the force that is orders of magnitude greater that works with you and for you. When paired with your discipline, willpower, and dedication, you become an unstoppable force. No longer will the working hours, study requirements, or early mornings cause you to begrudgingly drag yourself out of bed every morning; you'll spring out of bed, knowing that what you are working on, doing, achieving, and the lives you are affecting is something so much greater than the bags underneath your eyes or the other comforts of life you've had to give up in order to follow your greatest passions and purpose. When you align with the truest version of yourself, which is synonymous with your purpose, **you become your purpose, and your purpose becomes you.** You become everything that you are, and everything unfolds in the most pleasant and enjoyable way possible. Any difficulties that undoubtedly enter your path will be seen as opportunities for growth and further development, improving your character and skills, as it prepares you for the next phase of your development, life, and success. When your true self and purpose are aligned, the difficulties you face will not derail or discourage you.

Relationships. Cruises. Cars. Houses. Jobs. Money. All of this is outside of us and elicits a feeling of satisfaction, though the feeling itself can **only be within us.** This is within our control through our choices, perceptions, and the paths that we choose. It isn't the path or the things along it that bring us pleasure and satisfaction. Our satisfaction comes from our perception of our choices and life that bring us the feeling of satisfaction, contentment, and joy. Should we believe that we must seek an external condition, whether a college degree or the "end" goal of helping others overseas, we buy into the illusion that our happiness is conditional on an external state. Once we obtain that goal, we may feel happy, but this feeling is always temporary. And, what if, along the way, something unexpected occurs and we are unable to achieve that particular goal? Will we forever be unhappy?

Did the individual in the example waste most of his life chasing something he didn't really want after all? Not at all, unless you choose to perceive it as a waste, in which case, it most certainly will have been. We all have a journey of self-discovery and growth; each of our paths looks very different as they are individualized and custom-tailored to our needs. While he may choose the perceptive model and belief that he wasted those years, he could instead **see them as the necessary elements that they were** to become so stressed-out that it allowed him to reach a breaking point that he may not have otherwise reached. Once he hit the breaking point, he was able to become aware, conscious, and mindful in choosing his next path or perceptual model. Without the breaking point, he may still be stuck in his subconscious loop of self-inflicting pain and torture. Therefore, he may choose to view the path he took as the best years of his life, rather than the worse, as they ultimately led him to the point of awakening where he could find the happiness that could only be inside of him while aligning with his truest self and purpose. Through this, we realize that even the seemingly unpleasant moments of life are necessary for our growth. They can always serve us, should we allow them to do so. If we view the unpleasant moments as the worst times of our lives, they most certainly are. If we view them instead as essential moments for bringing us to greater states of consciousness, awareness, purpose, peace, and satisfaction, they most certainly are. Remember, the proverbial glass is simultaneously half-empty and half-full. All realities exist at once. It's the one that you choose for yourself that you create within your subjective reality, your life, and your world.

Should the path we desire require lots of effort, like medical school, we must choose a perceptive model that allows us to enjoy the journey rather than suffer in agony as we await the destination, which may never come. If you cannot enjoy the present moment and the journey you are on, you must either adjust your path or perception. There is no future; there is no later; **the time of creation is always right now.** Do not wait, do not delay, or hesitate. It's never too late to make a new decision, no matter what others tell you or how deeply invested you may already be in a particular path. If you are not receiving fulfillment or acting out from a place of passion in what you are currently doing, **change your path.** If you cannot reliably change your path at this time, **change your perception.** With a change in perception, you may be able to leverage your existing life and opportunity to expand to the next, or perhaps you realize that you didn't need to make a change in your path at all, and only the perceptual change was required after all, and you can find happiness, satisfaction, and contentment exactly where you already are.

What is your purpose? Surely, it isn't to become a doctor, own a sports car, get married, end poverty, or become president. **These are not purposes** and are only part of the rat race of illusions that can never truly satiate you. The exclusive and direct pursuit of these external goals will only create dissatisfaction in your life and disconnect you from your true self. Instead, you must **focus on the feeling** of what you wish to achieve in alignment with your true self. As in, imagine yourself achieving what it is you most desire with the greatest amount of detail, similar to the exercises presented in the chapter, "The Blue Sunflower." In this, you imagine having already accomplished what it is you most seek and desire. You can smell it. You can taste it. You can hear it. Imagine the relationships you would have if it were already here. Imagine the daily routines you would be performing and the schedule that you would hold. Imagine every detail of what it would be like to be already who you intend to be, and in that, you instantaneously become who you intend to be. You can feel it as if it were already achieved and residing with you in your present moment. From this place of pure imagination, you have received the very feeling that you seek but have begun to feel it through your thoughts and intent alone, without relying on an external condition. Therefore, you can now **focus on the feeling** and bring it into your present moment. This feeling has now been detached from the accruement of any external condition. From this place, your path will begin to form. For it can never be the external condition that brings us peace and joy, but the inner condition. Though, we must express caution. If, in pursuit of our purpose, we develop a mindset that we are not happy yet but will be as soon as we arrive wherever it is that we wish to go, we have missed the mark. When mindful enough, we can concurrently find peace and satisfaction where we stand while enjoying each step of the pursuit towards our ideals.

Maybe you feel you don't have a purpose, or don't amount to much, you aren't smart enough, or capable enough. If any of these thoughts or feelings have entered your awareness, spend some time unraveling your current motivations in life. Why is it that you are doing what you are doing? In any moment that you become present and conscious enough, analyze and observe yourself. Your thoughts. Your state of mind. What are you feeling? Are you happy? Are you satisfied? Why or why not? If you begin to externalize blame and responsibility in this stage, **do not deny this**, as it serves as your guide. You cannot change your feelings if you do not first acknowledge, respect, and love them. Follow the thread wherever this takes you while applying the principles within this book. Always lead with love.

Follow the feelings and do not deny them.

MANUAL FOUR
(IV)

12. STRENGTH IS A CHOICE

What is strength? Strength is a choice. The word strength, when used in this context, acts primarily as an arbitrary indicator of the level of difficulty we've assigned to making a particular type of choice. In other words, the amount of perceived strength required to make any difficult choice is assigned and selected by us through how we choose to view the pending decision and our willingness, or unwillingness, to make it. One might suggest that they are not strong enough to make a particularly challenging choice, but this is only because they have made this assumption based on their own belief about themselves and that they lack the strength necessary to carry it out. Unlike physical strength when participating in weight training that requires a progressive overload of weight week after week as muscles rip, tear apart, and rebuild to become stronger and larger over time, developing strength with your choices differs in some very key ways.

When faced with any difficult decision, you might be tempted to choose the easier option, even when it directly conflicts with your core values and goals. The level of strength "required" is based on your **perceived level of difficulty that you have chosen** to assign to this particular choice. Then, instead of making the choice that you know you ultimately desire to make based on your own best interests, you make the subpar choice and tell yourself that you lack the strength necessary to make the more difficult choice, despite it being more in alignment with your core values and true desires.

If you **decided** that you were not strong enough today to make the difficult choice, at what point in the uncertain future do you envision yourself to be strong enough to make the tougher choice someday?

What steps or series of actions have you laid out for yourself to build the strength necessary to make the more difficult choices in life that require this seemingly unattainable strength?

What **condition** or moment in life are you waiting for to elapse to obtain this ever-evasive strength that you'd like to possess?

Perhaps, you may say to yourself, when you are married, or when you have kids and become a parent, or when you're ripe in your middle age, or when you get that promotion, or some other **external condition** is met. When viewing strength and our own perceived weakness in this manner, we will never accrue or develop the strength we deeply desire. But, when we are being honest with ourselves, we already know this to be true. We've told ourselves this story for most, if not all, of our lives. Yet, the desired strength to make challenging decisions has not yet arrived upon you. We can never obtain strength by waiting for an external condition to occur; **strength must be actively chosen by us**. We tend to get bogged down or otherwise discouraged when presented with these difficult situations that require strength; however, we can make a decision in the present moment to shift our perspective any time we desire.

Think of someone you know that seems to have the strength to make difficult choices. This person can be someone you know personally or even a fictional character. Once you have someone in mind, what is it about them specifically that makes you think that they have the strength to make difficult choices? Most likely, you've arrived at this conclusion about this person or character based on witnessing or otherwise being familiar with them making a challenging choice during a difficult time. This is how you have defined them as strong, based on their track record or performance when confronted with **d**ifficult choices. You would not see them as strong without first seeing them faced with adversity, as you watch in awe as they chose to overcome it. What prerequisite quality do they possess that you seemingly do not?

We may see ourselves as inferior in some way as we begin

to make excuses and list all of the reasons we believe to be lacking the required strength to make difficult choices. This mindset and perspective suggest that this other person carries some special trait that we somehow haven't yet developed, or worse, we weren't provided with at birth. Consider taking a moment to make a list of all the reasons you think you are not strong enough to make difficult choices. In precisely the same manner this other person has shown themselves and others to have the strength to make difficult choices **by demonstrating it in the very moment it was required**, you can **choose strength** for yourself **at any time**. In fact, you can only ever be strong within the very moment you are presented with the situation to show strength. You cannot show strength at any point in the uncertain future; it must be now, **it can only be now**. In the future, you may be presented with another moment to show strength and define yourself, but you will be experiencing that future moment just as you are experiencing this current moment, which is experienced as something that is occurring "right now" that you are consciously aware of and participating in. By putting off your decision to choose strength in some future moment, you are only delaying or prolonging the only moment you ever truly have to choose strength. No other moment will ever arrive that will make your current moment easier for you to make difficult decisions. You can only define yourself and create your strength in the very moment you are presented with the decision to choose it for yourself. Just as we cannot demonstrate bravery or courage without first coming into contact with fear and choosing to move forward despite the presence of it, showing strength through difficult choices operates in the exact same way. It is in the very moments of adversity when we are faced with a difficult choice that we get to choose who we want to be. **Strength is your choice.** Rather than dreading the opportunities that present you with a difficult choice that you don't feel strong enough to make, consider celebrating and embracing them. If it is truly your desire to have the strength to make challenging choices or decisions, **this moment is the one you've been waiting for** to finally define yourself as a strong person. Without these difficult or challenging moments, you will never be able to demonstrate to yourself or others that you are a strong person. Leverage these moments to **choose** exactly who you want to be.

Contrary to the physical building of strength, building strength with your choices over time does not require a progressive overload approach. As in, you do not need first to tackle smaller or easier choices that progressively become more and more challenging as time goes on. Though, should you believe the smaller steps and choices are necessary for the building of your strength, **you will have created this self-limiting and requisite condition for yourself**, and it will be so. Instead, it is about encouraging the habit of being conscious and aware enough in the moment you are faced with adversity to not only realize that you do have a choice in this moment but also to choose strength over weakness and bravery over fear. As previously defined, choices that **we think** require a certain amount of strength are an arbitrarily assigned value by ourselves, meaning **we create an illusory level of difficulty** and assign it to the choice based on our own internal willingness, resistance, or fears. With this in mind, there is no order of difficulty between various choices, including the choice to **choose** strength or to **choose** bravery in any given circumstance. Once you've chosen to become more of who you always knew you could be by choosing strength, the benefits you receive compound as you encounter one victory after another. Your old story was one in which you told yourself that you were weak and lacked the strength. Once you realized that strength is your choice that could be made at any moment and acted on it, you've now adopted a new story for yourself. You now see yourself as a strong person, rather than a weak one, and in that, you have become so. You will have developed your own track record for yourself to lean on should you ever doubt yourself or your abilities in the future. Even now prior to making any decision or life change, you must know that **you are already strong**. This strength has never left you, for it has always been with you. The greatest strength is already yours. You have access to it, and it can only be inside of you. And to access it, you must only decide to **choose** it for yourself.

13. DEAR DIARY

I'm smart.

I'm dumb.

I'm sexy.

I'm a loser.

I'm a nobody.

I'm a hero.

I'm below average.

I'm a good person.

I'm not a slut.

I'm generous.

I'm kind.

I'm patient.

I'm a good friend.

I'm a good husband/wife/spouse.

I'm brave.

I'm fearless.

I'm weak.

Do any of these resonate with the ways that you identify yourself when looking in the mirror? Think about who you really are when you are alone with just your thoughts and how you classify yourself.

- What other descriptions might you add to this list that you feel define you?

- When in social situations and considering the relationships you hold, how do you describe yourself to others and desire them to see you?

- Is this in alignment with who you **really** are or an inauthentic representation?

- Is the way you view and define yourself when you are looking in the mirror in alignment with how you position and posture yourself to others?

- Is the way you view and define yourself in alignment with how you **think** others see you?

Oftentimes, we attempt to use others in our feeble attempts to transform into something greater than our fears, insecurities, and doubts. We do this by pretending to be something we are not by imposing these ideals for ourselves onto others, believing that should enough of them buy into our game, that it will indeed become so. There are elements of this that may bring some success, but it is temporary until the change is rooted inside of you.

We attempt to use other people for this, whether or not we realize or admit this to ourselves. Our real identity is inside of us and can only be changed from within, never from without. Therefore, if you really knew who you were and made the changes within yourself, would you feel it at all necessary to put on an elaborate dance for others to convince them of your persona? This desire to dance and persuade others comes from the insecurities we hold upon realizing the image we see inside, though we often fail to admit the rawness of the image we perceive and instead defer to the externalization of our attempts to resolve our internal identity crisis.

Independent of what you think about yourself, your purpose, or your relationship to the world, you've chosen to give yourself a story, whatever story that might be. Overwhelming, this story has been created by you and you alone. While your story, narrative, or view of self has certainly been impacted and developed as a result of the life circumstances you have experienced, **you are wholly responsible for everything that you believe yourself to be in this very moment**, from perceived imperfections and insecurities to your strengths and positive qualities. We all do this; it's natural, and there's nothing inherently wrong with this coping process as we deal with and interpret the life we observe around us. The disconnect arises when we mistake our conscious selves for this manufactured identity. We then believe the manufactured self to be our definitive self. Lastly, we select this illusory self as the operator for the dominant narrative we've chosen for our life story and purpose. We may see this fabricated self as something that, more or less, has been preselected for us in the physical body we appear to occupy or as a direct product of the life experiences and situations we've faced that we could not control. As in, we feel that our story, our excuses, our weaknesses, our identities, and so on, are something that has happened to us, rather than something we have **actively participated** in **choosing** to create for ourselves with our own best interests firmly in mind. Though, even this analysis is partial and does not provide the full context of how we've arrived at this moment in time with the story and narrative we have provided for ourselves and our lives.

We give ourselves a story, a purpose, a reason to live, or perhaps, a reason not to live, with internal thoughts, dialogs, phrases, beliefs, and expressions, such as:

"I'm a victim."

"I'll never recover from this."

"I'm not smart enough to pursue that career or obtain that promotion."

"I'm screwed up because of how my parents raised me."

"I'm insecure because I was bullied heavily in school."

"I lack confidence because I was beaten or abused as a child."

"I'll stay in this abusive and unhealthy relationship because it's comfortable. We've been together for seven years, and it's not **that bad.** I really don't think I'd find someone else anyways. I fear being alone."

"I do so much for everyone else, and people still treat me poorly. I feel empty; they don't seem to care about me in the same way that I care about them."

We also provide ourselves a life purpose, whether grand or insignificant, alongside excuses or reasons why we haven't yet achieved it or why we're predestined to remain stuck with an insignificant purpose. Perhaps of even greater concern, we settle and convince ourselves that living an unhappy, depressed, and unfulfilling life is "good enough." We stay stuck in a **perpetual loop of discontent and unworthiness** until death inevitably arrives at our door. All the while, we complain about our life, our financial situation, our friends and family, but do not do anything to change it. Though, we think we do. We may even convince ourselves that we are doing or have already done everything that we can. **This is a great deceit that we have played on ourselves.** We won't ever change it if we continue to defer responsibility for who we think we are and the story we tell ourselves. We most commonly defer to life situations or the actions of other people, whether currently present in our lives or someone from the past, living or dead. Yet, the story we've chosen to accept for ourselves and our lives goes on despite this, even if what we deem as the primary influence for our story has been out of the picture as an ongoing influence within our lives for many years. Even if the influence(s) are still actively part of your life, **you have conceded your power to choose who you think you are to an external entity.** When was the last time you got to choose the narrative and story for someone else's life? Why would we ever give up control of how we view ourselves to someone else, who has their own life to live according to the way they want to live it? This cannot affect us **unless we allow it** to by accepting it as our own story and narrative.

The story that **we create for ourselves** from our perceived limitations, insecurities, fears, and unworthiness is a direct result of what we believe to be true about ourselves. Surely, we've been impacted to some degree by the words, actions, perceptions, and judgments from others, but we have mistakenly given others jurisdiction over the creation of who we think we are and the story that we've accepted as our own. We must step into the realization that **we alone are responsible for the story** that we have chosen to believe about ourselves. The responsibility or liability for the story that you've created and accepted for yourself cannot truly be deferred to anyone; it is exclusively yours and yours alone. Until you accept this and truly believe it, you will never become anything more than the story you have created for yourself or the story that someone else has created for you. Regardless of the origin of the story you have accepted, you must realize that it exists because you chose it. Whatever story you've given yourself, whether a hero or a victim, **you are exactly what you think you**

are, and your actions will align in direct accordance with it. The very way in which you perceive yourself and the world around you is based on this internally contrived and highly subjective version of your reality. Though you may never become anything more than what you believe yourself to be as long as you continue to hold such a belief, when you **take full ownership and responsibility for the story and purpose you have given yourself**, you provide yourself with an incredible opportunity to change it. This opportunity and choice have always been yours to choose. We always have the power to choose, create, and modify the internal stories and narratives of our lives, who we believe we are, and what we imagine we could become, along with the truly magnificent things each of us can achieve.

When we **choose** to change our story, **we change** our perception of life.

When we **choose** to change our perception of life, **we change** our emotions and feelings about our circumstances and situations.

When we **choose** to change how we feel about life, our actions begin to change and align with how we see ourselves. Should we stay this course consistently, **our lives will transform in accordance with the belief about ourselves**, our abilities, and our story. This is a certain and inescapable result, should you **choose** to take responsibility and accept it.

To begin the process of changing the story you've given yourself, we must first understand that this is **never about denying our past experiences**, but contrarily, about fully embracing them and choosing to see them differently in a way that empowers and grows us rather than tearing us down. This is not ignorance, this is not denialism, but instead, a refactoring and repurposing of our experiences. When we accept full responsibility for how we choose to view our past and story, we immediately step into our ability to reshape our attitude and mindset about it without limits. Choosing to create a new story from past experiences, especially traumatic ones, can be difficult and take time to emotionally heal as we face things that may be very uncomfortable and painful. Though the past may not be materially changed, we always have the ability to change how we feel about it, as well as how we learn, develop, and grow from it. We have the choice to decide how it defines us, and to what degree, if at all.

The story we have accepted and provided ourselves with based on past experiences affects our very belief about ourselves, our worth, our purpose, and our potential. In turn, this affects our perception of the world we see in the present moment. How we choose to view our story defines how we view and value ourselves. This gives birth to our uniquely beautiful, 1-in-7-billion perception, which directly influences the very manner in which we interpret the seemingly objective stimuli and the world around us.

Your experience in life is very real and should never be discredited, nor should you allow another to discredit your own experience. Be advised, this is a non-negotiable two-way street that **applies equally to both directions**. No one's experience is more valid, more real, or superior to anyone else's. Regardless of how accurate you personally feel your version and interpretation of events are, you have inevitably perceived and filtered these events through a highly subjective and biased lens based on the chosen story and beliefs for yourself. It is of vital importance to understand the subjectiveness of your unique version of reality and the perceptual bias you invariably hold. For each life form on this planet to possess the ability to uniquely interpret and perceive the otherwise objective physical universe is an incredible phenomenon. While we ought to celebrate this incredible diversity of thought and perception for the true beauty that it is, we instead tend to get frustrated, annoyed, argue, or actively discredit and silence the perceived reality of another individual, while promoting the validity and accuracy of our own.

Just for a moment, temporarily set aside any bias or pre-existing belief you may presently hold about yourself, your purpose, other people, life, and the universe as you currently believe it to be. Now, let's assume together that all of existence and the matter contained within at the deepest and most fundamental levels consist only of atoms, molecules, frequencies, waves, and patterns of vibration. Everything in the known and unknown universe would involve various combinations of these elements as they came together, wiggling, dancing, giving, and taking to create things we are capable of perceiving and interpreting like air, sound, light, colors, plants, animals, temperature, stars, and heartbeats. With the universe consisting of a seemingly infinite randomization of these items, there would be an absolute and decisive way in which all of these could be observed, analyzed, and understood. Essentially, this could all be measured and examined in a purely objective and irrefutable way. Yet, even with a seemingly objective world encircling all of us, we perceive and interpret the world and the situations we encounter very differently from one another. If everything can be boiled down to objective data points, how could this be possible? Perception creates our reality, which often varies greatly from another's perceived reality. **Perception is a product of a choice** we've made to view ourselves and the story we've assigned and accepted, as well as our chosen belief structures.

IN PLAIN SIGHT

Consider for a moment the trippy artwork known as stereograms or auto stereograms. These images are known for their ability to hide pictures inside of other pictures. For those unfamiliar with the term, these pictures often look like patterns or other imagery at first glance, but only after staring at the picture long enough and adjusting your gaze are you able to see the hidden picture within. Though this hidden picture may not be noticed straight away, in actuality, it was there all along; you just didn't know where to look or how to see it. With stereograms, some people may not even know a hidden image exists and will take the artwork at face value until someone else tells them about the existence of the hidden image. With this knowledge that a hidden image exists, many will still fail to see it even as the supporting party attempts to guide them by pointing to seemingly random locations around the image as they declare the various points to be "this" part or "that" part of the hidden image you are presently unable to see. Even with expert instruction, the hidden image cannot simply be shown to the viewer; it must be something that the viewer sees and experiences for themselves through concentrated effort and a true willingness to see it. Once you see it, it's difficult to unsee, and you wonder why it took so long to see it in the first place as it sat in plain sight this whole time. After mastering this particular stereogram, you may be capable of switching your perceptive gaze on command to see both the patterned image and the hidden image. Our perception of the world is no different from the stereogram, though many of us are unaware of the impact our perceptual biases have on our interpretation of the world. In this, our lives and the world are riddled with hidden images and meanings, should we only know where to look and how to adjust our gaze to see what it is we desire to see. By adjusting your gaze and perception in life, you are not training yourself to see something that isn't there, but instead learning to see the various hidden images, meanings, and perspectives around you **that have been there all along.**

If someone didn't tell you that the artwork was a stereogram, would you have spent the additional time to gaze upon it intently? Or would you have simply written it off as a tacky piece of art and moved on? Even if informed it was a stereogram, how long would you stare at it before resigning your efforts, should you not see what another tells you exists within the pattern?

There are many hidden patterns and images in life, often nested deeply within one another, seemingly without limits. There is not a strict right and wrong way to view the images and patterns of life. Though, should you see things that you don't want to see, don't ridicule the stereogram; you must only **adjust your gaze.** Not all will see, and not all will try, it must be a choice, and effort is required. If you see one thing in the stereogram, do not expect another to see precisely the same thing that you see in the same way, or even at the same time, as the viewing experience is unique to the viewer and is seen through the lens of their own subjective reality. Our realities are highly subjective, and therefore, cannot be directly compared or contested.

To continue illustrating how the story we choose for ourselves affects our perceptions and, in turn, our realities, we will explore the following simple example. If you have given yourself a story and belief that you are unattractive, you will interpret everyone who looks at you as you walk through a public space as them judging you. You feel that you stand out, in a bad way, and when people look, they are thinking critical things about you, your appearance, or even questioning your worth or value as a person. You may think that they are whispering things behind your back, are unkind, rude, or stuck-up people. In this way, this **perspective has become your reality**. Therefore, whether or not it is true in the objective world of atoms wiggling and dancing with one another, **it has become true in your reality**, which is the only reality that can ever be true and real to you. However, if we take this same objective scenario and swap out your belief for one that you instead believe yourself to be highly attractive, you will instead interpret everyone looking at you as complimentary and flattering. Perhaps, you believe that you are so attractive that people cannot keep their eyes off of you, for this is the reason that they look at you. You would also believe that when you enter the space, people not only notice, but they envy you. Everyone that you catch taking a glance is very kind, approachable, and friendly. You smile, and they often smile back.

Nothing of material significance changed between these examples, and in each scenario, the objective reality maintained consistently the same. The only thing that did change between these two scenarios was your belief in who you think you are and the story you have accepted for yourself. With this, how you personally interpreted your subjective experience of an objective world was vastly different. When you hold a belief, whether consciously or subconsciously, it creates a subjective interpretation of the world. Rather than challenge a core belief, we tend to operate on autopilot and instead choose to see things that further "validate" our beliefs and our understanding of the world around us, locking us deeper inside our already biased view of "reality." As was the case in the prior example, when you believed you were unattractive, you found validating evidence to support that particular belief. Though when you believed yourself to be attractive, you also found evidence to support that belief. **We see what we choose to see**, even when looking at the same objective world. We always look for things that back up whatever belief we hold, and with that, we will indeed see what we seek. We will make excuses for our beliefs, justify our actions, defer blame or responsibility, change the story, censor information from our own memory (repression), or any other number of behaviors to defend and protect what we "know" to be true. Everything we see and experience "must" fit the mold of our core belief and self-accepted narrative, even if it means violently shoving a square peg into a round hole.

With this...

- How can we ever know with certainty that our unique perspective of the world external to us is factual or objective when so much of what we feel, see, and experience is vulnerable to subconscious bias, much without our conscious awareness?

- Whose unique opinion of reality is more accurate? Yours, or someone else's? Can anyone's be superior? If not, can you set your own narrative, story, and perceptions to whatever you'd like?

- If your belief and view of reality are susceptible to bias and misinterpretation, wouldn't everyone else's also be in the same exact way?

- What if you believe your interpretation to be true, but five other people disagree with your opinion? Are they more right and have dominance over your personal view of reality or your opinions? What if that number increased to 50? Or 1,000? Or 1,000,000?

Though notable and significant, something superficial like physical attraction may not be so consequential in the grand scheme of things. However, the greater point about observing the same patterns and waves in varying ways is both relevant and substantial. To be able to change our story is not to deny our past experiences, but to **fully embrace them** and choose to see them differently in a way that empowers and grows us, rather than tearing us down. For example, if you were abused as a child by an alcoholic parent, though undoubtedly tragic, you must realize that as you read this now in this very moment, you have an incredible choice. It's a simple choice, albeit a difficult one that requires strength and willingness to execute. You can live the rest of your life broken and defeated as a result of this traumatic experience, always limiting yourself and never pushing for greatness due to feelings of unworthiness or defeat, or you can choose to use this experience to grow and develop yourself into something so much greater. Your story can be:

> *"I'm an alcoholic, and I can't hold a job because my father was an alcoholic and abused me."*

Or instead, your story can be:

> *"I was abused by an alcoholic father, and it really made things very difficult for me while greatly affecting my self-confidence and self-worth. I don't want to live like he lived or abuse others in the way he abused me. I will rise above the example he set. I am not a product or victim of the actions, words, or abuse of another."*

You may even decide to take this empowerment and choice a step further by starting a podcast, a national toll-free helpline, writing a book, or hosting a support group for others who are still coming to terms with and accepting the toll that their traumatic abuse has had on them. You may even decide to work directly with those struggling with alcohol and substance abuse, as you know first-hand the impact the actions of the addicted have on those around them. Similarly, when losing a loved one to death, it's very painful as we undergo the grieving phases. Over time and with some effort and support from others, we learn to carry on in life. We eventually smile again, we learn to laugh again, and perhaps, we may even open our hearts to love again. Though, no matter how far we've come and no matter how much time has elapsed, when we sit in silence and think about the person we've lost, we will likely experience feelings of sadness, as we will always miss them dearly. This pain lives with us forever, like a scar on our hearts, but we have the ability to choose what we do with it. We must never ignore or discredit our pasts, our traumas, or our experiences. Contrariwise, we must face them. When we face them, we give ourselves a choice on what we choose to do and make from those difficult experiences. For the loss of the loved one, you can choose to possess the overwhelming narrative of sadness, how much you miss them, and how the rest of your life will be a miserable existence until the day that you yourself perish. On the other hand, you can choose the narrative that you are enormously grateful for the time you had with this individual and the incredible moments that you shared together that not everyone gets to experience. You can be grateful for the special connection you had with this person. You can also work to enjoy life once again, as you know this person would have deeply wanted to see you happy after their passing. In no way is any of this a denial of the traumatic experience, but simply, a refactoring and repurposing of it through a choice, which yields a shift in your perception. This shift ultimately allows you to create a new reality in which to reside, one that is filled with optimism, gratitude, joy, and love. In this way, you write your own story. You create your life through the narrative you choose to adopt.

If you hold the ultimate authority over the way in which you view yourself as well as the story you provide for yourself, **how will you choose to experience life**?

The **choice** is yours.

Your life is yours.

14. THE CHOICE IS YOURS

You always have a choice. There is never a situation in your life that robs you of your ability to make a free choice. The single greatest lie in the history of all of mankind involves the brilliantly corrupt deception that we do not have a choice or that we must select from a limited menu of society's pre-approved options. We "must" follow the incoherent laws erected before us. We "must" pay taxes to which we don't agree. We mustn't speak about certain things. We mustn't think about certain things. We "must" adhere to the structures of religion, society, or culture. Even expressing our truest thoughts and feelings may be unacceptable in a society or culture, ultimately leading to a condition of internal self-betrayal and suppression. In many cases, we don't feel like we have a choice, and we are instead victims of our environment, the government, some societal hierarchy, or bound by laws and the rules of religion. Some people inaccurately feel in control of their lives and truly believe that they are making free choices, at least in certain areas of their lives, when in true reality, they are likely not. Whether we feel there are situations where we **think** we don't have a choice or feel that we are in complete control of our free choices, this is the result of sophisticated illusions and the conditioning from our influences and upbringing. Initially, this may not sound like it applies to you and your choices. You may feel like you are in control, or perhaps, you feel that you do not have control. Regardless, as we explore various examples and dig deeper, we'll demonstrate the construction of choice and the unconscious deferment of our power and personal responsibility.

There is much that can be taken away from you as you experience life: material possessions, friends, limbs, good health, achievements, status, and even your current mortal experience of life as you know it. Anything that can be obtained or gained can also be lost. Anything that someone else can take, use, or reassign upon your death does not truly belong to you and never will. However, the one thing that no one can ever take from you is your power of choice. The word power, when used in this context, is not to be taken lightly, as this is among **the most powerful of forces in the entire universe**. It's a power that you possess that can never be extracted or taken from you. We all possess this incredible power, but the overwhelming majority are unaware of it. Those that are aware are only partially aware and do not understand the full scope or breadth. They have been deceived out of their power and have placed it in the hands of another. By its very nature, this power may only ever belong to you and you alone. You may choose to hand it over to another, whether consciously or unconsciously, but it can never truly belong to another. It is often misplaced or misunderstood, but it's always yours, and it never leaves you. The very moment you become consciously aware of it, you instantaneously retain full use and control of your power, immediately removing it from the hands of others in which you may have unknowingly placed it. **This power is everything**. This power is your happiness. This power is your peace. This power is your joy. This power is your free will. This power is your free expression. This power is your emotional, spiritual, and mental freedom. This power has the ability to transform your life into exactly the life you choose to live, whether by purpose, passion, or divine assignment, it's yours to explore and yours to use.

The very syntax of the language in which we speak has only contributed to the confusion surrounding the power of choice that exists within you. It has been widely misinterpreted and misunderstood. Therefore, to simply communicate to you with words that you possess this incredible power is not enough. We must explore various examples, one after another, to begin the process of separating your intellectual and conditioned attachments from the true intent and meaning. There is nothing that can be shown to you in this book that will give you your power, **for it already is within you**. Through your willingness and conscious choice to identify your power within, the examples provided may help guide your journey through yourself as you begin to realize the incredible power that you alone hold. At first, some of the examples may seem too soft, irrelevant, silly, or out of touch; however, they have been carefully selected for a specific purpose. You may use the provided examples as a guide to get started on your journey to your ultimate realization, though it is often very beneficial to use your own life and the situations you are presently in. Regardless of which examples from your own life you choose to analyze and reflect on, the one fundamental element must always remain all throughout: you **always have a choice**.

OWNING YOUR CHOICE

Though it may appear backward at first, we can start identifying our ability to make free choices by taking ownership of the choices we have already made. We tend to defer responsibility for not only our choices in and of themselves but also the pain, frustration, anxiety, depression, or fatigue we experience. We will reassign responsibility for our feelings and our choices on anything and anyone rather than ourselves. We rarely take full accountability and responsibility for our decisions and everything that they entail, such as the pros, the cons, and the consequences. We have been conditioned to play the victim role of life, and we justify it, when in reality, **the complete opposite is true**. The world isn't responsible for your pain, suffering, depression, financial woes, or your dead-end job. You alone are responsible, and you alone have made your choices.

We've accepted that going to school, getting good grades, and a good job is what life ought to look like and that anything outside of this model and expected template is irresponsible or out of touch. The word "accepted" in this context requires a choice, as you cannot ever accept anything without first making a choice to accept it. There are many things that we have accepted as functioning and "responsible" members of society that we are oblivious to or unaware of. Though this lack of awareness and identification of the presence of this in our lives is due to the conditioning and pressures to make these choices, so much so that we have forgotten there was even a differing choice to make. As is the case of fish unaware that they are in water after spending their entire lives in it, we too are unaware of the many choices we've made in accepting the environment that we've been presented by the world at large. As we step through the lighter examples to illustrate the power of choice inside of you, we will also begin to unravel some of the choices you've unconsciously made long ago that have become part of your core beliefs about the world, which affect your perception of reality. For example, if you greatly dislike your job, why are you still showing up to work? Why do you clock in, clock out, while being chronically stressed-out, and complaining about it not only during but after working hours? The real answers are not likely the first few that may have popped into your head. The immediate answers you may have initially considered are **the result of a response that you've been**

conditioned to provide to yourself and others. This, on its own, has caused you to surrender your power. Let's explore this more deeply to begin our understanding of the process of making choices. If you abhor your job, you've **consciously made the choice** to continue going to your job, **no matter what**. Even at this point, there is not a single excuse or argument that can be made to the contrary, and any attempt to excuse your responsibility for your choice to attend your job is a subconscious surrendering of your power. You must fully accept, without deferment of responsibility, that attending your job and any other situation you find yourself in stems from a choice you've made, one that you can never be forced into.

When you make a choice, you must also accept the pros and cons of **your choice**. By making the choice to attend your crummy job, you've **accepted** your subpar salary or hourly wage. You've **accepted** your commute. You've **accepted** your boss' raging narcissism and unfair treatment of you and others. You've **accepted** Karen in accounting, who won't stop talking about the new outfit she dressed her dog with for this week as she aggressively places her phone in front of your face to share the pictures you didn't ask to see. You've made the choice to be there. You must completely own your choice and acknowledge to yourself that it was and always has been your choice to make, and yours alone. When we make choices in life, there are almost certainly pros and cons associated with each available choice.

Whatever choice we make, we must immediately accept all of the pros, the cons, and the consequences. In regard to this example, what choices do we really have, and what excuses do we make for ourselves that we think acquits us from taking responsibility for the consequences and the ownership of choice?

- **Situation:** I have to go to work at this job that I hate because I have bills to pay.
    - **The Pros:** I will make money, which will help my financial situation and allow me to pay my bills, even if just partially.
    - **The Cons:** I'm underpaid. I'm stressed. My boss is rude. I don't have enough time for my hobbies, passions, and family. I still make barely enough money to get by.
    - **The Choice:** I've decided that the pros of the situation outweigh the cons. I'm choosing to put up with the cons entirely and put in the hard work in pursuit of the pros I am seeking from making this choice. Given the choices between going to this job, or not going to this job, I choose to go.
    - **The Delusion:** Okay, so I guess I technically have a choice, **but** if I don't go to work, I'll get fired, I'll lose my house, my car, and I won't be able to provide for my family. Though I might have a choice, my hands are tied. It'd be foolish or

irresponsible to make any other choice than the one I am already making.

- o **Alternative Options:** Find another job. Live in a smaller home. Obtain new skills and education. Stand up to your boss. Tell Karen you aren't interested in her dog's outfits. Get a cheaper car or sell it and start taking the bus. Ask for help from others. Live with family or friends as you develop the next round of skills you might need for a new career. Change your spending habits. Adjust your lifestyle. Move away from the area to another with a cheaper cost of living. Become a minimalist. Live in a tiny home. **The choice is never binary,** and the options available to you are limited only by your ability to **imagine** them.

- o **Choice Ownership:** I am fortunate enough to make a decision for myself out of all of the potential options that I have available. Out of my infinite array of options, I choose to keep going to my job. I choose to accept the disrespectful behavior of my boss. I choose to keep my mouth shut and not stand up to him. I choose to accept my subpar salary. I choose to accept my stressful working conditions. I choose to accept my commute. I am grateful for the opportunity to make any choice that I want to make, and with this recognition, I take full responsibility and ownership of my decision, knowing that it was mine to make and mine alone.

Despite what you might initially think or how your current situation may appear, the choices available to you are **never** binary. The only binary thing about choice is whether or not you choose to realize you do indeed have a choice, then once realized, choosing to make one for yourself. What you choose, or how you choose it, is truly infinite. This is something only you can do and that no one else can do for you. Whether it's occurring right now, or it happens later on when faced with an active moment of decision, your preconditioned internal dialog may start speaking to you to convince you out of this realization. Whenever you are aware enough to realize the moment that this dialog is occurring, ask yourself this question: "If I am aware enough in this moment to notice this negative self-talk, emotions, or feelings, then **who am I** as the observer if **I am** capable of observing the occurrence of this happening?"

If you are indeed capable of observing your thoughts and feelings, then you must not be your thoughts and feelings. Your thoughts and feelings change often, day to day, hour to hour, or even second to second. Yet, even with these sometimes-radical shifts, there stands this unaffected version of your being that is capable of remaining constant and aware of everything going on.

This is a higher level of our own consciousness that transcends emotions, feelings, core beliefs, and our own personality. When you mistakenly identify with your fly-by-night emotions and feelings, you also buy into the limiting beliefs, pain, and suffering that are associated with that particular thought, feeling, or idea. When you identify with this higher-level observer that is yourself, even if only very briefly in a flash of true awareness, the ability to make a true choice outside of the constructs of any particular belief, idea, or emotion becomes not only possible but practical. When you rediscover this higher self, you will recognize it as **it is you**. It is not an external entity or being. It's you—untethered from your own mental constructs and limiting beliefs. It's been with you all along, but forgotten, ignored, misplaced, suppressed, or discredited. And once you become aware again of its existence, you'll be able to, in ever-increasing frequency, pull yourself out of any particular emotion or state of being and take on the role of this unbiased observer, who is not capable of judging or criticizing anything or anyone. From this point, you can begin to see the world, yourself, and your present situation for what it truly is, not what it appears to be, through the eyes of a subjective interpretation of reality and your preconditioning.

THE GRIND

As we get back to taking ownership of our choices, we must accept and embrace the pros and cons associated with each. This is paramount to begin the actualization process of the power you already hold. We can drill down further into any one of the choices mentioned in the above scenario. As we explore, we will begin to see the infinite array of choices that we actually have in every situation and every moment of life. We will see that the choice is far more than just choosing to put up with an unsatisfactory job or to quit the job, though that might be the choice we are currently distracting ourselves with and actively blaming for our unhappiness. Everything in this scenario involves an elaborate series of simple choices, in which we forget that we hold the power to make these choices in every single moment. For instance, if you are absolutely dreading the moment that Karen joins you in the break room, knowing that she is about to interrupt anything that you are doing, you've already made a series of choices prior to her imminent arrival and subsequent bombardment. You've made the choice to return to the break room, once again, where she frequently invades your time and space. No one is forcing you to use the break room. You might think, "Well, the break room has all the good snacks and drinks, and the only other place I can really go for privacy and a nice break is the restroom or my car." On the surface, this appears logical, but do not allow this reasoning to distract you from your responsibility and ownership of the **choice**

you've made. You've decided, based on what you believed to be your available options, that the break room was the best of the choices that you presented to your conscious mind. You weighed the pros and cons and selected the best-case scenario for yourself. In some way, at this point, you've been able to exercise a type of power within you to make this choice. If this is the decision that you've made for yourself and on your own accord, what could there possibly be to complain about? Would you have found something to complain about regardless of the decision that you made? If you chose to eat your snack in your car instead, would you still be complaining about Karen invading the break room, which is seemingly forcing you to eat in your car, continuing to shift the blame to her? Have you ever told Karen you don't want to hear about her dogs or see pictures? If not, why not? Is it because that's offensive, rude, or might hurt her feelings? Very well, and that's fair if that's what **you choose**, but again, that's still **your choice**. You have the ability to ignore her, to tell her that your break room time is your personal time to unwind and unravel, but you are choosing instead to keep quiet and "play nice" not to possibly hurt her feelings. Yet, you continue to complain to yourself and others about Karen. Though you avoid her, you continue to blame her and her actions as she seemingly forces you to your car through **a choice that you have made**. What does Karen have that you do not, that she is able to force you to a place of internal suffering, discontent, frustration, and ultimately to your car just to avoid her? What power and responsibility have you yielded to her, through a seemingly unconscious choice, to allow her to control your internal state, life, and peace to this incredible degree?

None of this is to suggest or otherwise lead you to infer what the "right" answer or decision is. There is no right answer; there is only the choice that you've decided to make. So long as it's truly a conscious choice and one that you've taken full responsibility and ownership for, there can be no "wrong" choice. On this, your religion, society, beliefs, or personal opinions might suggest otherwise. After all, how could there be no "wrong" choice? At the very core of your acceptance for the religion, societal standards, or belief you identify with, was your choice to accept and embrace it, along with its rules, boundaries, and the moral compass inherent to the chosen opinion or belief itself. Thus, at its essence, there can never be a right or wrong choice without there first being a choice made to accept what is and what is not within the confines of your chosen reality. Only then, through the intellectual adoption of manufactured standards and beliefs, may one arbitrarily classify the apparent morality of any **subsequent choice** in terms of "rightness" or "wrongness." Every choice carries with it pros, cons, and consequences, yet you always have the ability to make a choice based on the available evidence and your unique interpretation of this evidence. If you choose to avoid Karen and eat in your car, celebrate the pros of the situation that you selected for yourself. Celebrate the fact that you made this choice for yourself to now have uninterrupted time to relax, someplace that Karen won't be able to bother you. Celebrate the fact that you even have this space to use that allows you to get away from others at work as you unwind and prepare for the next part of your day. **You've made the choice**, so own it and take responsibility for it. Under the same breath, when we take full responsibility for our choices, **we forfeit our right to needlessly complain** about the cons we've accepted as part of our choice that we do not like or agree with. There is nothing wrong with acknowledging the cons that you've knowingly accepted as part of your authority to make a choice, as there are not many choices in life that do not carry some undesirable or unwanted effects on you or others. But to incessantly complain about something inherent to the decision you've made that cannot be changed requires the mental absence and the deferment of responsibility that this con you have failed to wholly accept only exists as a **result of your choice**. Whether the choice is a material one or merely how you've chosen to perceive a particular situation, any resistance, grumbling, or complaining about a choice you've made and accepted in your life is a fruitless endeavor. Any overwhelming or unsatisfactory feelings and negative associations with the cons of a particular choice also imply that you have not taken absolute responsibility for your choice after all. With this, enjoy the best parts about your decision while completely accepting the cons that you chose to accept as part of the decision-making process. If you don't like the cons, make another decision. If there doesn't seem to be another decision, think outside of the box, as there is always another decision to be made.

In some cases, the decisions that can be made may not be material, or it appears on the surface that they are binary. Instead, the choice that you always have available to you is how you choose to perceive and interpret the situation. Should you decide to view Karen as a friendly but very lonely woman who is hurting, sad, and lonely, you'll no longer grit your teeth as you hear her very specific way of constant sighing as she approaches the break room. Instead, you may see it as an opportunity to bring light, love, and companionship into her life, knowing that she is just lonely, sad, and broken. In this way, you now genuinely care about Karen and see all of her obliviousness and bombardment as a symptom of her internal suffering and pain, rather than a blatant disregard for your personal space. You may view this as an opportunity rather than a chronic inconvenience that will ruin your day and lose sleep over as you toss and turn in frustration about her. Perhaps she isn't hurting or in pain, but she just doesn't grasp social clues as well as others might or as well as you'd like her to. With this, you can choose to set boundaries and tell her that you need time to yourself at work to unwind, and if she chooses to be offended by your boundary-setting, that would be a choice that she made based off of your choice. You are not responsible for the choice of others, though you are entirely responsible for your choices and actions, just as others are for their choices and actions. This is where the line often becomes a bit blurry in our society, as our choices may have the unintended consequence of hurting someone else's feelings. But at the same time, if someone chooses to become offended or hurt by something we've said or done, whether intended to be malicious or not, that is still ultimately **their choice** to perceive you and the situation in such a way. Now, this isn't necessarily to be misinterpreted as a free pass to treat others with blatant disrespect and then disregard the other person's feelings as we arrogantly claim that they've made a choice to be hurt by our actions. We must still take full responsibility for our actions and choices but understand where the lines of responsibility are drawn. Ideally, we'd treat others in the way that we wish we were treated, though this is seldom applied as we are often unable, or perhaps unwilling, to see things from another's point of view. Even when we make an honest attempt to see the world in a way that we'd imagine aligns with how this other may be seeing the world, this attempt can only be made from the cockpit of our own version of subjective reality. Regardless, what you put out into the world, you will get back. If you put out frustration and anger, you will feel it and receive it. If you see love and send love, you will feel it and receive it.

In the case of your boss treating you poorly and unfairly, this may be a case of blatant disrespect. He may know that he treats people terribly, and he doesn't seem to care. He might possess a superiority complex of some kind and is someone who enjoys treating others disrespectfully, knowing that he has the power to fire them should they stand up to him. Regardless of his intentionally unfair treatment of you, there are still many choices to be made. While some choices seem more reasonable or practical than others, you cannot ignore the fact that you always have options. Whether or not the options you presently are aware of seem like common sense or not is irrelevant to the root of the discussion, which is that you always have a choice to make.

You do not have to live a miserable, sad, angry, or frustrated life as a result of someone blatantly treating you disrespectfully. In this particular situation, not only do you have many materially applicable choices to make, but you also have many perceptual choices to make. If you choose to sit quietly as your boss verbally abuses you and others, you have also made the choice to feel angry and helpless about it. If you choose to rise up and yell back, you have also accepted the possible outcome that you may lose your job. You can choose to physically strike him in the face and knock him to the ground, and you'd also be choosing to accept the likely consequences that come with that particular choice. You can choose to covertly rally together coworkers that mutually feel abused by his constant verbal abuse, sign a petition for his removal, record video and audio of his verbal and emotional abuse, and send it to a corporate office or leak it to the media.

As we all live in our own versions of subjective reality, let's follow this thread of exposing your boss' behavior publicly that may lead to his ultimate dismissal. If he was fired as a result of this exposure, do you think he would return to the office, sincerely apologize to everyone he hurt, and be a changed person from here on out as he begins to treat others with love and respect? This is an unlikely outcome. But why? His subjective reality and personally assigned narrative will tell the story of how he was misunderstood by others, how he was under so much stress to keep the office in order, and that his high level of discipline and aggressive personality was required. In fact, he might even be the hero of his own story by telling himself that they should all be grateful for him as he was able to **keep** everyone working hard, which made this particular office branch highly successful financially and allowed the office to employ as many people as they had. He may continue to argue that would it have not been for his tough, but fair, leadership, others might not even have a job to go to, period. He might paint everyone as a slacker, how he ran circles around them all with his own hard work, and that it was everyone else who lacked character as they went behind his back and betrayed him, despite all of the great things he has done for them over the years with his "tough-love" approach. Would this suggest that a coup shouldn't have been formed to expose his abusive behavior as it may not be effective at enacting the desired change within him? Not necessarily. This is only to pull on the thread to its end by acknowledging the **simultaneous realities occurring at once** in every single moment as they exist inside each of us individually and often shared collectively as a group. If your goal is simply to get rid of the mean boss, this might be a successful approach, but that is beside the greater point. In his subjective reality, **he is absolutely correct** that he is the savior of the office, and this treatment of him by his subordinates was undeserved and unwarranted. It is likely the same story that he has told himself about who he is and the role he has within the world, even outside of this particular work environment. Anything presented to him, or any of us, simply with our preferred view of our chosen subjective reality will be met with haste and defense. He may call everyone else ignorant, blind, or ungrateful, and really mean it and believe it. However, imagine for a moment that there are elements of truth to his subjective reality that you were unable to see based on your view of reality as you remain seated comfortably within your own perceptual bias. What if it were true that, though he was blatantly rude and brought a lot of stress to the office, he did increase the productivity of the office, which allowed the office to employ more people? What if it was true that he held many roles and had a lot of stress that was passed down to him by his boss, **because he cared very much**, but didn't know how to express it in a healthy way? Remember, each of our realities is subjective. We can never see the whole picture, nor can we see things for what they truly are. All interpretations of all events occur solely within us individually. Though there is a true, boundless, and objective reality that we all live in, the only reality that feels true to us is the one that we have chosen to live in. Whether this choice is made consciously or unconsciously is irrelevant, as it still can only ever be our choice. To each of us, **there is no truer reality outside of the one we've accepted**, but many other realities exist concurrently in the minds of others that are just as true to them as your unique one is to you.

Just as was the case with Karen, you have the ability to change your perception of your boss as well. Perhaps you ponder to yourself why your boss feels he must treat others this way. You begin to speculate that he might have been raised in a broken home and was physically abused. He hurts others as a defense to hide from his pain and vulnerability. He believes that if he puts on a big enough show for everyone and himself, no one will be able to hurt him anymore. So long as he is the one inflicting pain on others, he subconsciously believes he is superior and cannot be hurt. If you choose not to get rid of your boss through an attempted coup and if you also choose to continue going to work and not quit, then it is your perception that you must change. We must realize that we've chosen to accept the cons of the decisions up until this point and must embrace them. Though you are underpaid, you can choose to be grateful for the employment opportunity that you have in a tough economy when others may not even have jobs. You can choose to see your boss as someone who is stressed and doesn't know how to handle his feelings properly. You can choose to respond to your boss with kindness. You can choose to tell him, "thank you" for caring so much about the office and looking out for everyone, but as a caution, you must have the proper perception and actually mean what you say. Do not be inauthentic or disingenuous. There's no deception here, only a shift in your perception that allows you to truly be grateful for the employment opportunity and for the positive aspects that your boss might bring to the table, even if they might be hard to detect or spot initially. What if all he needs is the recognition that he so desires? What if people in the office began to change their perception and treat him with respect? Would it be possible that his behavior would change in response to the love and kindness being sent his way that finally provides him with the validation he internally craves? Choosing to step outside of what is initially seen and experienced through our limited perspective of life may provide us with an opportunity that we didn't notice upon our first observation. When we find peace within ourselves as a result of our perception, and as we take responsibility for our choices, decisions, and actions, we ultimately arrive at a place where we realize that **others cannot hurt us**, nor can situations. Others cannot make us feel bad or insignificant. Others cannot force us to retreat to our car for our snack break in frustration and anger. These only stem from our choices and perceptions. We can never truly control others, nor should we try. By changing ourselves and our perception, we can choose to see situations and life very differently, which can bring us peace. When we are at peace, **we are peace**. When we are peace, we can share peace openly and graciously with others, without expecting or requiring anything in return.

We indirectly change the world and others around us in a material and beautiful way by focusing our efforts within rather than without. Perhaps even with the greatest internal effort, it may appear that the world around us still fails to change. This might sound discouraging at first; however, you must imagine that if your internal efforts were successful, your subjective reality and perceptions of the world would have changed as a result. When your subjective reality changes as a result of shifted perceptions and the internal work you do on yourself, you will personally yield and experience more peace, abundance, joy, love, and acceptance in your own life and reality. If you are at peace and fully content with your life and with the subjective reality you've created for yourself through choice, did the world or others ever really require changing? Or was it only yourself that required a reality alteration? Let's say you could have forcefully made a change to Karen, your boss, and your work environment. In this, you might manage to find momentary peace as you've moved stresses out of the way, but this peace will only be temporary until the next life situation or next difficult person crosses your path. It will be akin to an endless game of whack-a-mole until your eventual death should you approach life with the intent of changing others rather than yourself. Should you truly change yourself, **the world will change with you**, including your past, present, and future. Your **past** and anything you've previously encountered effectively changes as a result of your renewed mindset, enabling you to perceive its purpose and significance differently and in an empowering way. Your **present** situation and your interpretation of it change as a result of your renewed perspective, as well as how your past had previously throttled your perception of the present. Your **future** changes as you are no longer stuck in a cycle of frustration and anger while waiting for the world to change, as it never could. In this regard, your choices empower you to become the creator of your life, **across various timelines**, through the choices available to you in the present moment. You choose peace, you choose love, you choose kindness, you choose patience, you choose frustration, you choose anger, you choose bitterness, you choose resentment. Whatever you choose, you also choose to actively experience the fruits your choice. This choice has always been available for you to make, and it's available to you right now. **The point of creation is always right now.**

As we can see, the choice outlined in this scenario was far from a binary one. We have only scraped the tip of the iceberg in the series of choices that had previously led to you living a frustrated and stressed-out life as a result of your subpar working conditions, which originated from **choices you made within yourself**, rather than the external situation in and of itself. In every single moment of your life, you always have a choice. If you feel sad, you have a choice. If you feel frustrated, you have a choice. This doesn't imply that you should ever engage in a state of self-denial or self-betrayal by ignoring your own thoughts or feelings. They are here for you, should you choose to use them and the invaluable guidance they bring. For example, if a loved one passes away and you begin to feel grief and sadness, this doesn't suggest that you should just simply choose happiness instead, and in the process, ignore the grief you presently feel. This is part of the human experience as we know it, with our ability to experience a vast array of emotions and feelings. Our feelings can be beautiful but also tremendously painful. Your reality, your feelings, and the world around you should never be denied. Instead, they should be **fully embraced and acknowledged**. If we try to hide uncomfortable or socially unacceptable feelings as we strive to ignore or reject them, this only does a great disservice to ourselves and others. **We must be honest with ourselves**, love ourselves, and express tremendous compassion for ourselves. Though our feelings can be painful or difficult, they are ultimately signs and symbols for us to analyze. They guide us to our deeper truths as we continue the boundless exploration of ourselves through all of life's experiences. They tell us a story about who we are, our current state of mind, what our values are, what's important to us, and how we are uniquely interpreting the situation at hand. When we remember that we are not our feelings, but the observer that sits above our feelings without judgment, we obtain the much-needed clarity into our state of mind and circumstances without the pollution of self-limited thoughts, ideals, and chemical compounds found within each of the emotions, thoughts, and ideas we choose to attach to in any given moment.

15. CHOICE DELUSION

We all choose to be placed inside of a box. Whether we think that we are in control and choose this box for ourselves or we feel that the box has been chosen for us by others, we have accepted the grand delusion of this illusory choice. What is this grand delusion? Is the grand delusion that we have chosen the box, that the box has chosen us, or someone or something else has chosen the box for us? **The grand delusion is that there is even a box at all**. This box only exists because you have accepted it into your reality. Once a belief in the box is established and accepted, the delusion becomes deeply rooted in your reality, and it becomes part of what we accept as our unquestionable truths. In this way, we still believe that we have a choice, when in reality, it has been taken from us. We have unknowingly accepted this but must revisit the existence of the box, where it came from, and why we have accepted the box into our lives. Any free person does not like to be placed inside a box; therefore, it cannot happen consciously. Further, the person must continue believing in the delusion that they are still free. After all, if they do not realize they are in a box, they do not question or re-evaluate their freedoms, as they believe their freedom remains. Even when you feel like you have the choice, must we only choose between the available boxes? Where did these boxes come from? Though we have the "freedom" to choose, who created these boxes for us, and why must these be our only approved options to select from? Would any truly free individual, free thinker, world changer, or powerful public figure ever be confined to a box? Place in your mind any free thinker or great influencer of history. Did they confine themselves to a box? Others may have tried to force the box on them, but they didn't accept it. They understand that boxes only exist if we allow them to exist and accept them into our realities. The existence of the box itself is a choice, your choice. This is what allows them to be free and greatly impact the world around them. But before we can become great influencers and take full control of our own lives, we must continue expanding our understanding of the incredible power of choice we possess, as well as the illusory choices we only think we are making freely, when they are still only confined within the very specific parameters provided by others.

Consider for a moment the classic Trolley Problem experiment by philosopher Judith Jarvis Thomson. For those unfamiliar with it, the Trolley Problem involves placing you as the participant in control of the lever that controls the tracks of a runaway trolley that is rapidly speeding towards a split. If you do nothing, the trolley may kill five people on the main track, but if you choose to pull the track lever, it will redirect the trolley to a side track where it will kill one person. This Trolley Problem has been switched out for many different variants, such as five individuals of advanced age on one track but a newborn baby on the other with its entire life ahead of it. It places the individual in the middle of an incredible dilemma. It provides them with a choice, one that most of us would likely never wish to encounter in real life. We can debate about the morality and ethical dilemma that this proposed situation entails and change out details to make this dilemma more interesting; however, that would miss the point entirely. As time begins to run out as the trolley ravages towards the split in the track, our hearts race. We try to consider the two choices that we've been presented as we scramble to justify whatever action we may ultimately take. We become so engaged in the dilemma and the excitement of the game that we forget that we are only in this game and "forced" into this uncomfortable decision **based on the initial choice even to play the game**. We believe we only have two choices because those are the two that someone or something else has provided us with, yet the real choice exists many levels deeper. **Do you want to play the game?** The people in this particular game are fictional and do not exist. Time may pressure you to make a decision, but the choice to play also involves the choice to accept the rules, boundaries, and limitations that exist within the boundaries of the initial choice, including that of the time constraint itself. Should you not choose the initial acceptance of the game, then the game does not exist, nor do the subsequent choices whereby you must quickly decide the fate of people's lives. In fact, it never really existed to begin with, and only lived in your imagination. When you accepted the rules proposed by another that had only existed in their reality, you brought it to life within your world, making it real. If we choose to play the game presented by another, we often cannot change the rules, as the acceptance to play the game involves the acceptance of the ruleset proposed. Once in the game, we may ask the moderator if we can have more time or if we can consider a third track option. However, this inquiry in itself only further validates the confinements of the game in which you have accepted the moderator to hold the ultimate authority of the rules and your pre-approved options of choices. If we have accepted the game, we have accepted the moderator. If we have accepted the moderator and their authority, we accept that they may not allow us to break or bend the rules without consequence or punishments, which we have also accepted. Should the moderator deny any requested rule changes or modifications, do you begin to question the moderator, or do you continue to operate within the confines of the accepted ruleset? Why are you playing the game? Do you have to play the game at all?

Now, let's raise the stakes a bit. Let's imagine that you are locked inside of a room with the moderator. The walls are bare.

There is nothing inside of this room aside from you, the moderator, and the game. The Trolley Problem is represented as a wooden toy track on the table with the inanimate victims scotch-taped to the track. **Must you now play the game?** No. You can still choose to refuse. **The choice is never binary**, no matter how it may be presented to you or appear. You are always in control of your actions and your choices, no matter the situation or circumstances. **There are no exceptions to this**. Though it appears in this situation that you must make a choice, you still possess your freedom, even as you find yourself confined inside of this locked room. You can turn around and not look at the wooden track as you protest in silence. You can tip the table over, rendering the wooden game useless. You can remove the tape affixing the helpless wooden men and women from the track. Or more aggressively, you can spartan-kick the moderator off of their chair for keeping you in this locked room and take their key to escape. But what if you aren't allowed to remove the tape from the future wooden victims on the track? What if you aren't allowed to leave the room or kick the moderator? Are we **n**ot "allowed" based on the very rules of the game we are presently protesting? What if you are threatened with an electric shock should you choose not to comply before the trolley hits the split in the track? If any of these excuses or similar concerns have crossed your mind, you have mistakenly conflated your power of choice with any perceived, or actual, consequence of a choice. Not only that, but you have also accepted the ruleset provided to you by the moderator of what you can and cannot do in this scenario. Any consequence, perceived or otherwise, must be completely detached from the choice itself. A consequence must only be seen as a **choice motivator or choice influencer**, but never as one with the choice. Furthermore, the consequence itself may also be illusory and only apply to the rules of the game, from within the game. As in, if you don't play the game, then you are told that you lose the game. Though, that logic only works should you accept the rules of the game as they are presented to you, the conditions established for "winning" and "losing," as well as the existence of the game to begin with. If you feel fine accepting that you are a loser of the game because you have chosen not to play the game, you have still chosen to subscribe to the imaginative reality of another by accepting the title of a loser, which acknowledges the existence of the game and its proposed rules, and that you did not win.

How many times have we made a choice based on the rulesets, boundaries, or limitations provided by another? A religion? A government? A society? The rules, laws, and boundaries only exist because we have accepted them into our lives, both individually as well as collectively in groups and pockets of individuals. However, the collective acceptance of any game rules does not make them any less illusory; they are still entirely fictitious and only seem to have any weight or gravity due to the collective buy-in and belief of the masses to accept them.

This creates them into existence that would otherwise not be so. How many members of the collective group have bought into the rules of the game only because it is what was presented to them by another or by the collective masses as they experienced it? Like you, they might have felt forced into the decision to accept the game rules because it was simply what everyone else was doing, yet everyone else was only doing it because it was what everybody else was already doing. We feel that we cannot challenge these rules, because as we do, we are called irresponsible, troublemakers, or even crazy. After all, **who are you** to challenge the established system of rules that everyone else seems to be following without question? Do others actually want to follow the rules, or are they only doing so out of obligation and because it is what everyone does if they want to stay out of trouble? **What trouble?** If the "trouble" exists due to the breaking of rules that only exist in the collective imagination of others, you will only be seen as an arouser of trouble to those that have accepted the imaginary rules. Should this same exact act or action defined as "trouble" occur in a region where these man-made rules have not been established or accepted by the masses, there would be **no trouble at all** for the **same** human action. The trouble, or consequence, only exists when we accept the rules of the game.

Both individually and collectively, we have forgotten our ability to make free choices and have accepted the game rules of another for our life. Much of this is unconscious, especially when we are born and raised inside of the offending fishbowl. It is akin to a dream, where you find yourself at the grocery store with your mother and your cousin that you haven't seen since grade school. You browse aisle by aisle, taking various treats off the shelf. You add your favorite brand of whole-wheat bread to the cart. You arrive at the cereal aisle, and just as you are about to turn the corner into the aisle, some kid knocks down a big family-size box of Cheerios that spills all over the floor. You decide to head down the aisle regardless. As you pushed your cart, the wheels crunched over the dry cereal until… wait, why are you at the grocery store with your mother? How did you get here? What did you do this morning prior to your arrival at this store? Which store is this anyway? And why is my cousin here, and somehow, he looks exactly the same from decades ago? At this point, you've caught yourself living inside the illusion. While you are in the illusion, you are unaware of it and make choices within it. You "chose" to still go down the aisle with the spilled cereal. You still "chose" to add your favorite bread to the cart. Oftentimes, it isn't until we wake up from the dream that we realize that anything was strange about it. During the dream, we operate within the confines, limitations, situations, and rules that are presented to us. When we are born into a society, culture, or religion with various beliefs, rules, laws, and expectations, this becomes just like our dream state, whereby we are unable to see what is imaginary or manufactured. **Manu**factured as in, created by **man**. These differ greatly from rules seemingly created by the universe, God, or otherwise. For example, if you choose to skydive without a parachute, but you don't believe in gravity or physical death, you might be in line for a rapid wake-up call. However, should you choose to drive and not wear your seatbelt when it is required by law, you will receive a ticket for this offense. This "rule" only exists in the world of man by accepting it into each of our realities. We can debate at great length about how enforcing the use of seat belts saves lives, or doesn't save lives, but this would be beside the point entirely. There is no natural law that requires us to wear seatbelts; it is a completely manufactured law, along with the legal consequences faced should we not follow the rules and laws that others have imposed upon us. Fines? Jail time? Suspension of your driver's license? These are all **arbitrarily assigned repercussions**, created by man, that we have accepted into our worlds. Even as the severity of the punishment may increase, perhaps even to that of a death sentence, this would not alter the manufactured and illusory nature of it and would only lure you further into the proposed illusion. Yet, if you choose not to wear your seatbelt because you don't agree with or believe in the law, you will still receive a ticket. Unlike natural laws, manufactured laws can always be challenged, should we be aware of their existence and understand that despite them, we still always have a choice. But what if the majority of people didn't actually want to wear their seatbelt, but they are all doing it because it's what the law says they must do? If everyone that didn't like or agree with the rule and associated penalties made the choice not to wear the seat belt, what might occur as a result? Would everyone be tossed in jail? Would everyone lose their driver's license? Surely not. Instead, the law would be revised, rewritten, or removed entirely. A control system of any kind may only successfully exist should the game rules be accepted by the individual, and ultimately the masses. Though, what are the masses, if not just a collection of individuals making semi-free choices? For many, the masses themselves create an illusion of their own, complete with boundaries and limitations, but only serve as just another artificial structure we've accepted into our own individual reality. When accepted into enough individual realities, it becomes the shared collective reality of the masses. At its core, this still requires the choice of the individual residing within the masses to accept or reject, which is **always a choice**, no matter the size of the masses or the threat they tease.

We are under the delusion that laws and rules define and restrict us; however, we forget that we ourselves are the creators of laws. Sure, you may not have personally created the seatbelt law, but by accepting it into your reality as objective reality and truth, only then has it become real. In this way, you have accepted the subjective creation of another into your world, which verifies the existence of a law or rule that once only existed in the imagination of another. It was spoken into existence by another, which still did not truly exist until others decided at some point to accept it as reality. Something that previously only existed in the mind, imagination, and spoken words of another, has become something enforceable based on the ideal of another's subjective reality and their interpretation of it, as they forcefully impose their ideals onto your life. As was the case in the scenario shared in the "Colliding Realities" chapter, a rule, law, or boundary might become real even if it was not initially founded in any objective reality or fact. Regardless of its existence in true reality, it has become real based on the acceptance of it as truth. Future generations then accept the manufactured rule, boundary, or limitation because it seems to be what has always been and always will be. When a manufactured limitation or belief exists long enough in the hearts, minds, and collective realities of enough people, it seems to become fixed, stationary, and unmovable, something that is no longer consciously seen or perceived. It becomes the bizarre world outside the grocery store walls in the dream, something that cannot be seen or acknowledged once accepted at a foundational level to accept it as it appears to be. Nothing can be accepted without first making a choice, even if accepted long ago in our infancy.

For this reason, **we must challenge everything**, as we ourselves may be unaware of the choices we've made and what we have accepted into our lives and for ourselves. With these foundational blocks, we operate in a mental autopilot mode and well within the mental constructs and game rules we've accepted for ourselves, seldom revisiting them, if ever. These rules and constructs only exist within our minds and what we have accepted as truth and reality. Recognizing and breaking past these mental constructs may be a time-consuming process, and they exist within all areas of our lives. For example, they exist in the way you see yourself. Are you important? Shy? Socially awkward? Attractive? Successful? What defines success without first buying into the social construct, expectations, and proposed game rules within our attempt to express it? Should you choose to redefine success in your own world as the measure of satisfaction in life, you might find yourself highly successful. Though, others might not think you are very successful as they point to your minimum-wage job at a fast-food chain and never-granted high-school diploma. They have decided to classify you as such based on the game rules and definitions that **they have accepted** as it had been presented to them, but their choice to accept the game rules does not require you to accept the same rules. You are always free to deny the rules and realities of others and create your own. After all, is that not precisely what they are doing themselves and to you? One million people who have accepted a particular set of beliefs or game rules that tease and torment you for not being successful according to their standards, adopted rulesets, and limiting beliefs **does not make your acceptance mandatory**. Should you choose to play by the game rules you'd prefer for you and your life, even if in the minority, then the efforts, taunts, and rejection from the masses need not apply or hold merit. You quite simply cannot be the loser of a game that, not only do you choose not to play, but you do not accept to be materially real in any way. In fact, the measure of success they impose on you is manufactured and is not a natural law of our universe. Therefore, it is subjective and does not become any more valid or real when the collective masses subscribe to this particular reality or belief.

It's important also to realize how one-sided the game rules are of those who intend to impose them on you forcefully. In the previous example, you are seen as an outcast and will be teased, tormented, and judged for not choosing to accept the ideals of another's subjective reality. Though, if you do not see yourself the same way within your own subjective reality, **they will not accept your rejection of their imposed rules**. **You** will be labeled the crazy one. **You** will be labeled the outcast. **You** will be labeled the rebel and the troublemaker. Regardless of the label others try to assign to you, these labels only exist within the world that they have accepted for themselves. Should you not accept their version of the world and associated rules, these labels are utterly meaningless. In the popular household game of Monopoly, it's as if you decided not to play, but this choice is rejected by the others. They say that your starting money allotment will be decreased by $100 for every minute you stall. If you still decide not to play, they state you will lose a turn upon every rotation. If that's not enough to convince you, your ironing board token piece will be placed in jail. At this point in the analogy, you can either decide that the punishment of an otherwise fictitious and imaginary game sounds severe enough that you'll be persuaded to play after all before you become too restricted inside the world that they created for you, or you will choose to bust outside of the boundaries they impose and reject them altogether. Society, religions, governments, and the masses do not like it when you don't play the game by their imposed rules. They will use every tool at their disposal to discredit you, but why does this occur? If the masses are no more than a collection of individuals with individual opinions and their own subjective realities, how can it be possible that their version of the world is superior to yours? How can it be possible for them to tell you what to do, think, act, or believe, but you cannot reverse the order and impose your way of life on them? Why is simply living your truest life unacceptable to them unless it fits into the mold that others have decided for you or what they want your life to look like? You may not even actively try to push your reality or rules onto them, but just the **mere rejection** of their reality by simply choosing another path is enough to send the masses into an aggressive frenzy. When speaking about the masses in this regard, it fosters the facilitation of what is commonly known as mob mentality or pack mentality. The ones within the masses must play by the rules, or they will end up like you, an outcast and rejected. They see how others who question the game rules end up and how they are ultimately treated; therefore, they comply and submit out of fear. This begins to develop the self-governing of others within the mob, with fear being the ultimate motivator and driving factor for ongoing compliance. The exact fear depends on the situation at hand, but ultimately, it may be simplified as a **fear of rejection** and any consequences associated with it. If not for the peer pressure and mob mentality, how many within the mob actually enjoy living within the mob's ruleset? Are they only continuing to live within it out of fear? Do they feel like they have chosen the mob, or has the mob chosen them? This is your life, and it can never belong to another without the surrendering of your power. Your life is defined by your choices. You always have choices, regardless of the consequences, perceived or actual. The consequence must be separated from the choice for the full realization of your choice to be seen.

16. STREAM OF LIFE

We must always lead our lives, knowing that we are the creators of them through our power of choice. From the various chapters and examples, we've explored how we are in control of our world, both inner and perceived outer, far more than we may have previously realized. Even with our power of choice and its ability to transform and shift the very way in which our lives are experienced, there are things in life that appear to be out of our control. Before we move any further, at all times, we must remember to keep in our minds that no matter the circumstance at hand, we always have a choice to think, act, and feel however we choose. There is no situation or person that can ever take this from us, for it is the very force of life that we all possess. There must be a distinct separation between "how" we feel about a situation and the substantive "what." In some cases, we can control both the "what" and the "how," but in others, we may only be in control of the "how." In these moments, we may have had control over the "what" in a previous moment of decision that we did not handle properly, which ultimately had set us up for the presently unpleasant situation. For that, we would have had control over the "what" previously, but not presently. Regardless, we always maintain control of the "how." When in the midst of a "what" that we seemingly cannot control now, it is not typically beneficial to defer attention away from the present "what" by resorting to blame-game tactics. We might decide to blame the "what" of a situation that we are currently experiencing on another. By staying focused in the present moment, we ultimately attain the much-desired clarity and wisdom into the situation by controlling the only thing that we can, which is the "how." We can use the situation presented by the "what" as a learning and growing experience for ourselves to master our craft of better defining the "how" in real-time, not only for now but for the situations we may encounter in the future. In this way, we indirectly create a new future for ourselves, regardless of external circumstances. We do this by redefining our ability to perceive the elements of the now, which is the only point at which any "future" can ever be created from within. Creation is always now, defined not by the "what" of our life, but our perception of the "how" in the now. This creates our future, which can only be experienced in the now.

If we revisit the Trolley Problem from the previous chapter, we can see that we had many more choices other than being forced to choose a track. The binary option we initially saw was to choose a track for the trolley to rush down. Though, we uncovered the deeper choice involving whether or not to accept the rules of the game, or any game, as it is presented to you. In this context, the word "game" is used as any form of establishment, rule system, societal conditioning, or beliefs, that arrive to you neatly wrapped with the constraints, punishments, expectations, and interpretations that it expects of you and from you. The Trolley Problem example was symbolic of many other choices we've made, often unknowingly, within our lives, which shape how we view the world, the games, and the "rules" therewithin. To know the rules, implicitly suggests there must be a game. To suggest there is a game, implicitly suggests you and others have chosen to play. As in, there could not be a game without the acceptance of it, which ultimately had created it into being. As we circle back to the principles within this example, we can reimagine it in a new way to further the topic of discussion into the "how" and "what" of life.

Now, imagine that the Trolley Problem is no longer only a wooden game that you have decided to play, but a very real situation indeed. Regardless of what decisions, choices, or actions by yourself or others occurred, you find yourself in control of the lever responsible for choosing the direction of a speeding trolley that cannot be stopped. Let's assume that there truly is nothing to be done to stop this trolley, and you have less than ten seconds to make a decision. We will also assume that you are the only one who can do it. If you do nothing, the choice is made for you through your choice to refrain from making one, as the trolley will continue along its current route. In reality, your decision is to either leave it as is, or change the trolley's direction. If we place ourselves at this very moment in time and space, we will see that spending time to speculate who might be at fault for the runaway situation, even if it was yourself, is truly irrelevant. **All we have is right now** and a decision must be made. What will you choose?

By placing ourselves inside the reality of the Trolley Problem, we find that it is symbolic of many things that may occur to us in life that we seemingly don't have control over. Things that we commonly view as unpleasant happen to all of us, often unexpectedly. One's home might burn to the ground with all of their possessions. The unexpected death of a loved one may occur. You may get hit by another vehicle while idling at a stoplight, leaving your car totaled and with little hope of your body being physically mobile again due to injuries. You may lose your job due to economic conditions or something else completely outside of your control. These situations often shake us to our core and leave us feeling vulnerable and helpless. While we ought to take responsibility for past choices and the consequences that might have led us to an unpleasant situation, we should not spend time sabotaging ourselves over things we seemingly cannot control. For example, if you were struck in your car while idling at a stoplight, it would not make much sense to blame yourself and think:

"If only I stopped at the grocery store first instead of going to the post office, I would not be in this position!"

Sure, you made the choice to leave your house. You also chose your route and the exact time you left your house. But the accident itself was not your fault. On this same note, it might make sense to become very angry or upset at the reckless or distracted driver that hit you and has potentially altered your life forever. In actuality, the fault may very well rest exclusively on the driver who hit you, **but even this is in the past now**. Assigning blame, becoming angry, or upset, does nothing to change the flow or stream of life that you presently find yourself living in. Whether you like it or not, you are operating the lever of the trolley track. You have the choice of "how" to feel and perceive this situation. In addition, you also have control over the "what" that happens next, but not the "what" that has just occurred. Remember, the time of creation in your life is always the present moment; it's always right now. If we spend our time living in the past, in regret, in blaming, and in anger, we are using our present moment of creation to revisit the past rather than to move towards the ultimate acceptance of the objective reality presented to us. When we become stuck in the past, we lose our ability to create something entirely new from it in this present moment of creation. This isn't to suggest that we should always find the "silver lining" of the cloud even in difficult situations, as that would minimize the greater points shared here. For starters, we mustn't ever deny our feelings. If you feel upset, or feel like crying, allow yourself to feel your emotions. Use your emotions as your guide to better understand yourself, your attachments, and your hang-ups. As you experience these emotions, rest with yourself, show yourself compassion and love. Experience the feelings for what they are. Do not spend much time attempting to justify them nor trying to fight them. Just be with yourself and let life flow through you as it is, without the unnecessary shame, guilt, or the anticipated pressures or expectations from others or yourself.

These are the unpleasant moments in life when we feel helpless and where we feel we have been robbed of our choice. It may be true that we were robbed of some of our options in life that we might have had access to otherwise. The options taken from us could have caused us to stray from the way we planned to live our life, but we can never be robbed of the only thing that we will ever have. This is the power of choice that resides above all, external to us, including our physical bodies. As stated in a previous chapter, our power of choice is the purest essence of what we are. When we separate the things that we possess from the things that we do not possess, this becomes clearer for us to grasp and apply within ourselves. In the case of the car accident, we cannot take this car with us beyond our mortal death. We cannot take our bodies with us beyond our mortal death. We cannot take our family or our friends with us. It's important to highlight here that the use of the word "our" is our emotional ownership, or perhaps in some cases, legally protected ownership of any possession, **but these things can never be truly ours**. As we place things in this greater perspective, we realize that even though the situation presents a challenge and may be highly uncomfortable or unpleasant, we still have the ability to choose how we feel. If we were to realize that everything we previously thought to have possessed was only being used or borrowed temporarily in life, we realize that nothing was taken from us at all, as nothing can be if it was never truly ours to begin with. We can be grateful for the time that we had with the various things that we had the opportunity to borrow for as long, or as short, as we might have been borrowing them. We can also be grateful for what's remaining of the borrowed goods, including our physical life, no matter how limited it may appear to be. Additionally, your power of choice always remains and can never be taken from you.

REDUCING THE LATENCY

What choices do we have when we seemingly get hijacked by this uncontrollable stream of life? We can start by choosing to accept the stream and flow of life for what it is and something that we cannot always control. Life is transitional in nature; there are no known exceptions to this. Life occurs in seasons, from sadness to joy and life to death. For can there ever be life without death, or death without life? Ideally, we'd all remember that life as we know it is only an illusion, or a dream-like state, that has been built off of our perceptions and core beliefs while being further established by our choices made from within our subjective realities. The moment we choose to change our core beliefs, our perceptions change, allowing us to view the same objective world in a completely different light. Whether that different light allows for a more pleasant or unpleasant perception of the world is a choice you always have. We must strive to live our lives from a place of acceptance of the flow rather than the rejection of it. The flow is what appears to be happening to us, through us, and for us. Should we view it for what it is without rejecting the elements of life that we cannot control, we'd free ourselves from much worry and anxiety. We'd begin to appreciate every single moment for what it is and what it isn't, knowing that everything in life is in a constant state of flux and transition. We can choose this perspective of life now and do not need to wait for an unpleasant or uncontrollable moment to do so. By choosing it now, you'll enjoy your present life much more while preparing your mindset for the inevitably unpleasant states that life will bring us all through.

If we simplify the example to a relatable modern-day annoyance, we may yield some greater insight into this particular point of learning to **reduce the latency of acceptance** towards the stream and flow of life. Picture for a moment that you are driving your vehicle and your tire blows out. The reality, or "what" of this situation, is that you are driving your car, and your tire has blown out. The "what" and substance of the situation presented to you through the stream of life has **just happened**, which now effectively **resides in the past, not your present**. There's no changing this reality; it already happened, as in the past tense. However, you still have a choice in the present moment to choose your next "what" and your present "how" of the previously occurring "what." Should you not already live a life in full acceptance of what "is" without stickiness or attachment, you'll already be well prepared to handle this situation by understanding these principles and applying them in your life. Until this mindset becomes your daily way of thinking, it must be consciously applied. For this reason, the sooner you can get yourself to realize that the tire blew in the past and there is nothing that the present version of you can do about it, you can switch your energy and attention towards accepting the situation and becoming the creator of your life, feelings, attitude, and emotions moving forward, starting in the now. You are always in control. You are always the creator. If screaming, yelling, and crying about the blowout aided the situation, allowed the tire to repair itself, or allowed you to get out of this situation sooner, this may not be a terrible strategy to execute. However, due to the lack of current evidence that this particular methodology works for your ultimate benefit and as it only seems to raise your cortisol levels while releasing other chemical cocktails in your body that cloud your judgment, it may be worthwhile to attempt another approach for your life. Every single moment you spend prior to the acceptance of reality as it had occurred to you is an unnecessary, unpleasant, and uncomfortable moment of pain and suffering that you are inflicting upon yourself. If you believe that life is maliciously out to get you by putting you through a situation like this, **you're right**. If you believe that life is presenting you with an opportunity to grow and develop yourself, **you're right**. This is your choice; there is no right or wrong choice, only the choice that you choose to make for yourself. This choice changes your perception, and ultimately, your experience of life within your subjective reality. There is no one to blame for your suffering other than the choice you have made to suffer through your refusal to accept reality for what it is, or more specifically, for what it was. When this is fully realized, understood, and integrated, you can choose to **reduce the latency** towards your ultimate acceptance of the situation. Imagine that you reduced the latency in any stressful situation that has occurred to you seemingly without your control, whether from a flat tire or being present during an armed robbery at a bank. When you accept the reality of the situation, you free yourself to focus on your next move, your next action, without unnecessary stress, fear, or discomfort. By living life in this state of rejection towards the stream, you are actively living in the past while the present continues to unfold and expand around you. Yet, you are not present enough to experience the constant unfolding of reality by attempting to strike an unwinnable deal with the past somehow as you beg and plead for it to reconsider through your rejection and whimsical protesting of it. When you effectively reduce the latency of acceptance regarding your car tire blowing out, you accept everything that the situation is. You choose to move forward by staying present in the now while continuing to create your future in the only moment that it can ever be created from within.

It matters not you are late to the most important meeting of your career.

It matters not you are already using your spare, and you do not have another.

It matters not your cell phone battery has just died.

It matters not you are on an abandoned highway in the middle of the night.

Surely, each of these specifics adds more logistical difficulty to the situation; however, **it matters not** what reality presents to you. It only matters that you accept the parts of life that are out of your control as you utilize your attention and focus on your incredible and limitless power of choice to create your world. You create your new "what" and your present "how" right here and right now. **There are no limits to this**. You may add any scenario you wish that occurs out of your control in the stream and flow of life. Undoubtedly, in every single case you picture mentally, you'll realize that anything that has happened, has already happened, and is beyond your control to stop or materially alter, as it has already occurred. By this, we can state that anything that you are actively observing and analyzing has occurred in the past. It is in your best interest to reduce the latency of acceptance towards the seemingly uncontrollable aspects of life.

RUMINATION ALTERATION

In the scenario with the flat tire, we might find someone or something to blame for the reality that is occurring, or more accurately, just occurred in our life. It's true that it might have been possible that a past decision that you made in a previously experienced present moment resulted in you being stranded on the highway with this flat tire. For example, you might have been told that your tires were starting to bald, and despite this knowledge, you didn't take action or take the time to resolve the issue. Or your current reality may be the result of someone else not doing their job properly that ultimately allowed this situation to occur. It's also possible that nothing could have been done to prevent this reality from occurring. Perhaps there was a small nail or screw in the road that would be impossible for anyone to see, yet it blew out your tire as your car hit the sharp object at just the right angle, causing an immediate blowout. Regardless, the why or how it happened is not important when in the context of the acceptance towards the present moment.

With that, we can always choose to learn from our mistakes in life, but that can only be done in the now, not the past. Surely, the poor choice might have been made in the past, but the fruits of that choice are only being experienced in the now. Additionally, how you respond to the happenings of the now, along with acknowledgment of your triggers, stressors, and anxiety, serve as an abundance of raw material for your personal growth and development. This is your training ground. Once you have mastered your present emotions and triggers by accepting the reality of now, only then should you move on to revisiting past choices and decisions that might have led you to this unpleasant moment. When analyzing and exploring our past choices, such as not getting the tires changed sooner even though we were warned about it, we must do so from a place of pure acceptance. If we have accepted our current reality, that must mean that we have also accepted our past choices completely and taken ownership of them. With acceptance comes understanding. With understanding comes the opportunity for true learning and growth. And with growth comes progression, which ultimately allows us to apply these life lessons humbly and make better choices in the future without the unnecessary stress, pain, or self-sabotaging rumination of past choices, which are unchangeable in substance.

If we change course slightly for a moment and assume that you knew your tires were going bad, but you hadn't the money to fix them, it'd be difficult to take responsibility and ownership for the choice. It may be a choice that you felt like you couldn't make, as you tell yourself that if you had the money, you would have changed out the tires. With this, have you taken the responsibility of choice from yourself? If you have, who or what might be to blame instead, if anything or anyone at all? As previously stated, playing the blame game only brings unnecessary pain and suffering and does not halt the reality of the situation from having occurred. If we have begun deferring responsibility, we must go back to step one and learn to accept the situation for everything that it is and everything that it isn't. Once accepted, we can attempt to dive back into the past choice that might have been possible to prevent this situation from occurring, if at all. If you didn't have money to change your balding tire out, it might be beneficial to ask yourself why you didn't have the money for this tire change.

How are you presently spending your money?

Do you have unnecessary extras in your life, like a smartphone, streaming services, or cable bill?

- How often do you eat out? See a movie? Go to a bar? Buy a coffee from Starbucks?
- Could you live in a smaller and cheaper place? Or live with friends or family? Sure, it may not be ideal, but could you?
- Where do you buy your clothes, shoes, and other accessories? How often do you purchase new ones?
- Is there any possible way to adjust your spending habits

and lifestyle to allow additional funds for other important things?

- Is there anything that you have that you do not need for your survival? Extra clothes or shoes? A TV in a room that you never use? A chair or other furniture sitting in your garage? That area rug in your living room? Wall art? We may enjoy having these things, but are these things more important than changing out a balding tire prior to a blowout?

- If any of these apply, even if only slightly, may it be within your realm of responsibility for your tire blowing out due to the ways you spend and manage your money and possessions?

Perhaps you find it isn't so much a spending issue after all, and instead, an income issue.

- Which job are you working?

- Are you **forced** to work at this particular place of employment for the salary that you've agreed on?

- What is stopping you from finding a new, higher-paying job? Do you place blame on someone or something else? Or is it the result of a self-limiting belief that you have accepted into your life that you are not capable of achieving something greater for yourself?

- What is stopping you from advancing your skills in another field of study to earn a higher wage?

You may or may not decide to spend much time trying to find the root of why you didn't have the money to proactively change out your balding tire, as it doesn't matter to the extent of accepting the reality of the situation. Though, it may matter in the sense of learning how to prevent a similar situation from repeating itself. After accepting everything as it was and is, you must ask yourself what steps you can take to proactively improve your situation for the future should another unexpected financial situation come up. You must be willing to do this without blame assignment and without bitterness for yourself or another. Instead, you can take these steps from a place of empowerment, control, creation, and peace. Would this not be the most beneficial use of your time?

If you are unable to imagine ever being in a position that you will not perceive yourself as the victim, you will be unlikely ever to escape your current situation. At first glance, this might sound harsh or discouraging, but if you cannot imagine what your life would look like being financially stable, how could you ever make the steps, moves, or decisions necessary to change or improve anything? It isn't enough to simply wish for more money; if it were enough, most of us would have the money we'd need when we need it. You must **deeply imagine** all of the things **in great detail** that would need to be present in your life and reality for you to be in such a situation. Use your imagination, and feel it, believe it, see it, and experience it as if it were a present fact. Once you have this locked in and you can experience the feeling now that you would expect to have upon being in such a situation, you have begun to develop your strategy for moving forward. Maybe you imagine being a successful CEO or a regional manager for the chain you currently work at. It matters not what you imagine, so long as you can imagine yourself with the financial freedom and lifestyle you ultimately desire for yourself. Sure, you may not know the exact logistical steps to take, but it is imperative not to allow that to influence your imagination and rob it of all of the things it is capable of doing to create the life you desire. Let the imagination do what it does best, which is, **imagine without limitations** what you think is or is not possible for your life. Once imagined and truly felt, you may now start taking steps, consciously or not, in the direction of that imagined life. Depending on what you imagined, you might know the immediate and practical steps to take, who to talk to, or which skills to develop. In other cases, you may not know where to start to make it all happen, but that does not matter. The purpose of this step is to create your goals and vision for your future, which you will begin to naturally gravitate towards as you keep your eyes out for opportunities that align with your desired goals. If you do not have goals and cannot imagine ever being financially free in your life, no matter the great opportunity that comes your way, aside from winning the lottery or similar, you will not know to utilize any other opportunity in furtherance of your goals, **as you had no goals to apply them to.**

We can choose to learn from anything that might have led us to this unpleasant moment in life in hopes of making a different choice later in life if presented with a similar opportunity. If we cannot identify what could have possibly been done differently, we can always look at how we felt and experienced the situation as it unfolded, especially if it took an excessive amount of time to reduce the latency of acceptance. Though, any time spent prior to reducing the latency is excessive, as any time spent in the state of anxiety and rejection is always unnecessary. From there, we can move onto what we could do differently to prevent it from happening again in the future. We do this by imagining what our reality might need to look like for us to be better prepared for similar situations. If we can imagine it, we can begin moving towards it. Even without the logical steps known to us, we will begin to gravitate towards the ideal reality by simply keeping our eyes open for opportunities.

Per a brief conversation taken from the Lewis Carrol novel, *Alice's Adventures in Wonderland*:

> *"Would you tell me, please, which way I ought to go from here?" said Alice.*
>
> *"That depends a good deal on where you want to get to," said the Cat.*

"I don't much care where—" said Alice.

"Then it doesn't matter which way you go," said the Cat.

"—so long as I get somewhere," Alice added as an explanation.

"Oh, you're sure to do that," said the Cat, "if you only walk long enough."

FLOW WITH THE FLOW

The stream of life carries all of us through the most unique landscapes. It might be tempting to classify or label certain parts of this journey or flow as "better" or "worse" than other parts of the stream, but regardless, every moment should be appreciated for the beauty that it is, should you **allow yourself to see it**. As with the natural law of opposites, we can only know pleasant experiences from our experience with unpleasant ones. Though the unpleasant experiences are often dreaded, these are the exact moments that present us with the opportunity for self-reflection, growth, and maturation. In the moments that bring us perceived bliss and excitement, we ought to be as present as possible and enjoy every single one of them, understanding that life is always in transition and even the most blissful moments may never last forever. This isn't a morbid outlook; in fact, it can be an enlightening and freeing one **if you allow it to be**. When in the midst of a beautiful moment, soak it in, and don't think about how long it may or may not last. Be fully present and allow yourself all of the goodness and pleasure of the moment. Be grateful for your life, for this experience. Be grateful for the unpleasant experiences that preceded this one, as, without those, you would not be here, right now, experiencing one of joy and bliss. When the moment ends, as every moment inevitably will, you're onto the next moment, which bears a purpose all of its own. Though the next moment may not provide you with the same bliss as the previous moment, it is still your moment to experience everything that is available to you. Will you use the new moment to step outside of your current present moment to live in the past, effectively rejecting the reality of now? Or will you choose to experience your new present moment and accept the reality it provides? Will you be grateful for the most recent blissful moment while also being grateful for the air you are breathing in the present one? This outlook is also beneficial not only to enjoy the pleasant moments more thoroughly but also to stay engaged when experiencing the unpleasant ones. With the understanding that every moment passes, whether perceived to be pleasant or unpleasant, allow every moment to flow through you, knowing that another one is already on its way. However, to experience any new moment, we must be willing to accept the uncontrollable aspects of our current reality and follow the processes outlined in the previous examples. Without acceptance, there can only be rejection. And with rejection comes suffering. Leverage the unpleasant moments for all the uncomfortable learning opportunities they provide without unnecessary or impotent blame assignment. Fully embrace the pleasant moments and rest within them, taking the much-needed breaks. We cannot have the pleasant without the unpleasant; therefore, do not deny yourself either. It is all part of your journey to experience, learn, and grow from.

Regardless of the situation, whether perceived by you to be "good" or "bad," **you always have exactly what you need**. You always have enough because you always have your power to choose. Food, money, shelter, friends, family, and possessions can never truly be ours. We often try to convince ourselves otherwise due to our societal condition, legal classifications of "ownership," or our emotional and physical attachments. We only have one thing, and that is our very consciousness. This provides us exclusively with the irrevocable power of choice that we hold. When we choose to hand that power over to another, event, or situation, we become empty and devoid of any meaningful experience of life. This unnecessarily subjects us to anxiety, depression, manipulation, or control. Fortunately, our power of choice is something that can never truly depart us, despite us unknowingly handing it over to another or life situation. It can only ever be a **temporary displacement**, which is returned to us instantaneously when we recognize this and decide to take it back.

REALITY-AGNOSTIC

You'll either choose to adopt a belief system and perceptual model that provides purpose to the unpleasant moments, allowing them to flow through you and into something greater, or you'll choose to reject reality as it has presented itself to you as you writhe in pain, suffering, and discomfort. There is no wrong choice, only the choice that you choose to make for yourself. You are in control of your experience of life through the choices you decide to make. If you believe you cannot change the unpleasant nature of life and actively reject it, **your experience in life will match your chosen belief** according to your attachment to the particular belief. The present moment is wherever the stream current has you, whether good, bad, or indifferent, matters not. You have a choice to be still and enjoy the uniqueness of every moment, even if "bad" or "unpleasant" while maintaining a full presence within it. **The true gift does not reside in the moment itself**, but rather, in your awareness and consciousness to experience this moment and any other. You choose how you perceive the moment and how you act upon it, either against it and in strife, or with it, in harmony, peace, and gratitude. You may also choose gratitude for the stream itself that carries you to and through your personal journey of self-discovery and growth. Without the stream taking you through the unpleasant, would you ever have consciously chosen it for yourself? Without the unpleasant moments, there would be no contrast. There would be no true growth, development, or realization. There would be no appreciation of the pleasant moments, as they would be all there was. **Reality in itself can never be pleasant or unpleasant**, for it is only our perceptions that can ever make it so. For any moments that we find unpleasant, these are only **representations of our internal state** and perspective of life. There are no exceptions to this, as it is universally applicable. We may believe that certain extreme or dire circumstances are exempt from this, but this makes it so **only to the holder of such a deterministic belief**. But should one understand the power that they hold and take ownership of it, we find that it is only our perception of life that can make it a pleasant experience or an unpleasant one.

If, while doing the dishes, a glass cup falls and shatters on the floor, we have a choice as to how we interpret this experience. Through perception, we can create a pleasant or unpleasant interpretation of a reality that does not otherwise define itself, but instead, has provided us with the power to **do** so. This world has allowed us to interact with it in such a way that it gives us the choice to live and experience it in the manner we most desire. For the broken glass, we can choose to curse at God, the universe, or even our own clumsiness, while mourning the loss of the now-shattered item. For this interpretation, you would not be incorrect with your perception of the situation when the choice to feel how you wish is solely yours, and in this way, **you can never be incorrect**. Though, with every choice, you must own what occurs within your own life as a result of your chosen perceptive model. Should you choose to express anger or resentment over the shattered item, you would also be choosing an increased heart rate, raised cortisol levels in your body, and potentially, to carry a short-fuse and general grumpiness for the remainder of your day. This choice is your freedom, but you must own every part of your choice by acknowledging everything that your choices entail. With a choice like this, though you are free to make it, how do you personally benefit or grow through the employment of this particular perceptual model? Is the broken glass worth the frustration, health issues, and the sabotaging of the rest of your day based on a broken item, in which no amount of crying, screaming, yelling, or fit-throwing can ever result in the reassembly of the broken glass? Perhaps this is the choice that you indeed decided to make, and by the next morning, you have moved on, and it no longer seems to actively disturb or distress you. Yet, while working in your kitchen the next day, another glass item falls to the floor and shatters. Are you any better prepared to handle a repeat of the same situation, given the opportunity yesterday had presented to you? What if, upon the first instance of the glass breaking, you instead chose to reduce the latency of acceptance? What if you used the opportunity to self-reflect and notice how upset you became at the glass breaking, which allowed you to realize your emotional attachment to material possessions? By allowing yourself to feel whatever comes up and observing it honestly, you are presented with the incredible opportunity to learn more about yourself and your beliefs about life that make a given situation or experience pleasant or unpleasant. We think it is life that is unpleasant, and we must only deal with it, but it can only be us that make it so. Possessing any other viewpoint can only ever be a deferment of responsibility, in which case, no learning or growth can be achieved. Without growth, self-improvement, or visibility into the elements of our belief system that cause unnecessary pain and suffering, we are bound to continue living unpleasant lives indefinitely. It isn't life that is unpleasant, but only our flawed interpretations of it. This isn't to suggest one engages in self-betrayal by pretending to be happy, pleased, or content with the glass breaking when you are really in a state of discontentment. You must never deny the reality you are perceiving or the feelings you are feeling. Through observation and the sincere challenge of our feelings and experience, we learn to understand ourselves better. Should we use the glass shattering and "unpleasant" moments of life for self-reflection while being grateful for them and the teaching opportunities they provide, our very experience of life changes. When the glass shatters, we are no longer focused on the glass but on ourselves and what can be learned. By choosing gratitude in these moments, you are making a choice to acknowledge and fully accept what is. There is no wrong choice, only the choice that you choose to make, which must be owned and accepted by you and the experience of your life that you provide yourself through it. In this way, **how will you choose to experience your life?**

What if the seemingly unpleasant situation holds more significance than the shattering of a glass cup? What if, instead, the item that shattered was a one-of-a-kind Ming vase that had been in your family for centuries? What if, instead, it was your house that caught fire and burned down, along with all of your possessions inside? What if, instead of possessions, you experience the loss of a loved one through their mortal death? Or perhaps, you experience something that is far worse than anything that can fit within any of these general classifications or categories; what then? Regardless of what becomes lost or what is taken from you, your entire experience of it is a perceptual choice by you. In which case, **there can be no improper interpretation chosen**. You are not denying reality, only choosing how you wish to interpret it. You can get to choose your experience of life by choosing your core beliefs and perceptions of it.

Should you choose to see everything in life not as difficult but as an opportunity to challenge yourself and grow through it, you will interpret the world and your experience of it precisely as such. This belief encourages self-growth through the opportunities that are presented to you. This belief also declares the difficulty of life, making it so.

Should you choose to see the universe, source, or God as being completely in control of things and believing everything happens for a reason and for the greater good and to your benefit, you will interpret the world and your experience of it precisely as such. This belief minimizes the pain and suffering one experiences while aligning one's purpose with something greater than themselves, as they feel protected and cared for as they journey through life and its various unknowns.

Should you choose to see the world as a dangerous place, where bad things continually happen to you and others, and most everything is unpleasant, sad, or depressing, you will interpret the world and your experience of it precisely as such. This belief yields a chronically unpleasant experience of life that will be reinforced through every moment of adversity. Even in the moments of positivity or joy, your experience of these will be limited, as you either fail to see the positivity altogether due to your perceptual filter, or you fail to enjoy them thoroughly as you actively anticipate the next depressing or negative thing that will inevitably come your way.

Should you choose to view the death of a loved one as an exciting next chapter for them, where they are free from the pains of their physical body and continue living in eternity, as they dance and sing with complete freedom, their funeral may become more of a celebration. You will shed tears not of sadness but of joy and true happiness, akin to a wedding or the birth of a new family member. This belief system has the potential to eliminate the anxiety surrounding death in your life while also choosing to view death in a positive and exciting way.

Some may suggest that choosing a belief system that allows one to incur more positive experiences in life requires one to live in denial; however, is that suggestion itself not rooted in a belief system of its own to the holder of such a belief to view the world in such a way? If we have the power to choose our belief system, which alters our perception, and ultimately our experience of life, why would we use this choice to create a life that is unpleasant, difficult, or depressing? Why not use this power of choice not only to overcome negativity and sadness but to **transcend it completely**? We mustn't need to overcome sadness, where a belief system of sadness in a particular situation does not exist. In the case of losing a loved one while holding a belief system that their death signifies a beautiful transitioning in life, much like a caterpillar becoming a butterfly, **there is no sadness to overcome**, as it has been transcended completely through this belief system. Should we instead believe that life sends us situations that elicit the feeling of sadness, so that we can become humble and more grateful for what we do have, this is precisely how we will experience life and what we will receive from it through this journey. We have made real the sadness through the acknowledgment of its existence, **as it does not exist in the world,** only in our interpretation of it. As a reminder, this isn't to deny sadness should you feel it or to inspire the feelings of guilt or shame for experiencing such feelings as the result of your chosen perception. It is only to understand that your experience of sadness is a direct result of a choice you've made. The choice to adopt a belief system that allows you to see sadness in the event you see and experience it is similar to the very way in which you have chosen to interpret the objective world around you. For those who have adopted a core belief early on in life, or one that they have chosen subconsciously, this may not seem like something that can be changed, as the current pain you might be experiencing is very real. For those in this position currently, the mere consideration that it might only exist as a result of something inside of you, such as a choice that has led to your subjective interpretation that ultimately results in pain or an unpleasant experience may seem as if it requires the flat-out denial of "reality" or the "real world." This process of transforming ourselves and our perception can take consistent effort over many, many years, or it can be instantaneous.

Whether or not you think this transformation is plausible for you, is **decided by you.**

The level of difficulty to obtain this perceptual shift is **decided by you.**

The amount of time it takes to achieve such a shift is **decided by you.**

If you have this free choice, so do others. If others choose to view life differently from you by focusing on the positives instead of the negatives, do you see them as out of touch with reality? If so, **you are correct**, as they are out of touch with reality, but only as you have interpreted reality to be through your chosen core beliefs and perceptual biases. In this case, **they are completely out of touch with it**. Meanwhile, they are completely in touch with their reality as they see it while experiencing happiness and joy regardless of their life situation or what happens to them. We all have this choice, and we all live life through our subjective interpretations of it, and therefore, who could ever be right? Can anyone be more correct than another as to how they choose to interpret life? One's chosen belief system may answer this question for them, which they have deemed inside of their reality to be the truth. Though, that is only a choice that they have made to view the world and others in such a way that **their truth is the truth**. Those who cannot admit this to themselves have so intimately identified with their chosen belief system that they cannot see outside of it. They fail to realize that they can only arrive at this **faux certainty** through their choice to adopt and choose such a belief system. This belief system provides them with the very framework that declares there can be no other way, truth, or reality other than the one they have chosen. **Therefore, the only valid and real interpretation of reality is the one that you choose for yourself.** Should others, whether one or many, attempt to coerce you otherwise based on their own chosen belief systems, is purely an action, based on a symptom, of precisely how they have chosen to view the world, as they strenuously force it, and you, to fit their desired mold.

- Does their happiness or satisfaction with life depend on your willingness to convert to their preferred belief system? Does yours depend on the actions or beliefs of others?

- Should you dance to another's tune for how they wish and believe the world to operate? Do you expect, anticipate, and desire them to dance to yours?

- Should you allow them to decide your role, behavior, attitude, and experience of life, all while sacrificing your power of choice to aid another's preferred version of reality, which can never truly be accurate or complete?

- Will you choose to "face the reality" of life and remain deep in sadness, depression, stress, and anxiety because that is what another believes you should be experiencing?

- Or should you choose to remain in positivity, optimism, contentment, and gratitude of all things, realizing it has provided you with an overwhelmingly pleasant experience of all things in life even if others have chosen to see things differently?

- Do you choose to conform to another's reality at the expense of your own suffering and pain to fit the preferred narrative of another? Or do you choose freedom to experience reality exactly as you desire to experience it?

There **is** no ignorance of reality in any choice made, whether the choice yields pleasant or unpleasant experiences. **Ignorance exists only in the belief that reality must only be viewed and interpreted one way by all.** But where does this belief come from, if not from a choice made by another through their own subjective interpretation of reality? How can one's view of an objective and unbiased reality be superior to that of another? Perhaps, you say, they are better educated, but to become better educated, they must have had to first prove this status through the adherence to the fabricated man-made structure known as the education system. This structure of education was constructed by another using their own subjective interpretation of reality, as well as how they believed intelligence ought to be measured or deduced. Therefore, this very measure of superiority ranking to measure the validity of one's interpretation of reality is incomplete, or at the very least, entirely subjective.

When we seemingly cannot control the circumstances of the world or the stream or flow of life, **we can only control ourselves through our choice.**

When we control ourselves, we control our perception of the world.

When we control our perception of the world, we choose our preferred experience of life.

If we choose to see pain or suffering, we will experience pain and suffering. If we choose to see light and love, we will experience light and love.

There is only one reality, the one that you choose to live in and experience.

Reality is experienced now, in the only moment it can ever be experienced in.

How will you **choose** to experience the only moment you have?

18. EQUIVOCALLY EQUAL

Civilizations have long used a ranking system of sorts to define the importance of one individual to another. This establishes superiority, inferiority, importance, value, and at other times, the rights each holds in direct proportion to the value they exhibit within the terms and expectations of the civilization to which they belong. Oftentimes, the value or importance may be assigned based on the contribution they may add to the greater society. In places where food must be hunted for and gathered, the individuals that are capable of providing food to their community may be regarded as more valuable or important than those that cannot. In any case, the importance and value placed upon another are based on a subjective metric inherent to the rules and expectations that govern that particular civilization. For those that do not meet the standards or add value in a way that's meaningful to the greater whole, these individuals will be seen as less valuable and less important. Though, what one civilization may deem as a valuable trait, another civilization may not. Therefore, the very metric of importance is subjective and varies from person to person and group to group. To be regarded as important in one society may not carry over to another. Does our value stem from our achievements and the value that we add to the greater whole, or is our value something intrinsic to our very being?

Think for a moment of the most important person that comes to your mind. Once you have one or even a few examples at the top of your mind, ask yourself the question:

What makes this person, or these people, important?

This is an incredible question to consider and one worth exploring for the many elements involved in the creation of the question, which will undoubtedly alter how the question is ultimately answered. At its surface, the question may seem to be a simple one to answer. It might have been very easy for you to answer, to which the answer or reply percolated to the forefront of your awareness almost instantaneously. In actuality, the answer will always return a dynamic response dependent on the subjective reality of the individual to which it was asked. By its very nature, the answer you provided to the question is wholly dependent on how you measure and define importance, as the concept of importance has been internally derived from your interpretation of your subjective reality.

First and foremost, we must establish that there are many ways to explore the concept and definition of importance, none of which can ever be definitive. The measure of importance is not only entirely subjective but also relative. The Oxford Languages dictionary defines the word "importance" as follows:

"The state or fact of being of great significance or value."

Let's consider this official definition as we continue through the subjective interpretations of the otherwise static definition provided. Now, let's assume for a moment that the person you thought of was a loved one, someone like your mother. You may have thought of your mother, or someone similar to this because your mother is very important to you. After all, she is responsible for your mortal birth into this world as well as the many years of nurturing and love that she has poured into you. If your mother was who came to mind, it also indicates that she is still very important to you in your life presently, whether or not she is still alive and with you. Perhaps she continues to support your dreams and encourages you, or she is a role model for your life. Regardless, you have your unwavering reasons as to why you would define her as someone of importance in your life. If you were to walk down the street and ask a random passerby if your mother was important to them, the passerby might be polite and kind, but your mother is simply not important to them as she is to you, for they have someone else of importance in their life. Perhaps they may even define the very word of importance differently from how you have defined it for yourself and chosen to express it. For this reason, the importance of your mother in your life came down to your own definition of the word "importance," as well as who she is relative to you in your life as your mother. To think of your mother as someone of importance, you may have defined importance as someone who is always there for you and cares about you. While your mother may be very important to you, she may be **just another human** on this planet in the eyes and subjective reality of another. It's also possible that this other person not only thinks that your mother lacks notable importance but may even view her as inferior to themselves or other people in this world, dependent on how they themselves define the word "important." Even in this, **they would not be incorrect**, as it is true for them in their subjective reality, just as much as you are correct that she is the most important person in your subjective reality. This very point highlights the incredibly subjective and also relative nature, definition, intention, interpretation, and phrasing of the word **importance.**

Let's assume that you thought of someone else of importance, such as a celebrity, historical figure, current or former president or politician, a researcher or philosopher in your field of study, the CEO of a well-respected company, or someone from the top 10 richest people in the world according to Forbes. Regardless of who you might have thought about and whether they fit into the categories provided or not, they will still be entirely subjective and relative in their alleged degree of importance. For example, let's consider the CEO of a well-respected company. One might consider this individual important to them, and this CEO serves as a personal role model and someone that they look up to and aspire to be, as they hope to achieve similar successes someday. Another might consider this individual important because they are very wealthy and have the financial abundance to retire at any time while continuing to provide for their family, their kids, grandkids, and beyond. Someone else might consider this individual important due to their responsibilities and duties for steering a large organization successfully, as they are well-educated and well-connected to business leaders and other important people in this world. Or even they may be considered important due to something else stretching much beyond their role or title, such as the greater impact and influence that this company is perceived to have on the planet when under this CEO's direction and leadership. For each person, it may or may not be a personal or relative connection to them, but it is always a subjective one as we continue to define the dynamic and individualized application of the word importance.

As we consider the variances in the meaning and subjectivity of the word importance, we will find that the word itself intends to **favorably distinguish** one individual from another. You mustn't **n**ecessarily hold a personally favorable opinion of an individual for them to be considered important; therefore, the word favorable, when used in this context, exists exclusively within a particular field when comparing one's responsibilities or duties to those of another. As in, for you to consider the individual holding the role of the President of the United States of America as important, it would be detached completely from your personally held opinion of him, whether favorable or unfavorable, while still recognizing the degree of responsibility and relative importance assigned to that particular role or position. In this way, you have favorably distinguished the responsibilities and duties belonging to the President of the United States from those of another individual who does not have the legal authority granted to him within the bounds of the United States Constitution and associated responsibilities. With this understanding, to define one as important, one individual must be more important, favorable, or relatively special to another inside of the particular framework and context considered. If someone is distinguishable enough to be considered important, then by default, **something else must be less important**. This may suggest that the important individual is, at least in some regard, superior to another. Alternatively, it may only mean that someone else is only more inferior when compared directly to the other. Thereby, this classification assigns the title of importance to the comparatively less inferior one. This wouldn't necessarily indicate that the individual who lacks the subjective classification of importance is inferior as a whole unit, though based on a spectrum of relative importance and the nature in which it can ever be made assignable, one must be more superior than another. Regardless of whether the inferior or superior terminology is utilized, expressed, or considered, it still suggests a varying value along with a standout trait or quality, even if just in the particular area in which they are directly compared. Though, even without a direct comparison between, say, two CEOs of competing organizations, "Company A" and "Company B," we may also compare the level of general importance from the CEO of a large organization to your mother, who may not have finished high school and never accrued more than a minimum-wage income her entire life. In this case, the answer received to the initial question of importance would greatly depend on the individual who is asked, their subjective view of the world, and the interpretation of the word importance.

A.I. – ARTIFICAL IMPORTANCE

Through the last section, we identified several variances of how the word importance may be interpreted through the observer's own subjectivity and relativity. In this section, we explore a deeper constraint that is based more so on our core beliefs, involving the very tests, standards, or measuring sticks utilized to come to any type of conclusion to determine or infer importance.

As humans, we are all created, designed, or birthed with equal natural rights, regardless of what any government, society, or religion might employ after the fact. To illustrate this point, we must first identify any assumption or bias we may hold to this point and break it down further. What could possibly make any human born on this planet less important or possess fewer rights or privileges than another, especially immediately after birth before the child has had an opportunity to make any decision, choice, mistake, or otherwise? Perhaps we can consider the gender route, whereby men, generally speaking, are more capable of obtaining greater levels of physical strength than their women counterparts. Straight away, this assumes that a measure of privilege or rights in this world ought to be compared and contrasted against the measuring stick of physical strength and stamina. If this is the measure we are using to decide, it's clear that men are superior. But what if the unit of measurement changes to those who are capable of childbirth, **w**hich is an absolute necessity for the human race to continue forward. After all, without the continual creation of humans through pregnancy and childbirth, the human race would cease to exist. In this case, women will be considered more important and superior to men. In either of these cases, or any other case that we can ever possibly bring forward, we've agreed upon and established that the measure of importance held by this new child or their right to equal privileges is solely dependent on something that is out of their control and decided by another. But to delve even deeper, in order to even present the battling cases for the male or female superiority and importance, we had to decide on the very way in which we measure importance, all of which are created, established, decided, and initiated by other humans. Even more so, we had first to agree that such a measure was **even necessary at all** to measure importance, or alternatively, that we as pre-existing humans have intrinsic rights over those who are new to this world to impose labels of superiority, inferiority, value, and importance. In this way, is the ultimate unit of measurement employed one that assigns the most importance to those that are the oldest among us and the least importance to those that are young? Therefore, with every passing day, hour, minute, and second, does one become more important, more valuable, and more significant until the day that they too possess the ability to impose the same ranking system of importance on another? **Why must a decision of importance be made at all**, or a comparison of any kind to begin with? **Who provided us with these rights to decide?** Or did the decisions of superiority, inferiority, and importance **predate our own births**? In this case, would it then be a societal construct created and fabricated by humans at some point in time, stretching far beyond even the oldest human presently alive? Would this indicate that the system of importance is built in such a way that it is not possible to reach the highest layers of it, no matter your achievements, gender, or advanced age?

Essentially, anything that requires the decision or judgment of another human to create and establish in a society can **only** ever be a **man**ufactured and artificial law, rather than a natural one. This is immediately evident in some countries and religions whereby, when sticking with the simplistic gender example, women are inferior to men in terms of privileges and rights. **In** more extreme examples, this even allows men to own women as legal property. For this standard to be adopted anywhere, it must have been created, initiated, and supported by humans in a society or religion. **O**therwise, this same limitation would inevitably have to exist everywhere on the planet objectively. This also indicates it would have to be undeniably evident to every single person. Because it is not universally known and applied, this can only make this a manufactured law, not a natural one. Surely, the societies or governments with this belief set may consider these laws natural rather than manufactured, as they are supported and pronounced by their chosen religious doctrine or ideologies. Though as we saw in the "Introduction to Core Beliefs" chapter in "Manual One," any belief requires first a decision to not only choose it but also to accept the associated assumptions and bounding boxes of the structure. In this particular case, this may be to accept the religious doctrine or related spiritual material as objective truth, **without the option to repudiate**. Only after electing to adopt the religious doctrine and words held within as objective truth would the chooser of this belief be subjected to a construct whereby expressing or demonstrating any doubts against the source material would be against the doctrine itself, potentially eliciting unwanted or undesirable consequences. These consequences may be legally bound by a government or society as a collective body or a spiritual punishment in this life or the next. This belief may suggest the rules and guidelines apply to those who adopt it and also to the ones that don't, but this is only according to those that do. To demonstrate this idea of understanding natural laws from manufactured ones in the context of importance, rights, and privileges, suppose there was an island whereby society, religions, or a government did not exist. For those newly born into this world, would the same privileges and rights be assignable by this rural population in the same way as other regions, governments, or religions? And if those on this island, who would otherwise be completely unaware that anyone else existed on this planet who might follow such laws didn't assign privileges and rights based on the gender discovered upon birth, would they be punished or otherwise experience consequences for the failure to comply with this "law?" Surely not, at least not legally or societally. However, when considering religious or spiritual consequences, whether applied in this life or the next, it is solely at the discretion of the chooser of this belief. Even if in a highly theoretical scenario whereby the religion and spirituality used in this context could be determined as objective truth, any consequences experienced in this life would not be interpreted by the uninformed island dwellers as direct punishments for their failure to assign importance, value, privileges, and rights based on genders within their society. They may very well perceive any negative consequences experienced in this life simply as "bad luck" since the very idea of punishments from an omnipotent God would not fit within their particular core beliefs, and therefore, could never be perceived as such.

ABNORMAL NORMALITY

In most societies, there are structures and hierarchies of power, governed by laws, which are enforceable by certain individuals and groups in positions whereby they can legally execute the duties assigned to them. For example, many societies have a form of law enforcement, like police officers and federal agents, that enforce the laws of the land. We've seen from previous examples that all manufactured laws do not exist in the objective world and are only created by humans, for humans, and can vary greatly from culture to culture based on subjective interpretations of reality and morality. Natural laws, on the other hand, never require the use of others in high positions of power or authority inside of a structure to enforce, as they are **automatically enforced through the pre-existing forces of the universe** that all currently known things are subjected to. The consequences attached to manufactured laws, such as fines, jail time, or even death, are also manufactured. To legally enforce the manufactured laws created by man, additional laws and roles must then be created to provide such authority to those in these new roles, such as law-enforcement officers. These roles are created and assigned the relevant authority by individuals with the legal capacity to create such roles, along with the "power" to distribute various levels of authority to those in these new roles. The "authority" for these individuals to achieve this has been granted to them from other manufactured laws, written by them or their colleagues possessing similar power and authority. With this, those in authority positions have directly or indirectly granted themselves the authoritative power to create laws, along with the means to create new legal structures and roles to enforce the manufactured laws. For this reason, any manufactured law must also be backed up by many other laws, roles, and authority, all of which are based inside of this entirely fabricated legal structure, to be enforceable and carry manufactured consequences to encourage compliance within the artificially built system. Therefore, for manufactured laws to ever become real, they must be accepted by the masses.

With everything discussed up until this point in the book and within this chapter itself, we begin to realize that any varying degrees of importance, significance, value, worth, or authority are simply a fabrication **not based inside of natural laws.** Furthermore, to define importance, value, or significance to one individual over another not only requires the fabrication of the subjective measuring stick or comparison tool, which can only ever be riddled with bias inside of another's subjective reality, but also the utilization of the forged concept that such a contest ought even to be necessary or required. When freed from the intricate depths of manufactured laws, ideals, and subjective realities of others, we begin to see that at the core, we are all created or designed equally, with an inherent and natural right to ourselves, our consciousness, our bodies, and our lives. It's only within a society, government, religion, or any other manufactured structure that any other reality could ever be applied. After all, we all have our own consciousness and essence that is provided to us upon conception. This also happens to provide us with our incredible power of choice, as detailed at length all throughout this book, as unique to you and something that can never be taken from you. **Only** a system consisting of manufactured laws could ever hijack your natural rights to employ your own mind, thoughts, feelings, and preferred ideals for the purposes of another. Then again, we have allowed this, albeit unknowingly and subconsciously, as our power can never be taken from us. Further, manufactured consequences are created to ensure compliance with the initiated ideals originating from the subjective reality of another who is **relatively more important**, powerful, or authoritative inside of the fabricated system. Effectively, the ideals and preferences stemming from another's subjective reality as to how they believe others ought to live their life overflows to the lives of others in a one-sided manner, as the individual citizen who might be subjected to these laws cannot manufacture and create laws in reverse order. This, of course, would violate the laws of the pre-existing manufactured system to which they have been subjected. In other words, the rules of the game suggest that there cannot be any other system that violates the rules of the game, but according to this game, **the rules demand it must be played.** If not, the manufactured consequences, such as fines, confinement, or death, become materially real, as they are imposed forcefully by those who have been given authority and power within the game to others without the "legal" authority to opt out. Once these ideals of another become integrated into a society through enforceable laws and with the authority granted to them from other manufactured laws, it creates a power hierarchy that limits and hijacks the natural laws, rights, and privileges. We hand over these rights that are otherwise provided to us upon birth through the illusion of rules, laws, and consequences. Additionally, the breaching of these laws implicates the individual citizen as immoral or unruly under the structure of a man-made and fabricated system not chosen by them. In this way, the hierarchy of structure itself concocts a semblance of authority available to certain individuals, who provide themselves and those with similar roles the power to create laws that are **designed to protect the integrity of the system itself.** This is further enforced through the fabrication of consequences as a **deterrent and classification mechanism.** Essentially, a self-enforcing system is created whereby the laws declare anything that challenges the integrity of the system or the authority granted therewithin as an act of **violence, treason, or even terrorism**. The classification mechanism exists within the fabricated system to define behavioral traits, actions, and even thought processes possessed by individuals and citizens as dangerous, illegal, irresponsible, psychotic, or immoral. This is done simply through the referencing of the manufactured laws and boundaries present within the system itself for the sole purpose of the system's self-protection. Those who are part of the system, whether consciously or not, often agree with the classification system and labels assigned to various behaviors and individuals. With the adoption of the system, rules, and classification mechanisms, the **seemingly erratic** actions fall well within the lines of something akin to terrorism or treason and align clearly with the laws that are already written for such protective measures. In this case, the labels and classification assigned to those who attempt to challenge the pre-existing system and authority are accepted and agreed upon by those residing in the system themselves, but never by those outside of it. To those outside of the system, they see the laws, authority, consequences, and boundaries as manufactured, existing only in the hearts, minds, and subjective realities of those who choose to hold it, but otherwise, realize it cannot hold any natural authority, merit, or truth.

What makes the subjective ideals of one more valid, moral, or enforceable than the subjective ideals of another? The pre-existing nature of a system dominates over any system that succeeds it, **but only to those who accept the pre-existing system and the associated game rules.** Surely, it is not quite as simple as choosing not to adopt an already-established system of rules, as the consequences, even though entirely manufactured, **become real when they are enforced** by those in the positions of authority granted to them through the system they have accepted for themselves.

Through our power of choice, we can always choose not to play, no matter the consequence, **but we must own our choices entirely.** Should we choose to play by the rules of the game, **we forfeit our right to complain** about the rules, as we alone are responsible for our choices and actions. As was the case with the seatbelt example from a previous chapter, if one individual decided not to adopt the seatbelt law, they would be punished according to the law of the land for breaching the artificial law integrated into an artificial society. However, should many more individuals realize and embody the natural power that they hold, **the power that each of us are intrinsically born with that can never be taken from us**, the laws and consequences will inevitably be changed and no longer apply. Though natural laws cannot be beaten or overturned, manufactured laws exist only **to the degree of the collective acceptance and adherence** to them. The very moment in which the collective masses simply decide to no longer adhere to a manufactured law or recognize authority figures who have **only been granted authority via a fabricated system** that has been designed to protect itself, the entire system collapses, and an alternative system that receives the collective buy-in from the masses will be used to recreate the society in which the individuals reside. When following the letter of the written law inside of a manufactured game, the power within each individual to reject the reality and rules imposed by another seems unlikely or difficult; however, **this is only part of the illusion created by buying into the game rules themselves**. Only upon choosing to step outside of the existing game rules can new rules be created. When the new rules become adopted by multiple individuals within a sub-society, this effectively renders pre-existing game rules belonging to a competing system or standard wholly irrelevant. Without a subjective reality in which to hold such rules, laws, or beliefs, the manufactured elements **dissipate and vanish entirely**. Much like a virus that infects a host, it can only survive in the case that the host remains alive. When the host perishes, **so too does the virus**, as it is without a host to leech its life from. If an individual, or a group of individuals, continue to choose to operate within the confines of the existing game rules in an attempt to overturn or challenge existing ones, the efforts to do so will be futile, as the **game rules themselves are designed to protect the structure and framework of the very system they support**. If manufactured rules can be arbitrarily created, they can also be challenged, rewritten, and entirely destroyed in precisely the same way.

Meanwhile, natural laws continue to operate independently and cannot be created or destroyed. In some cases, natural rights can be temporarily hijacked and derailed through the enforcement of manufactured laws and consequences, but only to the degree individuals allow such promulgation into their own personal realities. **Acceptance of anything into one's subjective reality always requires a choice.**

TRUE EQUALITY

We've explored how manufactured laws differ from natural ones, as natural ones are intrinsic to your very being. Natural laws can only be infringed upon through the use of manufactured systems of influence, such as governments, religions, or even the forced subjective reality of another when paired with fabricated consequences. We've also identified that "importance" can only ever be assigned subjectively and relatively, which must always employ a unit of measurement originating from a core belief or manufactured law of society. In which case, we are all born with the same natural rights, privileges, ideas, and internal freedoms to express and explore ourselves. **Anything that attempts to separate us from this realization can only be a manufactured law.** After all, how can anyone ever be considered better, more valuable, or more important than another without the decision to utilize a fabricated or subjective metric in which to compare? Even the decision and human urge to create a hierarchical system that requires comparisons from one to another first require the assumption that such a system is even necessary, required, valuable, or important to have.

With all this considered and when only natural laws are realized, **we are all created equally with equal privileges and rights** that are completely independent of race, gender, religion, governments, and anything else. It matters not if one individual is smarter than another, as "smarter" in this context suggests the allegedly superior individual's stellar ability to consume, memorize, and regurgitate material provided to them from an academically focused society structure. In this, they are measured by their ability to score highly on tests using subjective weighting metrics and to obtain a passing letter grade that was designed within the bounds of the fabricated system. This all intends to **effectively demonstrate competence at playing the game** better than another, within the framework and world of the game itself. After all, what is the purpose of a society's academic system, if not for it to be merely a training ground for individual citizens to become better players at a game that has been imposed on them? In this system, they learn to understand better the rules, expectations, and measures of success within the society they've adopted. Even the attendance to such a reformatory is a **mandatory requirement** as dictated by the manufactured and self-protecting laws therewithin. It matters not if one person is a high-ranking politician and the other a single mother in a rural town, as this important political status first requires the acceptance of this manufactured construct of a society, government, laws, and constitution, all of which provide importance, value, and authority within that particular framework only. Outside of this framework, they were both born into this same world in the same way. They each have their **own consciousness** as well as their natural ability to make free choices and decisions. They have their own thoughts, ideas, and unique expressions of themselves seen and experienced through their subjectively interpreted realities. Some may suggest that one is more privileged or has worked harder than the other; however, the idea of working harder or being more privileged only leads back to the manufactured system in which such a consideration can be made. Once again, this requires the use of a subjective and fabricated metric of comparison in an attempt to determine importance, value, and authority over the life of others.

With these considerations and when revisiting the underlying theme of the entire manual involving your power of choice, **there is no individual greater or more superior to you**, nor can you ever be more superior to another. Manufactured laws and structures attempt to cloud this reality through the use of common elements such as social status, titles, laws, consequences, academics, and wealth. It's only when we fully comprehend the great power inside of each of us and possess the ability to see through the illusions of hierarchy, power, and control inherent to all manufactured laws and structures that we can truly rise above it and retain what is and always has been ours:

Our beauty,

Strength,

Uniqueness,

Desires,

Thoughts,

Emotions,

Feelings,

Reality,

Experience,

Lives,

and **Choice**.

In a world of **true equals** provided by the natural laws in which we all reside:

There is no one greater than you.

There is no one more superior than you.

There is no one more capable than you.

There is no one more deserving than you.

There is no one more valuable than you.

There is no one more important than you.

There is no one more powerful than you.

There is no one with a greater claim to your experiences.

There is no one with a greater claim to your reality.

There is no one with a greater claim to your life.

There is no one with the authority to claim your **choice**.

Anything that invalidates any of the above assertions, or otherwise suggests directly or indirectly that one could ever be more superior, important, worthy, or valuable than another **may only ever exist within the constructs of a manufactured system** of ideals imposed through the lens of another's subjective reality. If such a system and its associated metrics can be spoken into existence and enforced through the subjective ideals of humans, it can also **just as easily be destroyed**, as it only ever existed inside the **accepted realities of individuals**. When such manufactured ideals no longer exist inside the subjective realities of individuals, it immediately ceases to exist materially in the objective and natural world.

19. WILD WILDER WEST

Upon understanding the illusory nature of all man-made laws and how they limit one's ability to make free choices, we may wish to challenge these structures, hierarchies, and laws in order to retain our natural birthrights to make truly free choices. But would a civilization without laws or material consequences be a civil civilization at all, or would it be more akin to living in the Wild West? Without rules, there would be truly free choices without consequences, aside from any social consequence that may apply collectively for a particularly unpopular action, but this would only be subjectively applied and on an ad-hoc basis. Therefore, are there laws that can be implemented that would allow us to retain most of our reasonable freedoms without unrelenting chaos? Is there a universal standard of ethics or morality that can be applied and collectively agreed upon that allows others to live freely without artificial limits within a societal structure?

To begin this theoretical analysis, we'll postulate a society that can collectively agree upon the merit of a singular rule: **Do not physically harm another.**

At the most fundamental level, the **intent** behind this rule may be shared among those that supported it. However, as we dive into the details, enforcement, and necessary exceptions to the rule, we identify how even the simplest rules cannot be agreed upon, as they also require additional laws or rules to support them.

In the case you live in a society where this singular rule is active, what occurs when a burglar breaks into your home and begins taking your possessions? If a singular rule exists not to physically harm another, then burglary is legal so long as physical harm isn't occurring. What options might you, the victim of this burglary, have to stop this burglar? You cannot shove him or restrain him, as you would be breaking the singular rule of said society as you induce physical harm upon him. Perhaps you can ask nicely and politely. Maybe you attempt to verbally reason with the burglar or offer him a trade or bribe of some kind. If this fails, perhaps you consider using a loud voice as you attempt to halt the burglar's ongoing actions to rob you. If you use a voice loud enough, he may claim that you have **physically damaged** his eardrum due to the excessive level of volume you've emitted, causing hearing loss. This, in turn, has made only you the criminal in this society as you have violated the only rule by physically harming him in such a way. Or potentially, as you speak to the burglar in a reasonable tone to leave your property, the burglar physically harms you and breaks the only rule of society. What occurs then? Who is responsible for enforcing this singular law?

The initial rule to not harm another had been agreed upon by every member of society, but any future rules may not be. In this case, must a new rule be made that designates new ones may be created or amended if they receive a majority vote? If this becomes the case, the society has already become split, and there isn't unanimous agreement or consent to laws and the associated consequences. At this point, we begin to stray from the original intent to maintain a universal law that is unanimously agreed upon to simply not harm another.

Perhaps a coalition is formed to assist in the enforcement of society's rules with the collective and unanimous support of the society as a whole. Where does the money to fund this group come from, if not volunteer effort only, if taxes do not yet exist? Or even, has this society agreed upon the value of any standardized monetary system, or have they relied on the bartering of services and goods only up until this point? Without additional laws or rules to regulate finances, there is only bartering. Assuming the newly formed law-enforcement group operates on a volunteer basis, would the police show up for an offense such as burglary that is technically legal under the current system? If the law-enforcement group does indeed show up to the scene, how might they be able to stop a burglar that is physically harming the victim if a society rule is in place that even they cannot harm another? For are they not citizens themselves who have only volunteered to help serve others? In this case, the rule would need to be amended to apply **only to citizens** with an exception made for individuals who are **granted such authority** from the greater society, with majority or unanimous consent, with the **right to legally inflict physical harm** to others for breaking the law of inflicting physical harm. The line of distinction must also be drawn as to when such exceptions apply to individuals. Are the exceptions indefinitely applied to those within this volunteer coalition? Or only when wearing a certain uniform? During certain hours of the day? What if the burglary occurred without physical harm to any of the parties involved? The law-enforcement group will not arrive as there is no law actively being broken.

Therefore, a **new law** is introduced to make the theft of another's property illegal, which must also inherently contain verbiage and clauses indicating what defines one's personal property and under what terms. How is ownership of anything defined? What can be claimed, what cannot be claimed? Can one claim their house? A plot of land? If land can be claimed and others are found walking through your property and gardens as they damage your growing food supply, but they are not taking anything or harming you, they are not breaking any law. People then decide to pass a **new law** involving trespassing and loitering restrictions on private property, which are also enforceable by the law-enforcement group.

Due to the increasing number of laws to enforce, the community decides to allow more power to the individual citizen who becomes a victim of certain events, especially where physical harm is involved, and the law-enforcement group may not be immediately available or arrive quickly enough at the scene. After all, if an individual physically harms another, the victim citizen is not presently allowed under the legal constructs to engage in self-defense, as this too would be causing physical harm, rendering them no better off than the instigator of such an altercation. With this, the society, either through majority or unanimous votes, allows the use of self-defense only if another law is broken and they become the victim of another's actions. But, what are the limits to this self-defense? If one is punched in the stomach, is the other allowed to engage in self-defense by breaking the other's legs and arms, or even, murdering them, all in the name of self-defense? Or should self-defense be exactly proportionate to the degree to which the instigator of such violence leads the way? Essentially, if the instigator punches one in the face, can one only perform the same action in return? In this way, the instigator will always maintain the upper hand as the victim cannot exceed the level of violence and physical force that the instigator employs; otherwise, the law is broken by the victim, effectively making the victim of the crime a criminal themselves.

Are the consequences and punishments for physical harm universally applied? As in, should one punching another in the stomach be reprimanded in the same way as one who paralyzes another? Or kills another? Each of these variations and degrees of consequences and punishment requires **additional amendments and rules** to solidify and clarify, in the name of fairness, safety, and protection for all.

Though there may be some debate on the degrees of physical harm and the consequences entailed, the society unites unanimously around another rule: **Thou shalt not murder.**

Additionally, the society also agrees on the consequences and punishment for this extension of the pre-existing physical harm offense, which requires the individual to spend 25 years in confinement for each offense committed, or death by hanging should the murder count exceed two. However, to initiate the consequence of **confinement** to any degree requires a **new law** to be formed that outlaws **kidnapping and holding one against their will**. To enforce this, further exceptions must be created for cases that particular laws have been broken while only able to be legally enforceable by those with the appropriate authority to do so. Additionally, **another exception** must be made to **authorize the murder of a murderer** without the stated consequence of death by hanging applying to those who are enforcing such laws.

Otherwise, they would be breaking the existing law restricting the murder of another and be subject to the same consequences and punishments.

With consequences now so severe for various actions and behaviors, the community realizes that there must be some protections for those who are accused of breaking a law but have not in reality broken any such law. This is for the protection of truly innocent citizens so that they are not inappropriately held in confinement. To ensure that innocent individuals are not held in confinement by a mere accusation, or in the case of the greater society believing that they are indeed responsible for the murder of another, a process must be put in place and agreed upon. This, ideally, would allow the accused to defend themselves while enacting a requirement of irrefutable proof or evidence for any accusation to be substantiated. But what qualifies as valid evidence or proof? A single eyewitness account? Multiple eyewitness accounts, and if multiple, how many? Does the age, status, health, occupation, or gender of the alleged eyewitness matter, which provides varying degrees of perceived credibility and validity? How is one protected against intentionally malicious accusations, or in a more innocuous case, protected against a case of mistaken identity? Therefore, new laws and authority structures must be initiated to provide a system akin to the modern court of the United States.

Up until this point, even with the relatively unrealistic assumption that most if not all citizens are in unanimous agreement with equal representation, there still remain additional clarifications that must be made. What if a citizen accidentally murders another? Are the punishment and consequence the same? What proof might be required to achieve the lighter charge that deems such removal of life as accidental rather than intentional? What if, through the act of self-defense, the once-victim accidentally kills the perpetrator during the physical altercation as he fights to honestly protect his life? Is this considered murder at all, given the greater or lighter charge of it?

Further, **the mere description of murder must be verbosely outlined**. For example, in much of the United States, if a pregnant woman is killed by another, the one responsible for the death will receive not one but two counts of homicide, **as the unborn qualifies as a life form**. However, should that pregnant woman have been on her way to an abortion clinic to have the pregnancy terminated voluntarily as a result of her own choice, she could terminate the unborn **without any penalty at all**. There would not be a penalty for murder, nor would there be a penalty for the physical harm unto another. In the same scenario of a pregnancy becoming terminated, one outcome is classified as murder, whereas one is not. This point is not unknown to many in the United States as it is a highly controversial topic in the ongoing and passionate "Pro-Life" vs. "Pro-Choice" debate.

Like other controversial topics shared within this book, this specific point regarding abortion is outlined not to convince any party one way or the other to change beliefs, but only to highlight the incredible difficulty in creating laws, hierarchies, and structures that are universally accepted, agreed on, and understood. Even with a community of well-meaning individuals who wish to create a better society for everyone through laws not to harm or murder one another, this quickly becomes a controversial topic whereby the once-unified community becomes hostile, combative, and in heavy disagreement. They begin to curse the laws and structures that have formed around them that they must all follow, even the ones they do not personally agree with and vehemently reject on the basis of their various beliefs. The hierarchical authority structures become bloated, as the means to enforce the rapidly multiplying set of laws becomes burdensome, while division among the members grows with every new law or amendment created.

LEVEL THE PLAYING FIELD

What if we consider the formation of a community whereby the only rule intends to restrict anyone from encroaching on the free choice of another? Initially, this seems to cover many other laws indirectly, such as physically harming or murdering another, but even this situation rapidly becomes paradoxical when considering

all parties involved. Additionally, does this law, which itself states that one cannot make a choice that robs another of their free choice, paradoxically rob one of their free choice by restricting how they may ultimately decide to use their own free choice?

In addition, **e**ven this simple concept becomes anything but when referencing the prior example involving abortion. As in, should the woman who carries the unborn have the power to choose what to do with her body and her life or does her choice with her body inhibit the choice of the unborn? If a law created by another restricts a woman from having an abortion, **does this not rob her of her choice to do what she desires for her own body and life?** Indisputably, regardless of one's personal opinion on the topic of abortion rights, this law restricts one's ability to make a choice of their own discretion and personal desire. Subjective ethics and morality aside, the implementation of a law that restricts one from making their own free choice by placing artificial limits upon it **inhibits free choice**. In another but related example, this law effectively makes an adult's choice to murder another adult illegal, as the murderer would be robbing the adult victim of their free choice to live however they wish without the unwanted interference from another. Though, does this law not also restrict the murderer's free choice and desire to murder another on whatever grounds they choose to partake in such an action? Does the law itself not rob one's ability to make a free choice, based on the subjective moralities created by another, even if through the collectively decided morality of the majority, but not unanimously agreed upon? The point of controversy exists within the context of whether the mother's ability to make a free choice inhibits the choice of the unborn, **should it be considered a life form**, or simply a relatively lifeless mass of fetal tissue unaware of its own existence, and unable to experience pain or feelings. Therefore, we must not only seek to define and clarify what is classified as murder and the exceptions to it but also to define clearly **what is considered life itself**. When should the unborn have a choice of its own? When does it officially become a life form with the right to its own choices and life? Does the "right" for the unborn to possess a choice of its own require the assumptive, subjective, manufactured, and **illusory barometer of life**, all created by man, that independent life only exists upon the natural exit from the womb upon reaching nature's predetermined incubation period at roughly nine months? At that point, is it only then to be considered an independent life form worthy of choice and a life of its own? Though, infants at **only 24 weeks of incubation** in the mother's womb have roughly a fifty percent rate of survival. This indicates that at even just 24 weeks, even if materially unborn through natural means and without first reaching nature's expected gestation period, it has the potential of experiencing life, awareness, and consciousness all of its own. In this way, to create a law that one cannot do anything that robs another of their ability to make a free choice first requires the declarative definition of what is considered an aware and conscious form of life. As to rob one of a free choice, the victim of such must be considered a form of life. There is no choice without life; therefore, we must clearly define life before we can define choice or the restriction to it as it otherwise exists in the natural world. The creation of such a declarative definition can only be created through the human intellect, **which can only occur from within the context of their own subjective reality**, perceptual biases, and chosen core beliefs. In the current climate in the United States, this particular argument on when a life form is considered a life form effectively highlights the crux of the debate. What is life? What is consciousness? Who has the right to choose the inevitable fate of another: the subjective law, the mother, or the unborn?

In any case involving an attempt to level the playing field for others, first, the subjective measuring stick, which can only ever be an illusory fabrication of man, must be determined. What is considered "less than" when compared to others? Once the method of measurement and comparison is decided upon, the equalizing rule may be applied. However, regardless of the equalizing method applied, **it will inevitably rob another of a free choice**. In one example, perhaps the community begins to consider the idea of assisting others in need, such as those with physical limitations. For this, handicap parking spaces are formed in front of all business establishments to aid those who cannot easily trek great distances physically. However, several society members find even this to encroach on their freedom of choice to park their vehicle wherever they'd like. As in, should they park in any spot they'd like, which in this case is a handicap parking space as it resides closer to the building they wish to enter, they will be subjected to a consequence for breaking a law that they do not agree with. They believe it invalidates their ability to make a free choice of where to park their own vehicle. In this way, to level the playing field for one, another must sacrifice something. Those that agree with this particular equalizer have made their free choice willingly to help others in this way, as it aligns with their core beliefs. While those that disagree have been robbed of their free choice for a cause to which they do not align.

For every equalizer employed, those that support it utilize their free choice to assist another, but this too requires a compatible belief set that those who will be assisted are deserving of such treatment or benefits. Those that believe these particular others are in need also believe that the ones who do not support the suggested equalizer are heartless, lack compassion, are selfish, or immoral. However, this classification and judgment **only apply when viewed through the lens of their own biased and subjective reality**, which is inherent to all of the perceptive limitations within the chosen belief structure. Thereby, this highlights another instance where a core belief or perceptual bias is confirmed within the realm which they presently occupy, complete with self-validating truths and ideals. Those who don't wish to make that same choice of lifestyle or possess the same moral beliefs will be punished as they are forced to comply or face punishment. One might suggest that the individual opposing such ideology still has a choice, to either comply and not get punished or fail to comply and face the consequences. However, it is important to outline that **this is an illusory choice**, one that only exists within the manufactured confines of a hierarchical system that they did not choose to begin with. **This is an element of the choice delusion**. Is this a matter of interfering with their free will, if only allowing others to "make choices" within the boundaries of a construct that they did not select for themselves to operate within? Is this not akin to playing by the rules of a game that you do not wish to play but still acting in accordance with such rules under the guise of free choice within those boundaries of pre-approved options? If you think that a person who does not want to save a space for a handicapped person is immoral, rude, or selfish, you must first revisit your own morality and definitions of those very terms. You may very well be classified as immoral or selfish to others inside of their world, as you self-govern the laws and standards that you hold for yourself as potentially superior or more objectively factual or true than another's interpretation of reality.

THE FREEDOM-BUBBLE EXPERIMENT

Can a community of individuals exist with simple, straightforward, and universally accepted laws, where all members maintain equal representation and not one person is forced to follow laws that they do not personally align or agree with?

For this, consider a theoretical approach to life whereby everyone that resides within fully autonomous and sovereign "bubbles" collectively shares the beliefs, values, laws, and consequences that each member fully supports and aligns with. In this way, a functioning society may exist where the laws are agreed upon, and each member willingly submits to the laws, regulations, and expectations within the confines of the bubble. Those who do not agree with the rules of the bubble may leave freely and enter a new bubble that aligns more closely with their personal set of beliefs. Though, once in a bubble, they must agree to the terms inside the bubble regarding their ability to exit or move freely between other bubbles, which may limit their movement to a degree. The terms of the bubble one chooses to enter must be respected, so long as it is the individual's choice to initially select a bubble of morals, ethics, laws, and behaviors. This ensures each individual maintains their free choice to enter the bubble to which they most align. With this, the individual effectively chooses a belief system and accepts any necessary compromises and restrictions inherent to any particular system. Some bubbles may allow their inhabitants to enter and exit freely without restriction, whereas other bubbles may have strict immigration policies for newcomers, population limits, or specific rules, restrictions, or processes for exiting their chosen bubble.

However, even this idealistic scenario of fully autonomous bubbles is inherently flawed. As in, would this concept not also require an overarching agreement from all other bubbles declaring that each must remain wholly autonomous from one another, without encroaching on the rights, freedoms, and choices of the other independent bubbles? Without this universal agreement from all bubbles, each bubble is subject to being challenged, destroyed, or overtaken by another with opposing beliefs or ideals. Some bubbles may unite humans that are threatened by the deeds, lives, or religions of another bubble. Whether the perceived threat is material or a fabricated result of their chosen belief system is irrelevant, as the threat is undoubtedly real to those who believe it to be so within their collectively shared reality. In this, they will seek to kill the others they believe are a threat to them, in servitude of their own core beliefs, as it may include disallowing others with opposing lifestyles to coexist peacefully. Specifically, if a bubble of individuals adopted a belief system whereby the way to a harmonious afterlife involves the killing of others who do not subscribe to the same belief system, then the freedom of each of the other bubbles becomes threatened. This occurs as the stated "rules" of a bubble only apply to individuals who have chosen to accept the rules of the bubble they entered but not to those outside of it with a different set of beliefs, opinions, preferences, and ideals. With this, a bubble may want to protect itself from those with beliefs that do not allow others to peacefully coexist independently from one another. To better defend itself from violent attacks from a more aggressive bubble, it might decide to engage in intelligence and spy operations to stay abreast of potential incoming attacks. This effectively infringes on the "freedom" and autonomous nature of the bubble of another, which is what the originating bubble had originally sworn to protect for itself and all other bubbles. This, in turn, may break their own rules, which states that bubbles must be fully autonomous and respected, as they wish their own to be protected. Therefore, they have broken their own rules and compromised their own values in service of protection of such values and freedoms. Where are the lines drawn? Is it acceptable to break the rules and sovereignty of another's bubble, in the pursuit of protection of one's own bubble? If the rules and beliefs of a bubble were to be followed at all costs with no exceptions, then the bubbles possessing the most aggressive ideologies would undoubtedly become superior to all other bubbles. The aggressive bubbles would either destroy all other bubbles until it was only their own that existed, or they would leverage the resources of the other less aggressive bubbles using a domination hierarchy through threats and fear to control others effectively. In this way, one bubble would then decide the rules for all others to follow as the dominating opinion, ideology, laws, and beyond.

We might think that any belief that requires the forceful domination and lack of acceptance of another's belief is incorrect, as it robs another of choice. But this statement only works under the assumption and core belief that we must all have an ability to make a free choice that cannot be infringed upon by others. In this way, what would be considered an infringement of another's choice or rights? As we saw earlier in this chapter, even the concept of not harming another or attempting to level the playing field for someone else becomes highly subjective and may be an infringement of the rights to others in itself. So long as bubbles with belief systems that challenge or threaten the sovereignty of other bubbles who otherwise desire to be autonomous exist, there cannot be independent pockets of individuals who share a particular belief in peace, harmony, acceptance, and love. Perhaps a bubble, or coalition of bubbles, decide collectively that the threats posed from the ongoing attacks of the aggressive bubble must be removed if the others are to ever live in peace and harmony. This would require the coalition of otherwise peaceful bubbles to **destroy the very ideologies that threaten their own existence**, as well as completely halt the distribution of materials that represent this ideology to prevent it from spreading around the world and to other bubbles. Though this would be done in the name of peace, self-defense, fairness, and justice, would this not be setting the preferred morality and ethics for others to follow on a world stage, which requires **breaking the sovereignty of other bubbles** all in the name of protecting your own bubble, freedoms, and desired sovereignty? Meanwhile, this indirectly requires the assertion that the philosophy and ideals of your bubble are superior to those of another to the extent that you would be willing to kill another and rob them of the free choice that belongs to them before they ultimately rob you of yours. Is this not exhibiting precisely the behavior of the bubble you scorned, whereby one bubble claims superiority over another and is willing to seek, kill, and destroy over?

To effectively ensure that such an aggressive bubble could never exist again in the future would require the **censoring of any information** that may lead future generations to the same conclusion. Without the active censorship of all information that may lead another to this ideology, it may inadvertently induce an eventual repeat of history. Further, it would also require the **ongoing imprisonment or killing** of anyone **who demonstrated or voiced these particular beliefs**, as they would still pose a threat to our own lives and autonomy should these ideals ever be shared among others. For the other bubbles that don't agree with the bubble coalition's actions that sought to destroy the aggressive bubble but aren't necessarily aggressive or violent types in their own regard, what may happen to them at the hands of the coalition should they do something deemed offensive by this coalition?

Would these other non-violent bubbles fear their own existence and sovereignty after the observation of other bubbles, in the name of harmony, peace, and coexistence, becoming exterminated by the people, ideologies, materials, and beliefs belonging to that of another seemingly autonomous bubble? Would this lead them to consider destroying the bubbles that state they are peaceful but have just demonstrated the destruction of another? If this was considered and perhaps acted upon, would this not render them identical in substance to the ones that they now abhor and are threatened by?

Which bubble was truly the most aggressive and least accepting of another?

As individuals with our own choices and consciousness are we, ourselves, not mere bubbles?

20. THE THIEF AND THE VICTIM

This book attempts to highlight the incredible power we all have within us, the power of choice. The power of choice is intrinsic to our being, granted to us through our consciousness and awareness. Our choices do not only dictate the seemingly insignificant, monotonous, or routine choices of life but rather, they create everything that is known within our lives, including the ability to destroy it.

We choose our beliefs.

We choose our perception.

We choose our happiness.

We choose our joy.

We choose our sadness.

We choose our frustration.

We choose our pain.

We choose our experience of life.

We choose our interpretation of life.

We choose our facts.

We choose our truth.

We choose our morality.

We choose our reality.

We create our life, through choice.

Others can attempt to persuade you away from your inherent ability to make free choices. Though, there is **only one** that can ever truly rob you of this natural birthright, yourself. When one successfully convinces or persuades another to surrender their choice, it still is the choice of the one who surrenders it to surrender it, as it can never be taken forcefully or materially, only hijacked. It can **only be you** to surrender it when you do not realize the true power you have always held and always will hold. Therefore, **there is no thief outside** of you with the capability to rob you of your choice, as it is only you who can rob yourself. In this way, **you are both the thief and the victim**.

No choice can ever be thrust upon us by another. Any attempt of another to persuade you away from your ability to choose freely means they have attempted to perform one of the **greatest deceptions and illusions of all time against you**. This attempted coercion is most effectively utilized when combined with the powerful element of **fear**. The fear of a consequence for making what would otherwise be, in the natural world, a free choice. Even when staring down the barrel of a loaded gun held tightly by a known serial killer, **you still have a choice**. Do not forget that you have a choice in every situation. You have a choice to laugh. A choice to cry. A choice to submit to another. A choice to stand against the ideals and preferences of another's subjective reality. No one can make you do anything that you do not want to do. You have the power to choose, and with each choice, there is always a cost. With your choice, you choose and accept the cost. Is the cost worth the choice? **O**nly you can decide this for yourself in the moment that such a choice must be made. When you defer responsibility and ownership of your choice to another, you have surrendered the one thing that makes you **uniquely you**. When you surrender to the ideals of another or choose to become the victim of your world within your reality, you surrender your feelings, you surrender your desires, you surrender your passions, you surrender your purpose, and most of all, **you surrender your life** to the subjective wills of another. Why must they have power over your life, but you cannot have power over theirs? Why must one ever have power over another? What is power, if present in the absence of another surrendering their choice? Without one's effective use of fear or societal conditioning to form a culture or expectation whereby the surrendering of choice is commonplace, there is no real power. What good is power or authority of any kind should the ones in power be unable to control others effectively? **Without others to control, the illusory hierarchy of power quite simply cannot exist.**

For power to exist, there must be a submission of it. Void of the submission of said power, there is no power over another, nor is there superiority or inferiority. As in, imagine a society where the taxes are high, and the citizens do not wish to pay what they deem to be unfair. Should a citizen decide not to pay the taxes, there will be a consequence of confinement or death. However, should all the citizens that do not agree with the taxes decide not to pay, would they all be confined or killed? Assuming the consequence was withheld uniformly despite the masses rebelling, what would this do to the "power" hierarchy that stands above, with no one or very few remaining to pay such taxes? With most citizens confined, or dead, how will the ones in power continue to make money or maintain control through over-taxation? Therefore, there is no power without submission of it. When we refuse to submit our power by acknowledging it as ours and ours alone, we **cannot be controlled**, not by a government, not by others, and not by life itself. For this reason, **you are responsible for the power hierarchies present in your life through your belief and compliance to them.** In the context of a greater society, you are also responsible, but there is strength in numbers, with fear used as a tactic to prevent many from making unwanted choices. When one rebels, an example will be made out of them in an attempt to discourage others from making a similar choice. The ones that hold such power over others understand that they themselves are always in the minority, and should the masses realize this, **the power hierarchy collapses**. With this, they ensure the consequences, punishments, fines, and treatment of those that rebel in such a way to discourage others from behaving, or thinking, in a similar way. **This is implemented to protect themselves** through the management of others using fear and fear alone. By choosing to avoid the fabricated consequences of a choice by following the rules set before us, we are choosing submission, control, and slavery to another, as we forfeit our right to complain about the result of our choice. We all wait for another to make the difficult choice, refusing to be the first, or the second, as those that lead such a movement face the greatest punishments and consequences. Though, it's when we realize that **we are responsible for our lives** that any real change can ever occur.

DANCE KITTY, DANCE

The greatest trick that those in our lives play on us, whether through personal relationships, governments, or religions, is to deceive us away from our true identity by enticing us to act in a manner that is not in accordance with our most authentic selves. Instead, they persuade and coerce us using fear to behave and live our lives in a manner that is preferred by another. Our ability to choose is intrinsically tied to our ability to think freely. **We are all wild jungle tigers** but conditioned by others to believe we are only domesticated house cats. When we remember that we are tigers, while thinking and acting from this place, we know that **nothing and no one can ever control us.** Nothing external to us can control our emotions, our actions, our thoughts, our feelings, our morality, our realities, our choices, or our lives. **We hold the ultimate authority over our lives** and must not be persuaded away from this. **We never cease to be tigers**, but we may cease to see ourselves as one and identify as such. We are the victims of our lives if we choose to be. We are a slave to others, if we choose to be. We are truly free, if we choose to be. What is this choice worth to you? Do you choose to live in slavery to another or risk consequence by choosing freedom? Should you believe that you are actively choosing freedom in life by avoiding a choice you'd like to make but are not making due to it carrying a consequence of death, confinement, or financial penalties, you are not living in freedom, but only "freedom" within the bounds of a concocted reality filled with manufactured rules. We must escape the boundaries and rules of another's reality and understand that **this is not true freedom**. Why must your definition of freedom, and experience of it, be described and classified by another, with limits, boundaries, and restrictions that would **otherwise not apply**?

Analyze the motivation for any decision that you make. Are your decisions rooted in fear, obligation, or guilt? Are you making this choice to please another, in order to not "rock the boat," or because it's a decision you feel like you should make? As in, if you feel like making one decision, but instead, feel that you should make another, where does this pressure to make a choice that is inauthentic to your own being and preferences come from? Are you cautious about what your friends or family might think of your choices to live your life however you choose to live it? Does it conflict with the religion or doctrine you choose to follow wholeheartedly, despite it possibly disagreeing with your sense of being, passions, and wishes in this moment? Essentially, are you making decisions truly for you or for another? If you make decisions for yourself, is that selfish? If so, why do you feel that way? Do you feel that way because you are told by another that it is selfish? Or perhaps you feel this way due to a chosen belief system or law? Would you feel selfish on your terms if this classification was not thrust upon you by something external to yourself?

I LOVE YOUR... VALIDATION

Even the most "selfless" actions, undertaken from what appears to be a place of love, can bring about tremendous anxiety, stress, and suffering. If you have ever found yourself being stressed, anxious, or even bitter about doing so much for another while receiving nothing, or very little, in return, are you truly acting out of a place of love? Could a true act of selfless love towards another ever bear such fruit? Does love require praise, recognition, or acknowledgment to be loving, kind, or compassionate? If you find yourself becoming frustrated with loving others when not receiving what you **expect** in return, are your actions driven from a place of fear, obligation, or guilt while parading under the guise and **deception of love**? If delivered from a place of pure intent and true love, there is nothing the receiving party can do, or not do, that can turn the love within you sour. When acting from a place of true love and pure heart, you can own your choice and action while embracing it as the authentic choice that is executed solely **by you and for you**. With this, you will have no reason or desire to complain, be resentful of yourself, another, or the situation at hand. **You are in control of your life, your actions, and your perceptions.** Regardless of the ultimate decision you make, when you make a choice for yourself while fully grasping the motivation behind it, this is not selfishness but empowerment. Inside this free choice, you can then choose how to define selfishness, or selflessness. When empowered decisions are made by you and for you without the pollution or influence from others, you act out from your **truest wills and desires**. This yields an exponentially stronger result in the choice you ultimately make while failing to carry the unnecessary resentment, bitterness, or regret, in knowing that this was a choice that you alone chose for reasons pure in intent and that were authentic to yourself.

THE PARADOXICAL CHOICE

We are both the thief and the victim when it comes to the choices that we hold, which is the facility within us to **create all things** experienced by us. When we surrender our choice to another, or become the victims of our lives and situations, we experience anxiety, lack of purpose, depression, or overall dissatisfaction with our life. We give up control as the creators of our lives and allow others to create our life experiences for us. Yet, we may only experience these unpleasant outcomes of life when we do not understand that it was always our choice to begin with, and that we have chosen to surrender it. When we do not realize even this, we also fail to realize that it was ever our choice. In this, we feel others have made a choice for us. **We cannot escape this version of our present reality without the realization that our power has never left us, as it can only ever be temporarily surrendered**. Even when unconsciously surrendered, it is never held within the hands of another but **remains inside us**. This allows us to instantaneously regain control over our path, perception, creation, and experience of our own lives.

We become overwhelmed by the unpleasant experiences of life and the actions of others when we forget our true identity and our ability to perceive our lives however we choose. When these feelings become too much for one to bear, one may consider taking their own life through the act of suicide. To consider taking one's own life, one must first lose sight of the gift and overwhelming beauty it truly is. They have lost sight of the incredible uniqueness that is their life, consciousness, and their **power of choice to create such destructive interpretations** of an objective and otherwise formless reality that encircles them. In this way, to feel the various stages of dissatisfaction and depression in life to the point that one would consider taking their own life; they have forgotten the power that they hold within themselves to choose the life they desire. They have instead surrendered it to others, situations, or the environment in which they live. Yet, in the very moment they fully commit to the act of taking their own life, they have simultaneously **taken back the power they had misplaced** while also **losing it in the same moment and through the same act**. They have finally reclaimed their choice, but in the moment of decision, they were unaware of their perception of reality that sits behind the fear, depression, and deep sadness that they undoubtedly experience. In the momentary awareness of their own consciousness and ability to choose their life, which had previously eluded their gaze and grasp, **they have both taken back their life and lost it**. Using this conscious life force that was always theirs, they have taken back their power but then used this power to **inhibit their ability to make further choices**, destroying the very life force that granted them this choice to begin with. It is this gift of life itself that provided them with the unadulterated ability to make free choices, and it is with this sacredness of life that they have chosen to take away the gift that provides them with such a choice. Instantaneously, they have rediscovered the freedom of their choice and life that they possessed all along to make any choice they desire, but in the exact same moment, they have lost their ability to make a choice. This is the ultimate **choice paradox**.

Author's Personal Note:

The following is an unedited and personal journal entry taken from the author immediately upon escaping from a moment of contemplation to take his own life, just prior to the decision to create this book. As a warning, this section may be disturbing for some. Please proceed with caution.

> *"Why did I myself contemplate suicide? I realized I lived in a bubble of lies, chasing material possessions, and being close to the midway point in my life and not having anything of* ***real value*** *to show for it. Everything I had worked so hard and so diligently for had crumbled, fallen apart, and turned to dust. I didn't want to 'start over.' I didn't want to try again. Nothing interested me, I didn't have passion. With everything material having crumbled away, including the ego-self that I myself manufactured and told myself I was for most of my lifetime, I didn't know who or what I was anymore. I'm just a middle-aged man,*

*who has failed at everything, and has nothing. **I forgot that I always have a choice**. That I can choose anything I want in this life. I can choose to appreciate life. To be playful. To have fun. To play this 'game' with a completely new set of rules. I knew that if I **chose to continue playing**, I could never go back to the old ways of thinking, living, breathing, and experiencing. This game could be anything I wanted it to be, if I so chose it to be. Through this 'near-death' experience of holding a loaded gun against my body, I was shown the beauty in my own consciousness and awareness, and the power of choice that I always have had. **This realization made the game worth playing again**, even if just for a little longer, and it's far more rewarding and fulfilling when you truly understand who you are in the deepest parts of your being."*

ARTICLES OF FURTHER CONSIDERATION

373

E1. AUTHOR'S JOURNEY

This chapter in my personal life has been the most difficult I've experienced, unlike anything to have come before it, or perhaps, even after. I have seen and understood things in ways that I most certainly lack the proficiency to verbalize or communicate effectively. Further, I am only able to communicate and share my thoughts to the degree to which I've experienced them and can process them within myself, which is a struggle all on its own. Through this, I feel as if I've been turned upside down, like a snow globe, and shaken vigorously. Even though, at times, the snow globe has been placed back onto a flat surface, the snow still flurries, making it difficult to see the figurines that reside behind the storm, a storm that I myself have created. Through a deep analysis of my perceptions, I've realized that the world is an illusion of my own creation. Therefore, to learn to live within the world of my creation, I must first learn how to assign purpose, morality, passion, and most of all, love, in a manner that cannot be swayed through the many perceptual shifts I experience. I have been completely disassembled, with every part of me laid out bare on a table, as it is labeled, studied, and analyzed. This has occurred more than once, so much so that I have begun to lose count. Upon each subsequent reassembly, I believe I have found the answers I deeply seek and desire, only to be disassembled, retooled, and repurposed, once again. For the things that I once believed I had wholeheartedly understood, without question and without doubt, have been challenged and seen from an entirely new perspective. Oftentimes, this is from perspectives that I did not know existed. Perhaps these perspectives did not exist until I myself created them. Perhaps the various parts of me are only parts of me that I carry because I have decided to identify with them while assigning a meaningful and significant purpose to each in order to justify the existence of them within me and the effort required to continue carrying them. Why must I associate with these parts, or any parts, at all? To associate with any parts seems to require the requisite assumption that I must always be a complete whole with an assigned purpose or that I must be reassembled in a manner that is stable, certain, and resilient to future deconstructive efforts.

But how is life purpose derived, if not through my own chosen beliefs, perceptions, and assumptions? At times, I fear that I have only assigned myself a purpose to mask the reality that I lack purpose, value, insight, intelligence, or usefulness. But is reality itself not formless, bound by my individual interpretation and perception, yet created from these very same elements that bind it? Therefore, how can I ever be "in touch" or in alignment with "reality" if separate and distinct realities exist within each of us? In this way, can one ever be out of touch with reality? Surely, one can be out of touch with another's reality while being perfectly synchronous within their own, but would this not be an internal choice entirely? After all, if one can choose a reality to which to align, why would anyone ever choose to be misaligned with reality when they themselves are the ones who create this reality for themselves? Perhaps when we become most aligned with our own reality, it is merely a self-soothing mechanism, not unlike a baby's use of their own thumb to pacify the journey through the unknown. Are we not afraid of choosing an inaccurate view of reality? How can the accuracy of one's reality ever be measured or verified? Should we choose the reality that brings about the most joy, purpose, and day-to-day fulfillment? Or should we choose the one of deep introspection, as we relive the attachments and pains of the past that no longer seem to materially exist within our present? Though, was the past ever materially real, or only through your perceptually biased recollection have you made it so? The past has been lived, has it not? Or is it only truly being lived now, in the moment of recollection and mental reconstruction of it? Are we not using the present to recall what has already been? By doing so, are we not foregoing our opportunity to create more? Or have we only now created the past through our choice to experience it in the present? But, what if we do not wish to create more? Must we only alter our relationship and attachment to the past, and our optimism, expectation, and anticipation for the future to enable a present where more is even wanted or desired? If one believes the future holds more, does this require letting go of using the present to relive the past, rather than being used to create this new future? Is our experience of the present the delicate balance of our recollection of the past and our optimistic desires for the future, both of which only exist in our concocted realities? In this way, our present experience is a direct reflection of the reality we have chosen to create for ourselves.

Is your present pleasant? Is it only pleasant as a result of your interpretation of it? As in, could it also be unpleasant given a different perceptual slant? If so, does your pleasant reality require ignoring or discarding the unpleasant reality also present? Or perhaps the unpleasant reality only exists the very moment in which you create it, but it otherwise does not exist. This would indicate that nothing exists until we create it within us. Can there be a "wrong" or improper choice with this freedom to create? Must we only create what is pleasant or what others collectively agree with and approve of? Or are we truly free to create whatever we choose, without bounds or limitations? Do the only boundaries and restrictions exist within us, should we accept them into our reality, but would otherwise not exist? Though, would they not need to exist in some way, even in the form of raw and uncompiled materials, for us to create with them and from them? For this, perhaps our chosen reality is created from raw ingredients, much like a cake that requires flour, eggs, and milk. The ingredients themselves do not constitute a cake, but together, they can become almost anything you desire. The ingredients are no more a cake than your reality is what it isn't, until you choose to make it such. Therefore, did the cake always exist, even in theory or potential, or has it been fabricated from within yourself entirely? The menu is limited, should you decide that it is, or limitless, should you decide that it is. Are the raw ingredients static, or do even the ingredients exist at all? Perhaps the ingredients are not present in the formless world for you to create within, but are exclusively within, and not without?

Why must we want or do anything?

To assert that one must enjoy life requires the assumption and requisite belief to validate this assertion.

To assert that life is about pain, suffering, growth, and evolution requires the assumption and requisite belief to validate this assertion.

Perhaps life is all of these things, or none of these things.

If it is all, what shall we choose, and how often can we adjust our gaze, path, and perceptions? Must we choose only one to navigate our life's present moments? If so, who determines the rules or guidance for such a recommendation? Us, or another? If another, why not us, if another is just like us, riddled with subjectivity and biases of their own?

If it is none, then is it not us that are the sole creators of our life experience, by creating what it is we most wish to see and become? If we alone assign meaning and purpose, is this not the ultimate freedom to create the life, experiences, and self that we most desire?

If the world is not formless, but instead static and certain, then is it not still our perceptions that create our subjective reality within us individually? For this reason, can one ascertain what static reality objectively is in a superior manner to another, who of which is limited by the same human senses and experiences as any other? Whether formless, or statically pre-created, our realities are created within us in the present moment only, through choice and perception.

With each of my personal reassemblies, I view myself, others, and the world, in a brand-new way, believing it to be the most accurate representation of the world. In this, I momentarily find incredible peace, joy, purpose, and satisfaction until the moment I realize that nothing in the world has materially changed, but rather, only my perception of it. Though, how can I ever become certain of even this? After all, how could I ever know if my view of the world is a direct result of my chosen perception of it? Therefore, my perception of the world is a result of my choice. If I believe the world has not materially changed, it has not. But if I believe it has, has it not? It indeed has, does, and will change, but only to the degree to which I believe it to be so. How can it ever not be what I think it to be?

E2. THE SUN'S GLITTER

What assumptions have you made to read, absorb, and apply the contents of this book?

Do you trust that the author is who he claims to be?

Do you believe his introduction and his personal account of his life story leading up to the writing of this book and the emotional journey through it?

How could this be objectively verified, if at all?

Have you simply taken his word for his personal story, which exists inside the covers of the book written by the author himself, effectively creating a self-validating circle of truth?

Is the author sharing his thoughts from a place of depth and servitude to others while carrying a heavy heart? Or is this only a marketing ruse?

Is the author intentionally set out to deceive, confuse, and manipulate those that read this book? How might you know the difference objectively?

Do you trust that the author's stated intent, which exists within the published book itself, to open the hearts and minds of others to bring peace, love, compassion, and understanding to the world? Or is this just a guise, with his ultimate objective to bring about more chaos and more division in this world?

How do you think you would, or could, know the difference definitively?

Did you personally align with anything written in this book as truth? If so, why and how so?

Did you blatantly disagree with anything written in this book? If so, why and how so?

Were you triggered or frustrated by anything in the book?

If so, do you assign blame to the author for writing such offensive statements, or do the frustration and anger exist only inside of you, as a result of your personally held core beliefs, perceptual biases, and blind spots? How would you know with undeniable certainty that the answer you provide to this question is accurate? If blind spots are present in your judgment and conclusion, would you not be aware of them due to the nature of blind spots in and of themselves?

How do you know that you mustn't externalize blame for your feelings?

How do you know the author hasn't only used this tactic to get "off the hook" for publishing frustrating, offensive, and emotionally triggering content while deferring his own responsibility for his actions and words?

In either case, whether classified as fact, fiction, love, or hate speech by you, the reader, what could ever classify any of the statements within the book as such when various individuals that consume the contents of the book might arrive at a different fact or fiction conclusion than you?

Is your conclusion of the book's contents and validity any more accurate or more aligned with reality than another's, whatever that conclusion might be?

Is your education, background, or life experience uniquely supreme or superior to another's that provides you with the necessary authority to ascertain truth above and beyond the capability of others?

If this book was for you and you learned from it in a positive way, could it also be for another?

If this book wasn't for you, can you imagine a reality where one might find the contents positively life-changing? If not, why not? If so, what type of individual or individuals might you imagine enjoy the contents of the book?

Would you assign a derogatory label to such individuals due to their inability to arrive at the same subjective conclusion or opinion that you hold?

What information sources have you trusted in your own life for the beliefs you presently hold? Further, are the beliefs that you hold deemed to be true for you due to the information source you have chosen to trust validating the truth within itself? As in, a resource claims it is accurate and true by its own version of its own story within its own reporting? Can you ever validate this for yourself, without making assumptions or trusting the words of the information source whereby it states itself to be true, and others to not be true?

TLC/LC

LITLB

CIE/EIC

POAS/NSA

WAG/WAC

PBKR

4DEL